P9-AZU-353

The sociology of youth culture and youth subcultures

The sociology of youth culture and youth subcultures
Sex and drugs and rock 'n' roll?

Mike Brake

Keynes College, University of Kent at Canterbury
Visiting Associate Professor, Carleton University, Ottawa

Routledge & Kegan Paul

London, Boston and Henley

First published in 1980
by Routledge & Kegan Paul Ltd
39 Store Street, London WC1E 7DD,
9 Park Street, Boston, Mass. 02108, USA and
Broadway House, Newtown Road,
Henley-on-Thames, Oxon RG9 1EN

Set in Linocomp Palatino by
Rowland Phototypesetting Ltd
Bury St Edmunds, Suffolk
and Printed in Great Britain by
Redwood Burn Ltd
Trowbridge & Esher

British Library Cataloguing in Publication Data

Brake, Mike

The sociology of youth culture and youth subcultures.
1. Youth – Great Britain – History – 20th century 2. Subculture
3. Youth – United States – History – 20th century
I. Title
301.43'15'0941 HQ799.G7 79-41228

ISBN 0 7100 0363 3
ISBN 0 7100 0364 1 Pbk

Contents

Introduction

In this book I have developed an examination of much of the disparate work on youth culture, subcultures and delinquency which has been researched since the early thirties. One major theme which is noticeable is that if the young are not socialized into conventional political, ethical and moral outlooks, if they are not programmed into regular work habits and labour discipline, then society as it is today cannot continue. What is central to any examination of youth culture is that it is not some vague structural monolith appealing to those roughly under thirty, but is a complex kaleidoscope of several subcultures, of different age groups, yet distinctly related to the class position of those in them. My argument is that subcultures arise as attempts to resolve collectively experienced problems arising from contradictions in the social structure, and that they generate a form of collective identity from which an individual identity can be achieved outside that ascribed by class, education and occupation. This is nearly always a temporary solution, and in no sense is a real material solution, but one which is solved at the cultural level. Youth cultures interact with manufactured popular cultures and their artefacts but I would argue against manufactured cultures being deterministic in the sense that they are uninfluenced by their consumers. On the whole, youth cultures and subcultures tend to be some form of exploration of masculinity. These are therefore masculinist, and I have tried to consider their effect on girls, and one distinct sign of the emancipation of young girls from the cult of romance, and marriage as their true vocation, will be the development of subcultures exploring a new form of femininity. Given the material place of women in society today, this is likely to take some time.

One of the most worrying signs of friction and alienation in contemporary society is the problems that racial minorities have to face. Their harassment by law and order personnel, the use of the conspiracy laws and the 'sus' law and their isolation from their white peers suggest that a whole generation feels betrayed. The present crisis in capitalism, and the high unemployment rate which particularly affects ethnic minorities and women makes the situation seem pessimistic. If we are to have a culturally plural society, then we need to develop a socialist culture which retains the progressive elements of the different subcultures which have been developed, and counteracts the reactionary traditional elements which manifest themselves most clearly in racism and sexism. This obviously involves not only a cultural struggle but also being involved in a class struggle against the oppression in our present society. Economic exploitation develops an oppressive culture which alienates and brutalizes large sections of our society. The class struggle necessarily involves not only the way forward to a material revolution, but also a cultural revolution.

Youth has always been a source of envy, nostalgia and lust to its elders, usually involving a projection on to them that they are enjoying a hedonism we were too respectable or myopic to pursue during our own youth. The only compensation for that is to grow old disgracefully. As a working-class adolescent, I was unusual in that I vaguely had an idea there must be a more imaginative and creative life than the one I experienced during the dreary fifties. I became a ballet dancer, but a serious accident returned me to the unskilled working class. After several mindless, routinized jobs, I sought upward mobility through the caring professions. I was an occupational therapist and a social worker. I then entered university as a mature student, but the mixture of libertarians, marxists and hedonists I came into contact with converted me from my respectability. I graduated in 1968, and so I was able to live through some of the events in this book both here and in the United States. I was fortunate in finding friends in and outside of academic life for whom class politics, sexual politics and deviancy was both an academic discipline and a personal project. Doubtless we will grow old together pursuing the contradictions of dissolution, sexism, socialism and our petty bourgeois class location, boring the young even more.

I am grateful to David Downes, who patiently supervised the Ph.D. thesis on which much of this book is based, and also Stuart Hall who was more than kind. I am grateful to Frank Pearce for many fruitful conversations, and to Peter Hopkins of Routledge & Kegan Paul. I am also grateful to my students, who as they constantly remind me, provide me with a living. There are many others, but I am particularly thankful to Nicola Hewitt.

I would like to dedicate this book to my mother who did not read it, to my father who probably will not, and my daughter who I hope will.

1 The use of subculture as an analytical tool in sociology

> Adolescents are grouped together by adults and defined as a problem, and yet we must ask ourselves whether this problem refers to something in the adolescent, or whether it is making a statement about our society. (Friedenburg E.)
>
> The young people of today love luxury. They have bad manners, they scoff at authority and lack respect for their elders. Children nowadays are real tyrants, they no longer stand up when their elders come into the room where they are sitting, they contradict their parents, chat together in the presence of adults, eat gluttonously and tyrannise their teachers. (Socrates)

Young people have always suffered from the envious criticism of their elders. Nowhere is this more apparent than in the vast amount of writing, both of a scholarly and a popular kind, that has been generated about the organization of their social life, and their allegedly wild moral values. This has resulted in the definition of them as a social problem, particularly since the end of the Second World War with the adolescent working-class male, especially, being portrayed as a 'folk devil'. The growth industry of youth as a social problem has involved many theories in different social science disciplines. Explanations which contain many latent and manifest ideas about the nature of post-war industrial society have included sociological theories about class, pluralism and social mobility, social psychological explanations about educational opportunity and inter-generational friction, social policy planning concerning leisure and delinquency, psychological interpretation about frustration, conflict and aggression, and popular mythology about affluence, boredom and lack of discipline. Problems then, that have their roots in the political economy and the social structure, have been subsumed into a focus on the residual category of 'youth culture'. It is hoped in this volume to consider the development and history of various youthful subcultures, and to relate them to wider structural problems, in particular, problems of social class. However, an important element of the results of structural contradictions is the effect upon the individual actor. All human beings have to face the problem of the differential fit between what one feels one is (basically an ontological problem), and how one feels one is perceived by the outside world (a meta-perception by 'significant others').

By a 'significant other' I refer to the concept originating in the social psychology of G. H. Mead, and developed by symbolic interactionist theory. It refers to the recognition that in a fragmented and differentiated world certain others that an actor comes into contact with have more important perspectives than social actors peripheral to his development. Significant others can be individuals (for example, parents), groups (for example, peers), reference groups (perhaps Hell's angels motor cycle groups), or even oneself. They can be real, imaginary or mythical, but they are important to the social actor. The social world is composed of a complex set of matrices, involving the actor's position in an ontological grid, as well as his[1] location in a complex series of stratifications and roles. The deviant faces the problems of developing an ongoing creation of self, which has to take note of the stigma which may be attached to his/her location in the stratification system, and his/her consequent deviant role. Criticisms of subcultural studies (McRobbie and Garber, 1976; Smart, 1976), by women have pointed out the apparent absence of girls in the studies. This will be dealt with later, but briefly this is not surprising because an examination of the studies reveals on the one hand a sexist perspective, but also that the subcultures traditionally have been a place to examine centrally variations on several themes concerning masculinity.

New forms of femininity for girls have come later than adolescence, at present anyway, and have come from more middle-class groups with a feminist perspective. Significant others for these young women are not in working-class subcultures. The deviant's position in the ontological grid involves a dialogue with how significant others perceive, define and judge him. As self is intimately related to, and defined in terms of, socially recognized categories and roles, any rejection of status is also a rejection of self. Where the significant others regard the actor with approval, then social action may proceed along comfortable lines. A significant other can also be the actor's projection of his future self. This may cause complications if it is in conflict with the perspectives of significant others such as parents, employers, teachers or even the general public. When an actor perceives or experiences the contempt of significant others, then a solution has to be found to this paradox. This can take an individual form, with attendant dangers of atomization and isolation, or a collective form drawing upon a new definition of the situation defined by the subculture. This can resolve the dilemma, because it can offer an identity which although deviant, is external to that ascribed by class or occupation, and which is effectively supported by the group solidarity of the subculture. (This explains why, for example, delinquent boys score high on self-esteem attitude tests, whilst still carrying on anti-social behaviour.) Subcultural or group support is therefore an important variable for deviant identity. It is possible for the actor to create a status hierarchy of self-images, so that the external world can be dealt with by a series of interpersonal strategies. A cognitive order is imposed upon the social world to assist the actor in acting upon it. In this way the actor or actors structure solutions to deal with problems posed by the external social world.

These solutions can be at an individual or a collective level. Individual solutions tend to take a defensive role and can be conceptualized as with collective solutions, as a response to attacks on self-esteem. As Plummer (1975), argues, labelling caused by stigma involves self-labelling by the actor. McAll and Simmons (1966), suggest that at the interpersonal level of performance, actors may wish to project a role identity using a prominent identity from his role repertoire to gain social support for his social self. The role chosen tends to be influenced by the actor's internalized notion of his ideal self. Deviant identity may be organized to resist internalizing social stigma. Individual reactions without subcultural support tend therefore to be defensive.

Individual and collective 'solutions' to stigma

1 *Individual 'solutions' to stigma*

These are not solutions in any positive sense, but strategies developed to deal with the problem of deviant identity and stigma.

a Resentment

The actor rejects the societal stigma, and wishes to confirm his independence from the source of the stigma. However, he accepts the social context in which stigma is generated and his response is resentment.

b Individual dissociation
The validity of the stigma is denied, and the actor tries to disaffiliate from the stigmatizing society. He perceives himself as alien and aloof in that society (in some ways this is a form of alienation), and yet in a way opposes the societal definition of his deviance.[2]

c Self-hatred
The stigmatized deviant accepts the perceived hegemony,[3] as valid. The stigmatized definition of the situation is never challenged and becomes internalized. There are severe problems where the self-image is experienced as unchangeable as with race or homosexuality.

d Psychological damage
This is less a strategy (although the role of mental patient may be a solution) than the result of extreme stigma, where the psyche feels under attack. The self in this situation feels damaged to the extent that action seems impossible, and there seems to be little conjunction between what the self feels it is, and how it feels itself defined by significant others and official agencies.[4]

Most of these strategies are of a passive, accommodating nature, as it is hard to attempt an activist strategy which challenges many basic tenets of social reality without subcultural consciousness, ideology and support.

2 *Collective 'solutions' to stigma*

These are by definition subcultural, but the form of subculture or social movement may differ.

a Delinquent subcultures
These are publicly the most threatening in terms of societal response. It will be argued below that they are developed particularly among working-class youth, as responses to collectively experienced problems.

b Cultural rebellion
Culture is used against the prevailing hegemony, either through *avant-garde* art forms (e.g. Dadaism) or bohemian and expressive

subcultures. Arguments can be focused through 'agit-prop', 'happenings', artistic form and style, and also life-styles.

c Reformist movements
Pressure groups are used to extend existing values to cover or protect specific groups of deviants. Tolerance within the existing hegemony is appealed to, usually to indicate the similarities between deviant and respectable groups. An ethical appeal is made to a higher order of uniformity between the two, such as humanness. The danger is that the less acceptable forms of deviance may be driven further outside the pale.[5]

d Political militancy
A high degree of consciousness leading to a consequent analysis is important to challenge the hegemonic apparatus. Questions concerning the political nature of the social reality engulfing the group suggests a radical solution granting not only equality, but political power and self-determination.

As can be seen, subculturization, the entry into a subculture, is important to an actor in that it assists the actor to redefine concepts of self, to redefine a problematic situation, and to develop a sense of legitimation concerning the relationship between subculture and self. Consciousness is raised, and in one sense subcultures use consciousness in the Marxist sense of progressing from a class in itself to a class for itself.

The concept of subculture

The earliest use of subculture in sociology seems to be its application as a subdivision of a national culture by McLung Lee (1945), and M. Gordon (1947). This emphasized the effects of socialization within the cultural sub-sections of a pluralist society. It drew on the notion of culture as learned behaviour, and this behavioural element owes much to the anthropological approach, as for example, Firth (1951, p. 27):

> culture is all learned behaviour which has been socially acquired.

Culture is, however, wider than this and as Tylor (1871, p. 10) notes, when

> taken in its wide ethnographic sense, is that complex whole which includes knowledge, belief, art, morals, law, custom

> and any other capabilities and habits acquired by man as a member of society.

This opens up many of the essentials of culture, including several which have been useful in studying subcultures. Kroeber A. L. and Kluckhohn C. (1952, p. 2), synthesized a definition of culture based on an analysis of 160 definitions drawn from different social sciences. They conclude:

> Culture consists of patterns, explicit and implicit of symbols, constituting the distinctive achievements of human groups, including their embodiments in artifacts; the essential core of culture consists of traditional (i.e. historically derived and selected) ideas and especially their attached values; culture systems may on the one hand, be considered as products of action, and on the other as conditioning elements of further action.

Ford (1942), offered the view that culture is 'a traditional way of solving problems', or a 'learned problem solution'. This problem solving element was to be explored as a major determinant of subcultures by Cohen A. (1955, p. 51):

> What people do depends upon the problems they contend with.

Culture is a cohesive force binding actors together, but it also produces disjunctive elements. The viewpoint which sees culture merely as cohesive, takes an ahistorical, idealist view of culture. In any complex society culture is divisive, because by definition a complex society involves various subgroups and subcultures in a struggle for the legitimacy of their behaviour, values and life-style against the dominant culture of the dominant class. A dominant class uses culture to legitimize its control of subordinate strata. Swingewood (1977), puts it well:

> Through the major social institutions (the family, religious, educational, political and trade union organisations), cultural values, norms and aspirations are transmitted, congealing into largely nonconscious routines, the norms and customs of everyday experience and knowledge. At the level of popular consciousness culture is never simply that of the 'people' or region or family or subordinate class. Culture is not a neutral concept; it is historical, specific and ideological.

We are born into social classes, themselves complexly stratified, possessing distinct 'ways of life', which are modified locally by region and neighbourhood. We influence, and are influenced by, the perceptions, values, behaviour, and institutions which affect the social relations of these groups. The values and social meanings embodied in these make up the culture of the group. We are formed and also form (collectively at least) a series of social relations necessary to reproducing our social existence. We start to build an identity contained in this nexus of social relations and meanings, and the culture transmitting this meaning to us both aids us to make sense of the world, but also retrains our development. We draw upon existing cultural patterns, and from this make ourselves, including our relation to the dominant culture. We create ourselves, but bound by distinct patterns of possibilities, we do not have freedom in any absolute sense, but a series of choices bound by a distinct social framework. This framework is related to the production of material goods, and therefore to the political economy. Marx reminds us (1951, p. 225):

> Men make their own history, but they do not make it just as they please; they do not make it under circumstances chosen by themselves, but under circumstances directly encountered, given and transmitted from the past.

There may be in society a dominant class, but it is doubtful if there is a dominant culture *per se*. This is not to deny that there may be a dominant value system, which groups may understand that they are supposed to subscribe to, but any major value system is never homogeneous. There are constant modifications to, and adaptations of, dominant ideas and values. There are often divisions within dominant classes and these have their effects on values, as for example the struggle during the early part of the last century between aristocratic and bourgeois morality. There is also in any complex stratified society several cultures. The major forms of these are class cultures, and subcultures can be conceptualized as sub-sets of these larger cultural configurations. Subcultures share elements of the larger class culture (sometimes called the parent culture), but are also distinct from it.

Subcultures also have a relationship to the overall dominant culture which, because of its pervasiveness, in particular its transmission through the mass media, is unavoidable. We can therefore distinguish a subculture, for example that of the hippies, which has connections with, but is distinct from due to its deviant life-style, the progressive middle-class culture. The hippy subculture also has connections with the bohemian tradition of the artistic *avant-garde*, but its use of illegal drugs, and its value of instant hedonism means it has connections with other urban, more delinquent subcultures. The hippy subculture is itself culturally stratified, for example into mystics and militants, with religious and political value systems. There are, in addition, problems with the political economy, and with the dominant value system (the straight world) which, depending on public reaction, may accommodate, alienate or destroy the hippy subculture. In addition, Downes (1966, p. 9), suggests that one must distinguish between subcultures which emerge in positive response to the demands of social and cultural structures, e.g. occupational subcultures, and those which emerge in response to negative response to these structures such as delinquent subcultures. Membership of a subculture necessarily involves membership of a class culture, and the subculture may be an extension of, or in opposition to, this. It may also closely merge with the dominant class culture, or it may form a miniature world of its own. There may be a clear subculture with distinct 'focal concerns'. These have been described by Miller W. B. (1958), as 'areas and issues which command widespread and persistent attention and a high degree of emotional involvement'. (p. 6) These differ significantly from accepted middle-class norms. If we use these criteria, then we can begin to develop some form of analysis of subcultures which are distinguished by age and generation variables as well as by class, and which generate specific focal concerns. We can develop a concept of youthful subcultures. Popularly this has been subsumed under the term 'youth culture'. However, this concept assumes some sort of structural monolith appealing across classes to all those under thirty. There is, instead, as we shall see, a complex kaleidoscope of several adolescent and youthful subcultures appealing to different age and class groups, involving different life-styles. These subcultures appeal to different self-images, values and behaviour, and they bear a close relation to their parent class culture. I shall return to this later, when I consider the symbiotic relationship between myth and reality in these subcultures.

Culture, then, may be seen as a source of potential meaning structures that actors inherit. Subcultures, by their very existence, suggest that there are alternative forms of cultural expression which reflect a cultural plurality in a culture which seems on superficial examination to dominate the members of a society. Culture has several levels: the historical level of ideas, the level of values, the level of meaning and its effects on art, signs and symbols. There is also the process of material production and the symbolic and material effects of artefacts on cultures. Finally, there is the personal, dynamic element of human action and the way it is interpreted between actors. Subcultures exist where there is some form of organized and recognized constellation of values, behaviour and action which are responded to as different from the prevailing sets of norms. An element of reference group theory is necessary, according to Downes (1966, p. 7), who argues the important notion that subcultures develop to resolve collectively experienced problems. They emerge

> where there exists in effective interaction with one another, a number of actors with similar problems of adjustment for whom no effective solution as yet exists for a common, shared problem.

Downes (1966, p. 10), also points out that subcultures which originate from within a society can be differentiated from those that develop from without, as with an immigrant group. A subculture has to develop new group standards and an essential aspect of its existence is that it forms a constellation of behaviour and values which have meaningful symbolism for the actors involved.

Subculture as a concept has much to offer sociological understanding of human interaction against a cultural and symbolic background. It takes role play and reconstructs it as an active ingredient in a dialectical relation between structure and actor. At the structural level it indicates how culture is mediated to and generated by a collectivity of social actors, and at the existential level it indicates how meanings are taken from a subculture, used to project an image and hence an identity. This has an effect on the internal labelling element of identity, and uses external symbols to develop a self-image which has a cultural and an existential reality to the actor. Subcultures negotiate between the interpersonal world of the actor and the dynamics of the larger elements of social interaction. However, as a concept it is not without problems. Clarke M. (1974), looks at the formal and substantive elements of subculture, and argues that if the term was introduced today it would be rejected. It has 'spongy' aspects, which reveal its vagueness over areas such as the cultural and structural elements of the concept, the definitions of subcultural boundaries, and the genesis, maintenance and change of subcultures. Subculture has two complementary perspectives which often become confused. There is the empirical evidence of what constitutes membership of a subculture, which is abstracted from the social structure. There is also the hermeneutic aspect of cultural analysis, what the subculture 'means'. Subcultural analysis involves examining an organized set of social relations, as well as a set of social meanings. A subculture is not the same as a sub-community, so problems arise as to why one sub-community and not another creates a subculture. These are problems of empirical and interpretative method, however, rather than a problem in the use of the concept.

Fischer (1975), suggests that subculturization is the result of urbanism. Fischer (1972), sees a link between community and urbanization. The concentration in urban areas of large heterogeneous populations leads to the weakening of interpersonal ties, primary social structures and normative consensus. Dynamic population density leads to a complex, structural differentiation with consequences of alienation, social disorganization, deviant behaviour and anomie. This may have some truth for those who migrate from the rural areas to the towns but the evidence of Gans (1962), Lewis (1952), and Willmott and Young (1957), finds that there are close-knit communities within towns with long traditions of social support and closeness. Liebow (1967), finds similar primary groups existing for unemployed men in the ghetto. Fischer, however, argues that urban groups are more likely to deviate from the traditional norms of society. The more urban the setting, argues Fischer, the more variety there is of subculturization. Subcultures develop which generate subsystems of a social nature which can protect and foster the subcultures against external threats. Unconventional elements of a subcultural origin become diffused into mainstream culture. This argument romanticizes urban tolerance towards the emergence of subcultures, but it does suggest that in specific urban areas, usually metropolitized cities (for example, Amsterdam, San Francisco or London) the diversity of urban population creates the atmosphere for the generation of various subcultures. There is usually in a metropolis a down-town or bohemian area which contains a neighbourhood where various outsiders, such as drug addicts, inter-racial couples, students, artists, minor criminals, immigrants, the gay community and so forth make up a form of bohemian, lumpen-proletariat underworld. Two things occur if subcultures flourish. An informal grapevine recruits outsiders from other areas into the subcultures. This has an effect on the subcultural boundaries, which may harden over time, especially if subjected to stigmatization which may give spurts to their collective life, or they may be assimilated and absorbed into mainstream culture. The boundaries of subcultures remain a problem, even when clearly delineated as with exogenous subcultures such as those generated by immigrant groups. As these become part of metropolitan life they develop endogenous subcultures, as for example with young Rastafarians in the London West Indian subcultures. The other effect of a multiplicity of subcultures is their diffusion into mainstream culture. This clarifies why what Rodman (1965), called a 'value stretch' occurs in society. This is a commitment to norms, values and cultural themes which seems ambiguous, ambivalent and contradictory. Because of cultural differences from the assumed consensus, people may hold at least two sets of values. The 'value stretch' bridges the discrepancies between consensual public values (or the central value system as structural functional sociology calls it) and privatized variance from these. We can see that there exists a situation of apparent consensus to appropriate, respectable values and behaviour, but because of class differences in culture, and subcultural deviation there can emerge, especially in urban settings, a situation of pluralistic social realities. Matza and Sykes (1961), suggest that there is a fundamental contradiction present in societal values. Co-existing with respectable values are a series of 'subterranean values', which are permitted expression during certain periods, usually officially approved moments of leisure carefully differentiated from times of work. An actor then may not only hold values of security, routinization and hard work, but also values involving a search for excitement, adventure and hedonistic, morally disapproved behaviour. Young (1971) suggests that certain subcultural groups do not hold subterranean values in abeyance until the prescribed time, but actually stress and accentuate them instead of more official respectable values. Yinger (1960), has argued that where subcultural norms are developed which are counter-values and central to the subculture, and which bring it into conflict with the larger society, a subculture can be designated as a 'contraculture'. Yinger wants to differentiate as a contraculture the emergent norms of a group in a conflict situation, retaining subculture to describe more traditional forms of sub-societies which have developed particular local norms (e.g. the Subculture of the American Southlands). Empirically, no study seems to suggest that there is a pure contraculture, except perhaps in a political subcultural context (such as the Black Panthers). Although oppositional norms may be developed in direct contrast to respectable norms, a subculture cannot survive for long which exists in direct conflict with the prevailing society. There are politically militant elements of subcultures among minority groups, gay people and feminists, but their success and continuation depends on a series of strategies involving avoiding direct confrontation, but often waging systematic cultural guerilla raids on the dominant morality. There becomes a struggle over what is and what is not permitted. This illustrates Erikson's (1966), suggestion that deviancy has the function of boundary definition and boundary maintenance for what is and what is not permitted in a society.

Subcultures and style

It has been argued above that structural conditions, especially persistent structural contradiction often experienced as class problems, are a basic generating force for subcultures. Cultural traditions, particularly those generated by social class, may interact with the apparent middle-class consensus, and assisted by neighbourhood traditions and specific historic circumstances, act in shaping the cultural form of a subculture. One cultural form common in a subculture is its 'style'. Cohen A. (1965), in an interesting article, which raises the questions of the relationship of social structure to social interaction, notes that an important aspect of a reference group such as a distinct subcultural group is the symbolic use of a style.

> An actor learns that the behaviour signifying membership in a particular role includes the kinds of clothes he wears, his posture, his gait, his likes and dislikes, what he talks about and the opinion he expresses. (Cohen A., 1965, *op. cit.*, p. 1)

Several important indicators are raised by style. It expresses a degree of commitment to the subculture, and it indicates membership of a specific subculture which by its very appearance disregards or attacks dominant values. Style I shall define as consisting of three main elements

a 'Image', appearance composed of costume, accessories such as hair-style, jewellery and artefacts.
b 'Demeanour' made up of expression, gait and posture. Roughly this is what the actors wear and how they wear it.
c 'Argot' a special vocabulary and how it is delivered.

An important aspect of style is the differentiation of work and leisure. Thompson E. P. (1969), has suggested that the values of leisure have always been traditionally feared by employers because they present a counter-thesis to work – in order to preserve industrial discipline, as for example the work habit, working schedules, the commencement of the working day, all of which in the traditional crafts were paced and planned by the worker. Work and leisure were strictly separated, so that leisure became channelled into acceptable by-products of the work ethic. Holidays involving hedonistic carousal were seen as an anarchistic attack on work discipline, and the values of austerity, thrift and production were emphasized. One off-spin of mass production and consumption is to create a semi-mythical popular elite, promoted by the mass media and advertising, which the purchase of clothing and artefacts brings within reach of the average consumer. In this situation, Burns (1967), drawing on the work of Italian sociologists Pizzorno (1959), and Alberoni (1964), suggests there is an attachment to this mythical elite by the imitation of style and clothing to an identity which stands outside of traditional class definitions. The working-class girl imitating cultural heroines such as Marilyn Monroe, feels she is part of a specific 'classless' group of other girls who look like Monroe. This can be obviously extended into subcultures which have definite imagery and style. Indeed, style is usually a predominant defining feature of youthful subcultures. The precious gains of working life, money and leisure, become invested in dramaturgical statements about self-image, which attempt to define an identity outside that ascribed class, education and occupational role, particularly when the latter is of low status.

A parallel may be drawn between the use of style and fashion in subcultures by considering certain forms of analysis in linguistic theory. It has been argued that there is a general science of signs, semiology (Sassure, 1960). Language is the most sophisticated form of semiology, but gesture, music and images can all be analysed. Sassure (1960), differentiates between a systemized set of linguistic conventions called 'langue' (language) and 'parole' – the selection and actualization of language – speech. Hjelmslev (1959), elaborates this further, by distinguishing between the formal standard usage of language, and its regional use. The formal set of syntax becomes transformed by social usage. We can also see that subcultural use of fashion is a rhetorical usage of formalized styles, a sort of slang or argot of the 'standard English' of fashion. Style ceases to be merely informative, or taxonomic (indicating a cultural system which indicates membership of class or subculture), and becomes open to interpretation of what it means both subjectively for the actor, and objectively in its statement about the actor's relationship to his world. A hermeneutic interpretation is possible in Ricoeur's (1972), sense of the meaning of cultural documents, in this case style. Style, then, is used for a variety of meanings. It indicates which symbolic group one belongs to, it demarcates that group from the mainstream, and it makes an appeal to an identity outside that of a class-ascribed one. It is learned in social interaction with significant subcultural others, and its performance requires what theatre actors call 'presence', the ability to wear costume, and to use voice to project an image with sincerity. Indeed this form of performance skill may well be tested out by other subcultural members.

Willener (1970), has shown in certain changing social circumstances actors can transform, invent and juxtapose imagery to create new cultural styles. The symbolism of appearance has been illustrated in the subculture by Willis (1970):

> The dress . . . was not primarily a functional exigency of riding a motor cycle. It was more crucially a symbolic extension of the motorbike and amplification of the qualities inherent within the motorbike . . .

The complexities of the use of costume have been well analysed by Carter (1967):

> The nature of our apparel is very complex. Clothes are so many things at once. Our social shells; the system of signals with which we broadcast our intentions, are often the projections of our fantasy selves . . . clothes are our weapons, our challenges, our visible insults . . .

We may use clothing to challenge dominant norms, but we also make statements about our environment.

> For we think dress expresses ourselves, but in fact it expresses our environment, and like advertising, pop music, pulp fiction and second feature films, it does so at a subliminal, emotionally charged non-intellectual, instinctual level. (*Ibid.*)

Style also indicates a life-style, and as such has an appeal to subterranean values which combine to make a visual challenge at both a structural and an existential level.

> and in their Neanderthal way, the Hell's Angels are obeying Camus' law – that the dandy is always a rebel, that he challenges society because he challenges mortality. The motor cycle gangs challenge society because they challenge mortality face to face, doing 100 m.p.h. on the California freeway in Levis and swastikas, no crash helmets and a

> wide-awake hat, only a veneer between the man and his death . . .. (*Ibid.*)

Briefly, then, style at a subcultural level acts as a form of argot, drawing upon costume and artefacts from a mainstream fashion context and translating these into its own rhetoric. The difference between conventional costume and imagery is deliberate. American street talk in the black ghetto has taken the language of the dominant white culture, altered its rhythm by introducing African pitch and tempo, and confused the outsider by a complex set of metaphors drawn from the black subcultures. In many ways this is what subcultural style has done. Clarke, Hall and Jefferson (1976), illustrate this:

> Thus the 'Teddy Boy' expropriation of an upper class style of dress 'covers' the gap between largely manual unskilled near-lumpen real careers and life-chances, and the 'all-dressed-up-and-nowhere-to-go' experience of Saturday evening. Thus in the expropriation and fetishisation of consumption and style itself, the 'Mods' cover the gap between the never-ending-weekend and Monday's resumption of boring dead-end work.

Objects and artefacts (both of a symbolic and a concrete form) have been re-ordered and placed in new contexts so as to communicate fresh acts of meaning. Where there is a re-assemblage of styles into a new subcultural style, as with nostalgic revivals such as the Teddy boys, the assemblage must not look as though it is carrying the same message as the previously existing one. A new style is created by appropriating objects from an existing market of artefacts and using them in a form of collage which recreates group identity, and promotes mutual recognition for members. There is also, as Willis (1972), suggests, a fit or 'homology' between objects, the meaning of these, and behaviour. There is, he argues, a homology between intense activism, physicality, externalization, a taboo on introspection, a love of speed and early rock music in such groups as motor-bike boys (or bikers). There is a homology between structurelessness, introspection and loose group affiliation and progressive West Coast rock music in hippies. This is near to the concept of focal concerns, but extends the analysis into the cultural elements of the subculture and its style. The analysis is now extended below the conscious level to consider the meaning of the symbolism. This approach offers a valuable extension to more traditional empirical findings which will be discussed later.[6]

Subcultures, social reality and identity

It has been suggested above that subcultures offer on the one hand solutions of a 'magical' rather than of a real nature to inherent contradictions in the socio-economic system experienced at some level by the actor. With youthful subcultures, this is perceived and responded to by the actor, as a generational problem. On the other hand, the style of the subculture allows an expression of identity through a deliberate projection of a self-image, which claims an identity 'magically' freed from class and occupation. The subjectivistic perception and interpretation of structural problems is personalized, and is limited by the parochial locale of the actor's social class position. In addition, these problems are further mediated by the community the actor lives in. Thus, for the actor, there is an apparent range of voluntaristic selections of subcultures to choose from. Entrance to the subculture, as we shall see from the empirical evidence, is however limited by opportunities related to class and education. Empirically, clusters of subcultural groups are found in specific locations of the social class structure, with a common experience in terms of background, class, education and neighbourhood. The degree of articulation of subcultural life-style, and commitment to it varies considerably.

The relation of subcultures and age is important, because adolescence, and the period of transition between school and work, and work and marriage is important in terms of secondary socialization. Berger and Luckman (1966, p. 77) have suggested that patterns of behaviour are legitimized and habitualized in socialization, through what they see as a basic confidence trick of cultural relativism:

> In primary socialisation there is not a problem of identification. There is no choice of significant others. Society presents the candidate for socialisation with a predefined set of significant others whom he must accept with no possibility of opting for another arrangement. Hic Rhodus – hic salta . . . . The child does not internalise the world of his significant others as one of many possible worlds. He internalises it as the world, the only existent and conceivable world, the world tout court . . .

Children, then, perceive the world without any idea of the plethora of alternative social realities present, and internalize attitudes mediated to them from emotionally charged social interaction with their parents, or similar significant others.

Social institutions are seen as part of a symbolic totality which Berger and Luckman call the 'symbolic universe'. Everything in the world makes sense in relation to the hegemonic apparatus; the received world is experienced as the only world. It is used as a paradigm of experiential explanation which assumes that the symbolic universe is social reality whose subjective features become transformed into 'objective' reality. This is the way we resist chaos in perception and cognition, and impose some form of order upon the world. Central to this stemming from hegemony, is an idea about how things are and how they should be. But, argue Berger and Luckman, because the universe is not tidy, apparent anomalies and contradictions have to be avoided. One of the functions of culture, the anthropologist Mary Douglas (1970, p. 102), reminds us, is to categorize the symbolic universe into publicly recognized patterns:

> Culture in the sense of the public, standardised values of a community, mediates the experience of individuals. It provides in advance some basic categories, a positive pattern in which ideas and values are tidily ordered. And above all, it has authority, since each is induced to assent because of the assent of others. But its public character makes its characters more rigid.

Consequently, Douglas M. (1972), argues an anomaly is relegated to the categories of good or evil, and may therefore be rejected, ignored, abhorred, venerated or respected.[7] This is why morality as Douglas J. D. (1972), notes, has an object-like characteristic in Western society which makes the rules of morality seem apparently independent of free choice. They contain essential properties which make them necessary to all individuals, who attribute them some form of eternal, universal absolutism. They become perceived as part of social reality, unproblematic and absolute. This is why Scott (1972), argues deviancy has a dissident side, it challenges the clarity of the symbolic universe. Deviants are seen either as outsiders, recognized as having left the communal symbolic universe, or else as with immigrants, they are ascribed outsiders who participate in another symbolic universe which originated in a different culture. This group, as Berger and Luckman (1966, p. 91), remind us 'raise the question of power, since each symbolic universe must now deal with the problem of whose definition of reality will be made to stick'.

A subculture, then, may give an ideology and a form to deviancy which threatens the apparent consensus of the symbolic universe. The subculture makes sense to the potential recruit because of this challenge to the symbolic universe, and the would-be subcultural member identifies with the subculture. The recruit uses the values and imagery of the subculture to alter his own self-image. Glaser (1966), calls this differential identification.

> The image of behaviour as role-playing, borrowed from the theatre, presents people as directing their actions on the basis of their conceptions of how others see them. The choice of another from whose perspective we view our own behaviour is the process of identification. It may be with immediate others, or with distant and perhaps abstractly generalised others of our reference groups . . . . Acceptance by the group with which one identifies oneself and conceptions of persecution by other groups are among the most common and the least intellectual bases for rationalisation by criminals . . .

Actors, then, attracted by subcultural reference groups, select those within the parameters set by the social structure, which contain an attractive self-image, and an apparent solution to structural problems. In this way actors enter into subcultural interpretations of the dominant hegemony, which presents them with a different perspective of social reality, or sometimes a different social reality. As such they are important agents of secondary socialization. They introduce the values of the world outside work and school.

We have noted that the symbolic universe is not only a concrete form of social reality, but also a moral paradigm. Subcultures which confront or threaten the symbolic universe mean that the moral paradigm used to explain social reality has to be developed and adapted to deal with any anomaly. Subcultures tend to be deviant anomalies within the symbolic universe. They usually accept its definition of reality, but nevertheless are anomalies within it.

The development of an analytical framework for the study of subcultures

Becker (1963), has suggested that a fruitful way of considering deviancy is by the means of a 'moral career', by a processual analysis. Becker (1963, p. 23), argues:

> All causes do not operate at the same time, and we need a model which takes into account the fact that patterns of behaviour develop in orderly sequence . . . we must deal with a sequence of steps, of changes in the individual's

> behaviour and perspectives in order to understand the phenomenon.

This is obviously useful to the study of subcultures. However, Lemert (1951), indicates that we need to use this model in a wider context. We need to consider the following points:

1 The nature of the deviation, which includes information on the ways in which the deviant and the non-deviant differ, the subculture's relationship to the larger society, and the patterns of interaction within the subculture.

2 Societal reaction to the deviant. This involves the general reaction of public opinion to the deviant, and in particular the reaction of the mass media. This means also considering the effects of these on the subculture. Is it accepted, rejected or stigmatized?

3 The natural history of the deviant, including his socialization and the reaction of significant others to his subculturization. This means recording crisis points in the deviant career, such as changes in self-concept.

4 Social participation of the deviant, including his occupational status and income, and the effects on these that deviancy has.

Any theoretical framework needs to consider the process of becoming a member of a subculture, as well as the relationship the subculture has with society and the complex social and cultural relationships the two have. Cultural symbols are important, as Denzin (1970, p. 93), notes:

> Central to understanding behaviour is the range and variety of symbols and symbolic meanings shared, communicated and manipulated by interacting selves in shared situations.

De la Mater (1968), suggests that a study of deviance also needs to consider the genesis of a deviant role or actor, and how that is maintained, the reasons why an actor engages in the deviant role, and the maintenance of an actor's commitment to a deviant act. This introduces several social psychological processes. Taylor *et al.* (1973), indicate that a theory of deviance needs to consider both structural and social psychological levels. Such a theory needs to consider the wider origins and determinants of deviance found in wider societal conflicts, as well as the immediate origins of a particular deviance. Only against this background can the nature and setting of particular deviant actions be considered. It is also necessary to consider the immediate and wider origins of societal reaction, and the effect this has on the individual's commitment and actions within the subculture. Bearing in mind De la Mater's and Lemert's suggestions, and applying Taylor *et al.*'s critique, the following analysis is suggested for considering subcultures:

1 The nature of the subculture.

a The historical development of a subculture and its relationship to the structural problems of the wider socio-economic structure needs to be analysed.

b The style and imagery of the subculture need a hermeneutic perspective which considers the meaning these may have for potential recruits. The problems 'solved' by the subculture are important at this point.

2 Societal reaction to the subculture. An analysis is needed of mass media mediation of the nature of the subculture. The immediate effects of this in terms of significant others is necessary, as well as wide societal reaction in terms of moral entrepreneurs and public and official guardians of moral order.

3 A natural history of the moral career of the subcultural member needs to be constructed, in particular paying attention to Glaser and Strauss's (1971), 'status passage'. That is, that any moral career needs to be considered in sequences or stages, which have contingencies and problems affecting the actor.

Glaser and Strauss suggest several properties affecting status passage, such as how central it is to the actors. The degree of association and identification is important because subcultural attachment may be part-time or full-time. Where it is the former it is important adequately to socialize its young urban work force. The young have to be socialized into sets of values involving their place in the work force, the encouragement of an early family, marital life to assist in the reproduction of that work force, and conventional political and moral outlooks concerning the world and their place in it. If this does not occur, then the young work force is not programmed into regular work habits, with values suitable to strictly separated schedules of work and leisure. The young have to be bound into society first by values, and then by the responsibilities of maintaining dependants, and finally by financial commitment which means that the situation can take care of itself. One reason why the majority of people in a work force are docile is that whilst they may not have a great deal to gain ultimately by the prevailing social, economic structure, they have invested in it to the degree that they may have a great deal to lose if there is a sudden disruption of that system. This helps us to understand why the majority of young people pass through adolescence without any particularly long-term overtly deviant behaviour. They have invested a considerable part of themselves in the prevailing system, and as such to deviate overtly or to oppose it strongly would have no advantage to them, in terms of their immediate situation.

Young (1973), has argued that

> Deviant behaviour . . . is a meaningful attempt to solve the problems faced by a group or isolated individual – it is not a meaningless pathology.

The same argument can be made for collective deviant behaviour in the form of subcultures. In a complex society one needs to know how other non-subcultural elements of an actor's life are dealt with. Important variables therefore are entrance into, and exit from, the subculture, participation in and commitment to it and the effects of societal reaction at the individual level. The social visibility and the deviant or respectable nature of the subculture has a distinct effect upon self-image. Negative reactions from a public source can lead to a series of effects such as legal restriction to stigma, depending on the degree of negative societal reaction.

4 The social organization of the subculture. This involves two levels, the subculture's relation to the structure, and the effects this has on the social interaction within the subculture. The values, norms, symbols, imagery and behaviour of the subculture need to be considered in terms of their organization.
5 The persistence or discontinuance of the subculture. The subculture is unlikely to remain unaltered, and the altering boundaries of the subculture as well as its changing form need to be considered. One interesting element is the way in which subcultures may continue thematic focal concerns, yet reconstruct imagery so that the contemporary subculture addresses new interpretations of perennial problems, but with a totally different style which reflects specific problems of a particular generation.

Youth becomes a social problem – the development of subcultures as a concept in delinquency, and the rise of youth culture

One problem facing complex industrial societies is how different forms of cultural plurality can coexist. A plurality of cultures does not mean that various cultural groups have equal access to political power or to imposing their cultural patterns on society. The rise of interest of subcultures in the United States, can be traced to the fact that historically the United

States was faced with the problem of an immigrant labour force. Disparate groups from different ethnic origins, speaking different languages, with different cultural backgrounds, were not conducive to the development of a common class-consciousness. The ruling American elite, white Anglo-Saxon Protestants, attempted to impose their own culture. The immigrants, wishing to find a new identity in a new country were happy to absorb much of this culture, but as successive generations were to come up against structural contradictions, the Americanization of low status groups failed. The way in which this process failed among the descendants of African slaves in the ghettos is discussed by Valentine (1968) and the development of African culture in America in particular in jazz, is discussed by Keill (1966). The exogenous immigrant subcultures certainly helped to make the pluralism of the United States one of the most complex in the world, and this had an effect on the development of endogenous subcultures. Subcultures call into question the adequacy of the dominant cultural ideology. For example, what does the 'British way of life' offer to a black unemployed teenager, born in South London, whose experience of the country he was born in is framed in overt and covert racism? Youth itself, then, is not a problem although certain of its subcultures may be seen as a threat. There are problems for youth, however, created for example by the conscription of the majority of the young into the lower strata of a meritocratic, educational system, and then training them for occupations which are meaningless, poorly paid and uncreative.

The young are subject to the impact of occupational, educational and economic changes at particular times in history. These are experienced not only in class terms but also in generational terms. For these reasons, most subcultures of a distinctly deviant nature have been working-class youthful subcultures. This is the group most vulnerable to economic changes. These changes amplify contradictions in the structure which are experienced not only in class terms but also in generational terms. What may be in fact a traditional problem of class is experienced differently by the new generation. These differences may be small or large, but each generation has to work them through against the cultural background of their own generational peer group and its particular received subculture. Cohen P. (1972, p. 7), suggests

> You can distinguish three levels in the analysis of subcultures: one is the historical . . . which isolates the specific problematic of a particular class *fraction*, secondly the sub-

> systems, and the actual transformations they undergo from one subcultural 'moment' to another . . . thirdly . . . the way the subculture is actually lived out by those who are its bearers and supports.

The solution offered by the subculture is necessarily 'imaginary' argues Cohen. It is an ideological attempt to solve 'magically' real relations which cannot be otherwise solved. The particular time in a young person's life that a subculture has an impact is also notable. It occurs in the period between, or near to, the end of school career, usually at a point when education becomes perceived as meaningless in terms of a young person's work prospects, and lasts until marriage. Working-class subcultures in particular infuse into the bleak world of the working-class adolescent a period of intense emotion, colour and excitement during the brief respite between school and the insecurities of the early days of first working, and settling down into marriage and adulthood. It is left to the personal life of marriage to provide the emotional element of adult life after the brief encounter of a peer group subculture. For the middle class the subculture may last longer, because subcultures for them are often as Berger B. (1963b), comments 'youthful', in the sense that they are the domain of the young in outlook rather than merely the chronologically young.

It is proposed to consider the growth of subcultures in terms of their traditions. Matza (1962), suggested that youth is a time of rebelliousness, and that three particular forms that are attractive to youth are delinquency, radicalism and bohemianism. These modes of rebellion accentuate also Matza (1961), suggests, subterranean values. However, he fails to differentiate important intra-group differences in these traditions. In the next chapters we will consider subcultures in terms of the following traditions and themes. The study of youth can be subdivided into four main areas.

1 *Respectable youth*

Obviously youthful rebellion is relative and, as Berger (1963), suggests, most young people manage to pass through life without being involved in any teenage culture, or at least those aspects of it seen as deviant. They may be involved in fashions, but not necessarily life-styles. This group is seen by deviant subcultures as a negative reference group, the conformists, or straight youth.

2 Delinquent youth

Barnard (1961), has pointed out the important fact that teenagers reflected the class cultures of their parents and that class pervaded all aspects of the teenage world in terms of its cultural elements. E. A. Smith (1962), also stressed this in his study of American youth culture. Delinquent subcultures studied have tended to be working class, usually affecting young adolescent males. Males have usually been involved with illegal activities such as theft or violence or vandalism, and females with sexual misbehaviour which has been used by courts to take them under legal protection orders. The bulk of empirical studies are concerned with this group.

3 Cultural rebels

This group tend to be involved in subcultures in the fringes of the bohemian tradition. They are on the peripheries of the literary-artistic world, being adherents to it rather than artists. They tend to be middle class, and where young subcultures are involved they tend to have middle-class educations.

4 Politically militant youth

This group are in the radical tradition of politics. The scope of politics may be vast, from environmental and community politics to direct militant action. They may be factions of political groups or a broad mass movement like the peace movements of the fifties. They may be ethnic groups, such as the Young Lords or the Black Panthers, broad-based civil rights movements, issue-oriented groups such as the anti-Vietnam war groups, pacifists, student groups, political factions or environmentalists.

These traditions may of course overlap, especially in terms of their tactics and cultural traditions. However, it is proposed to examine these traditions in detail.

To summarize, it is argued that the study of subcultures is useful in the field of collective deviance and that subcultures provide particular functions for the young.

1 They offer a solution, albeit at a 'magical' level, to certain structural problems created by the internal contradictions of a socio-economic structure, which are collectively experienced. The problems are often class problems experienced generationally.

2 They offer a culture, from which can be selected certain cultural elements such as style, values, ideologies and life-style. These can be used to develop an achieved identity outside of the ascribed identity offered by work, home or school.
3 As such, an alternative form of social reality is experienced, rooted in a class culture, but mediated by neighbourhood, or else a symbolic community transmitted through the mass media.
4 Subcultures offer through their expressive elements a meaningful way of life during leisure, which has been removed from the instrumental world of work.
5 Subcultures offer to the individual solutions to certain existential dilemmas. Particularly, this involves the bricolage of youthful style to construct an identity outside of work or school. This is particularly employed by young males for reasons I will discuss later, and therefore subcultures have tended to be masculinist subcultures, especially working-class subcultures.

Adolescence and early adulthood is a period for reshaping values and ideas, and exploring one's relationship to the world, and is therefore an important source of secondary socialization. The young can explore, within the parameters of their immediate class situation, certain elements of achieved versus ascribed identity.

Analyses of youth culture and subcultures can be summarized by dividing them into generational and structural explanations. The first analysis is concerned with the continuity/discontinuity of inter-generational values, and the second with the relationship of youth to social class, the mode of production and its consequent social relations. The generational explanation has focused on age as a specific factor, and is basically concerned with functionalist and neo-functionalist explanations about socialization. As Woods (1977), suggests, generational theories are summed up in the structural-functional models of Eisenstadt and Parsons, and the generation unit model of Mannheim. Society is formed of inter-related subsystems, and the educational system prepares actors for a place in the economic system, which reflects the stratification system, which in turn participates in the political system. Inter-generational conflict (the 'generation gap') is a socialization dysfunction, resulting from weak integration between society and age groups. Age is the basis of social and cultural characteristics of actors. Youth, especially adolescence, is a preparatory stage for an adulthood based on the division of labour. In pre-literate societies adolescence is replaced by rites which mark the end of childhood and the beginning of adulthood, but in industrial societies transition is complicated. Youth is not central to the economy and has become isolated as a dependent, economic liability. Youth for Eisenstadt (1956, p. 28), is 'a transitory phase between the world of childhood and the adult world'. Youth groups in the structural-functionalist model appear at moments of 'disintegrating' with a 'reintegrating' function. They do not seek to change society, but to re-enter it. Parsons has also taken a similar view towards youth culture (Parsons, 1954), seeing it as particular to American society, with an emphasis of a possible dysfunctional nature, of having a good time, emphasizing 'its recalcitrance to the pressure of adult expectations and discipline'. Mannheim (1952), prefers a generation unit; within a youthful generation are groups which 'work up the material of their common experience in different specific ways' (Mannheim, 1952, p. 304). The collective experience of specific historical moments is more intense during rapid social change. The more rapid the change, the greater the gap between generational sets of consciousness, but for Mannheim youthful response contains positive and creative qualities. In this sense Mannheim allows for more impact on social change than traditional structural-functionalists. It has also been argued that disadvantaged youth (working class) is not anti the prevailing social order, but seeks a place within it, whilst middle-class groups actually seek social change (Woods, 1977), and that therefore the Mannheimian perspective has been more useful because it allows for a structural context. A functionalist approach seems to have been implicitly followed by official youth programmes which have appeared in times of crisis. These are not only the Scouts and the Duke of Edinburgh's Award, but also state schemes. The Manpower Services Commission set up in 1974 (under the Employment and Training Act 1973) implemented the 1975 Job Creation Programme, creating 'temporary jobs for those who would otherwise be unemployed' with an emphasis on jobs 'of value to the community', as well as subsidizing employers to find work of a temporary nature for youth under twenty.

Elements of Mannheim's historico-political moment and generational experiences are present in class-based explanations. This traces back subcultures and youth cultures to the relation between the class 'parent culture', hegemony and contradictions in the socio-economic structure. This involves a material as well as an ideological dimension. These issues are discussed later, and involve community and the local economic system, class-based cultures and values, and traditional class problems experienced generationally at particular historical moments. Youth is conceptualized as a particular generational response to a wider class problem involved with structural elements such as housing, employment, future prospects and wages. As we shall also see, these problems have other dimensions for subordinate groups which are in addition to class and age, such as sex and colour. These have a potential across class lines, but any collective solution will ultimately be complicated by class.

Not all subcultures are concerned with age, obviously. For the young, however (and of course not all the young are involved in subcultures), subcultures assist them to deal with both structural and individual problems. Some of them, especially in working-class youth subcultures, are transient solutions to specific problems. Others are of a more enduring nature leading to social change. Subcultures address themselves to structural problems, and implicitly contain a critique of society, admittedly often inarticulate and tangential. This has been explained away, especially in neo-functional models, as the problems of a transitional phase in adolescence.

> The concept of a 'transitional phase' in adolescence is often employed as a palliative for society's functional problems of recruiting and integrating youth into adult worlds; if it is merely 'a stage they're going through', then adults frankly need not confront the problems their behaviour raises, because after all, 'they'll grow out of it'.

as Berger (1963a, p. 407), notes. If, however, some of them are not going to grow out of it, but develop a pride in what they are, feeling little in common with the laws of a society they feel alienated from, then there is a serious problem for that society. Subcultures offer something to working-class youth that middle-class youth sought in the university. This is a moratorium, a temporal and geographical space, which can be used to test out questions about the world and their relationship to it. Identities and ideas can be experimented with, and possibilities for social change considered. Subcultures are rebellious, and usually no more than this. But they do contain the seeds of a more radical dissent which could erupt into an action threatening society.[7] It is this which moral entrepreneurs sense. Where this rebellion has a moral edge to it, it threatens the hegemony of the state. The reaction to this is a cry for law and order, and as long as this rebellion can be reduced to a social problem, or an adolescent phase, then it can be successfully excluded from adult society.

Notes

1 For brevity, I shall use the masculine pronoun and adjective when discussing the social actor, especially as most empirical studies of youthful subcultures are about males. The feminine gender could be substituted in cases save where I am discussing females and where I therefore use the feminine gender.

2 This strategy is imaginatively described in Isherwood C. (1974), where the novelist brilliantly examines the experience of an ageing, expatriate homosexual whose lover has recently been killed. Individual dissociation in literature is further considered in Brake M. (1978).

3 Hegemony is used in Gramsci's sense of a ruling group imposing its moral, political and cultural values on the majority. This has implications for the prevailing concepts of 'normality' and 'human nature'. Commonsense thinking about the social world becomes 'naturalised', that is, non-problematic because it pre-empts the notion of social change. This is broken, as Gramsci (1973, p. 366) notes

> when we succeed in introducing a new morality in conformity with a new conception of the world.

4 These processes in the phenomenon of mental illness have of course been dealt with by Laing R. D. (1966) and Becker E. (1964).

5 I have discussed elsewhere (Brake, 1974) how this process acted within gay subcultures. The societal reaction generated by mass media coverage of paedophiles during the autumn of 1977 caused many respectable homophile groups to insist that paedophiles should not be confused with 'real' homosexuals.

6 This form of cultural analysis has been valuably pursued by the Centre for Contemporary Cultural Studies at the University of Birmingham, and its findings can be found in Hall and Jefferson (1976). See also Mungham and Pearson (1976), Murdock and Phelps (1972), Murdock (1974) and Murdock and McCron (1976) in Hall and Jefferson, *op. cit.*

7 These groups contain a potential political force, but it must be noted that they can be either extreme left or extreme right wing in their affiliations.

2 Street-wise – the delinquent subculture in sociological theory in Britain and the United States

During the early 1920s, there was a considerable interest in youth as an urban social problem. Both psychology and education had previously shown concern with youth, but in the field of developmental psychology and pedagogy. The British psychologist Cyril Burt (1929), took the Durkheimian view that delinquency was normal, but that it was determined by a multiplicity of causes, involving an interaction between hereditary factors and environmental influences. Whilst there was no generable observable cause, poverty was stressed, but for Burt this was not so much material poverty, but moral poverty, particularly in the area of family life. He also noted an important factor, and that was that the delinquent was a poor scholar, probably due less to low intelligence than to under-achievement. The anthropologist Margaret Mead (1928), introduced a note of cultural relativism, to theories of adolescence with evidence that the traditional stage of storm and stress seemed to be a Western phenomena. There was the drawing together then of the relationship between a social problem, and a social situation of cultural and psychological poverty, and a concentration on adolescence as a social phenomena. The Depression meant that youth became perceived even more as a social area of concern, in particular youth residing in the slums, the ghettos and the down-town neighbourhoods. The work of the Chicago school was to develop ethnographic studies of the relationship between neighbourhoods, life-styles and youth. These were through the work of other theorists, to raise questions about the problems of material deprivation and cultural pluralism in contemporary industrial society.

The Chicago school and the social ecology of the city

During the 1930s considerable interest was shown at the University of Chicago about the features of urban life-styles, and they adopted a mixture of urban documentation, crusading reformism and detailed empiricism based mainly on the interview as a research method. This reflected one of their major scholars, Park, training as a journalist. The model adopted was based on plant ecology, and adapted to the city. Human beings lived together in a state of symbiosis, similar to plant life, with different species living in the same habitat. The social scientist's task was to seek out the well-ordered, mutually advantageous equilibrium known in plant life as the biotic balance, which was postulated to be present in urban life. As Matza (1969a), suggests, the Chicago school were aware of social diversity, but as they were committed to a model of society as in equilibrium, they were faced with the problem of resolving disequilibrium without an appeal to the psychologistic notion of individual pathology. They resolved this by introducing the concept of social pathology – social disorganization. In certain urban neighbourhoods, the balance between competition and co-operation has upset the biotic balance, so that the values and cultural patterns of these neighbourhoods seemed socially disorganized. Causal features could be, for example, unchecked migration into the neighbourhood. The social system of the neighbourhood is thrown out of balance by urban growth, so that social solidarity and social control break-down.

What had been recognized, is that the slums and ghettos had their own social structures with specific norms patterns of behaviour. Urban expansion had had an effect on city areas, so that the poor were ghettoized, and the respectable artisans joined the lower middle class in the suburban areas of large cities. Park R. E. *et al.* (1925), attempted to isolate those features of urban life which ecologically encouraged delinquency. Park used the concept 'natural area' to attempt to trace relationships between specific geographical areas, and the physical structure and social organization of those areas. The 'natural area' was a small residential area with recognized boundaries and inhabited by distinct cultural groups. A city was a collection of these natural areas, which became divisible into zones, extending concentrically from the centre to the periphery, reflecting industrialization and urban sprawl. Morris (1957, p. 71), writes

> Originally the population of the city lived around the business central district, but this area was the most obvious choice for the location of the new commercial and industrial enterprises. As industry moved in, the wealthier inhabitants moved out, and as the area declined in terms of desirability

> of residence, this depressed rentals so it became the obvious choice for newcomers to the city, usually poor immigrants in search of housing at lowest possible cost. The respectable artisans were as a result encouraged to move out, and they in turn began to displace the well to do who moved further out still.

Where an area was in the throes of transition from one phase to another, these were 'interstitial areas'. The social ecology model was adopted by scholars interested in gangs and delinquency (Thrasher, 1927; Shaw and McKay, 1927), or in the social organization of street corner groups, such as Whyte (1943), who carried on the tradition in the post-war period. Thrasher focused on the urban gang, found in the changing urban areas as a result of social disorganization. He looked at a particular area of downtown Chicago, the Loop district which he describes as (1927, p. 20)

> The central tripartite area of the gang occupies what is often called the 'Poverty Belt' – a region characterised by deteriorating neighbourhoods, shifting populations and the mobility and disorganisation of the slum . . . . As better residential districts recede before encroachments of business and industry, the gang develops as one manifestation of the economic, moral and cultural frontier which marks the interstice.

Methodologically Thrasher felt it necessary to enter the world of the delinquent, using his definition of the situation to understand two things. One was the delinquent's serious endeavour to make sense of his life, and the other, to distinguish the fantasy life of the gang (which was only too often confused with reality). Although it is only implicit in his approach, Thrasher emphasized the meaning that the life-style of the gang and the neighbourhood had for the slum corner boy. In slum life, the street is a crowded, exciting and dangerous place, where children daily perceive illegal activities. Confrontation with adult authority quickly forges the street play group into a gang. For Thrasher the adventure and play activities of delinquency were important, often motivated by nothing more complex than hedonism, a factor often overlooked for more complex causes. In working-class neighbourhoods the street is of great cultural importance, as is the market and the public house. Informal interaction offers a social life to the old or lonely, gossip and rumour provide information and drama. The street is the backdrop against which a scenario can be constructed and performed. The street is the playground of the delinquent, and where there is little else to take pride in, it can become a defensible territory. It offers escape from adult surveillance, and an apprenticeship in peer group deviancy. Brown (1967), describes his own childhood in such an environment, in the streets of Harlem, and the desperate attempts by busy ghetto mothers to keep their children in front of the house to control the corrupting influence of street life. Thrasher's view that the street was an adventurous free area, in contrast to the antithetical constraining agencies of social control, seen as weak, dull and unattractive by kids, was shared by Shaw and McKay (1927). They argued that delinquency rates in an area remain constant, despite substantial alterations in the composition of their populations. This Durkheimian perspective was explained by the view that delinquency was not determined by the physical location of an area, but that it was inherent in a community with a competing system of contradictory values, and weak community and family controls. They argue (Shaw and McKay, 1927, p. 26):

> The common element (among social factors highly correlated with juvenile delinquency) is social disorganisation, or the lack of organised community effort to deal with these conditions.

Important seminal elements are to be found in the social ecology model. There is the important link between neighbourhood, culture and community, although these are not spelt out with any sophistication. There is the point that whilst there may be a delinquent tradition in an area, this tradition is not radically different from more respectable traditions, a point elaborated later by Matza (1964). There is the hint of a differential association thesis in Shaw and McKay, that where there exists opportunities to learn deviant actions over respectable ones, there will be a variable delinquency rate. This occurs according to them in the disorganized neighbourhood, a point Merton (1938), was to link with a disjunction between goals desired by, but unobtainable to the poor, which Cloward and Ohlin (1960), were to link directly to the delinquent subculture.

Criticisms of the social ecology model. The problems of pluralism – class, conflict and power

Several criticisms have been made of the social ecology model. Downes (1966, p. 71), points out the tautology of the social disorganization thesis:

> the rate of delinquency in an area (is seen as) being the chief criterion for its 'social disorganisation', which in turn was held to account for the delinquency rate.

The emphasis on diversity runs into a problem, because of the suggestion that the socially disorganized neighbourhood lacks a coherent set of cultural norms. They resolved this by developing a theory according to Taylor *et al.* (1973, p. 115), where

> each specific area could be seen to represent the territorial base of a differing tradition. Social disorganisation became translated into differential social disorganisation.

The thesis suggests that a particular neighbourhood forms the territorial base of a type of differential social organization, a theme found in A. K. Cohen's (1958) typology of semi-professional thief, drug addict and conflict oriented subcultures, and Cloward and Ohlin's (1960), similar typology. These pluralistic elements are present in differential social organisation, but absent in the social disorganization model which takes a structural functionalist stance, opens up the possibility of conflict within a neighbourhood. The conflict may be present in two areas – first in the local political economy over scarce resources, such as housing, income, education, health and employment, and second, as we shall see, over cultural interpretations and ideological solutions to structural contradictions arising from policy over the first conflict.

This interpretation of the possibility of the differential organization model means we need to consider the material basis of this in a pluralistic society. Bourgeois theories of pluralism confuse the empirical presence of several cultures and subcultures based on class and ethnicity, with political pluralism. They make the assumption that these groups have the possibility to wield similarly important influence on political, economic and social policy. It does not follow that because there is a culturally rich and varied differentiation of social life in a complex, industrial society that the various communities have any basic influence on major political and economic decisions. The formation of interest and pressure groups is cited as a necessary part of the democratic process. The economy of Britain and the United States is not however distributed pluralistically. Concentration of material wealth in the United States is in a few corporations (Edwards *et al.*, 1972; Christoffel *et al.*, 1970), whilst in Britain a similar concentration is among wealthy elites (Atkinson, 1975; Reid, 1977; Urry and Wakeford, 1973 and Westergaard and Resler, 1975). This gives an approximation in the United States of 1 per cent owning 40 per cent of the national wealth, and in Britain 2 per cent owning 55 per cent. A minority who are related by wealth, corporation interests and often kinship, sharing a common background can hardly be presented as one interest group among many others. A ruling class or influential elite would seem more appropriate, and as Quinney argues (Taylor *et al.*, 1973, p. 194):

> Whilst pluralists may suggest that there are many diverse and conflicting interests among groups in the upper class, what is ignored is the fact that members of the ruling class work within a common framework in the formulation of public policy. Superficially groups within the ruling class may differ on some issues. But in general they share common interests, and they can exclude members of other classes from the political process entirely.

The political, ideological and economic control of the ruling class extend, admittedly in a diffuse and mediated way, into the local urban structure. The ecological model of 'natural areas' is improved by a consideration of this effect in public policy, the local economy and political system, and the exercise of social control through the police and magistracy. A stable social order is in the interests of the ruling class, and essential to this is a docile and contented work force. Criminal law is important in this, because it is recognized as making an appeal above the interests of specific groups to the neutrality of justice. Deviancy and delinquency can be separated off, as can any dissident elements as dysfunctional to law and order, and thus used to deal symptomatically with a problem which may exist structurally. In an empirical study of Glasgow's Easterhouse, Armstrong and Wilson (1973), have suggested a relationship between city politics and delinquent neighbourhoods. The built environment combined with local demography to structure the pattern of youth relationships, which already had a long history of their own in Glasgow. Factors such as policing the area from outside the district, the official designation and consequent stigmatization of Easterhouse as a 'problem area', and the social visibility of local street corner groups escalated problems of police control and local youth. The problem of violence and vandalism became a local party political issue with vast media involvement. This fed back to local youth an image of their neighbourhood's reputation and their part in it, leading to a situation of deviancy amplification, kept alive by local political controversy over delinquency. This is in direct contrast to Shaw and McKay's conviction that a delinquent neighbourhood is not the result of local social control. In fact the local corporation and the local authority are directly involved in Britain in what is seen as best strategy for dealing with what is conceptualized as an essentially local problem, and law enforcement directly reflects this. Morris (1957, p. 57), has suggested that police attitude to offenders is importantly related to neighbourhood. Local neighbourhoods and communities have a definite reputation, depending on their class and ethnic composition, and local administrative decisions, subject to middle-class pressure groups, directly reflect these. Indeed, it is at precisely this level that pressure groups have an effect (see C. Wright Mills, 1957), rather than at top decision-making level. Local ratepayers bring pressure to bear where particular community projects are to be sited (for example, centres for alcoholics or the mentally handicapped), or which housing estates are to be used for 'problem families'. Neighbourhoods are ranked in the public mind according to social desirability, and this affects property prices and investment: once stigmatized, the self-fulfilling prophecy operates with a district's reputation living on, as with Glasgow's Gorbals, long after it has been redeveloped.

High rates of criminality and delinquency in down-town areas contain an interplay between respectable and deviant values. Whyte (1943), found in his Chicago slum, that the street corner boy subculture was not simply delinquent. The street corner was a social milieu for the local boys to organize their social life during unemployment. Infractions of the law occurred, but these were situations where the law was seen as irrelevant. Delinquency in these areas is a normal form of behaviour, supported by a mixed set of values, giving rise to a differential learning situation framed in a normative context differing from respectable middle-class values, and allowing for apprenticeships into deviant careers as well as respectable ones.

The social meaning of territory in the working-class community

Following from the social ecology model, but ignored by it, is the social meaning that territory has in the local working-class neighbourhood. Physical space is not merely a simple territorial imperative, but symbolic of a whole life-style. Central to it is the status of the local neighbourhood but this needs to be understood in the context of the wider struggle for decent housing.

The inner city tends to be inhabited by impoverished, stigmatized groups, often from ethnic minorities and the immigrant work force. However the zoning suggested in the social ecology model is far from new. Engels (1962), writing of Manchester in 1844, notes zoning in

> all Manchester proper, all Salford and Hulme . . . are all unmixed working people's quarters, stretching like a girdle, averaging a mile and a half around the commercial district. Outside, beyond the girdle, lives the upper and middle bourgeoisie in remoter villages with gardens . . . in free, wholesome, country air, in fine comfortable homes, passed every half hour or quarter hour by omnibuses going into the city. And the finest part of the arrangement is that members of the money aristocracy can take the shortest road through the middle of all the labouring districts without ever seeing that they are in the midst of the grimy misery that lurks to the right and left . . . they suffice to conceal from the eyes of the wealthy men and women of strong stomachs and weak nerves the misery and grime which form the complement of their wealth.

G. S. Jones (1971), reminds us that in Victorian London, the fear of disease, and a repugnance concerning the poor caused them to be ghettoized, which meant that already impoverished boroughs had to pay a larger poor relief, whilst the wealthier ones avoided any obligation to the poor. Large thoroughfares and wide open spaces separated off the poor. In areas of high rents the poor cannot afford transportation, so where they reside is also dictated by access to employment, as in the Northern textile towns. No competition to the rich, they reside in unfashionable districts, unless these districts become perceived as possessing a picturesque charm, which puts up the prices. The last to arrive in a working-class neighbourhood are usually relegated to the ranks of the 'unrespectable' working class. In modern cities these tend to be immigrant workers, who because of a desire to preserve their culture, reside in a particular area which consequently they find difficult to leave. They become blamed for the deterioration of that district, as Downes (1966, p. 217), in Stepney, in London's East End, suggests:

> Virtually barred from council flats, the 'blacks' inevitably resort to this deteriorating property. Local white residents link the onset of deterioration with the arrival of the blacks, and blame the newcomers for the deterioration.

Rex and Moore (1967), in their study of the relations between housing scarcity and racism in Birmingham, favour a 'class struggle for housing' in the Weberian sense, rather than the social ecology model. The situation described in Downes was complicated in Birmingham by the use of political power by interest groups to gain access to housing. This disadvantaged the new immigrants, who, relegated to deteriorating neighbourhoods, became blamed for their decay.

Territory also has an importance symbolically in youth subcultures among the working class. Pride in the local territory becomes an expression of conservatism, with the protection of it flaring into prejudice and racism. Symbolically it can also manifest itself in the defence by the violent of its 'turf', or in aggressive support for local football teams. A typical example was the concern over Millwall F.C. in 1978. This local London team developed a reputation for violence among its supporters which seriously began to affect its gate. Three local youth groups made up the terrace fans who caused concern. The eldest were a group of young men, the 'F Team': they were seen as a bunch of 'nutters' who got involved in 'rucking', and would on away games visit other London home grounds with the intention of fighting. The 'Halfway Line' were teenage hard-core supporters who followed the home and away games, and were prepared to 'steam in' on the 'aggro', and finally the youngest group, who were a mini-version of the 'Halfway Line'. A career was possible through support on the terraces, from age ten to about thirty years old, with a pride taken less in the team (a rather indifferent local one) but in the fans' ability to fight, and the claim 'Millwall don't run'. 'Steaming in' on other fans was a test of support for the territory. This sense of local pride, if undermined by the decay of the district and its local economy, is replaced by a conservatism of a working-class form, which can take a highly reactionary stance against outsiders.

The statistical presence of delinquency in working-class neighbourhoods

One main argument favouring the social disorganization model was the high level of delinquency in down-town neighbourhoods. Certainly official statistics suggest a close relation between delinquency and young working-class males. Box (1971, Chapters 3; 6), discusses this, citing Lander (1954), who found home ownership and ethnicity correlating to delinquency,

Bordua (1967a), who found home ownership the most important variable, with overcrowding and education next and Polk (1957), who found a correlation between delinquency and ethnicity and hence poverty. Even Gordon (1967), who disputes these findings on computation grounds, finds a correlation between social class and delinquency. An important element, though, is law enforcement policy. In all 'rough' districts there are complaints by working-class youth about police surveillance, or 'heavy manners' as young West Indians call it. Police on the job screen possible offenders, and this is related to particular types of youth. In America, Goldman (1969), found 65 per cent of blacks and 34 per cent of whites referred to court, although the rate evened out for more serious offences. The London Metropolitan Police in 1978 suggested that 42 per cent of theft was by young blacks. Piliavin and Briar (1964), found demeanour an important element in police-juvenile interaction, with those being arrested who were older, black, 'greasers' or undeferential. The study suggested that the police concentrated on the urban ghetto and indiscriminately harassed citizens, a complaint now heard in the ghettos of London and Birmingham. Werthman and Piliavin (1967), noted the importance of territory, with gang boys seeing the streets as their 'turf' and the police as enemies enforcing a law supported and produced by an external power structure which suppressed minorities and promoted racism. Their contempt for the police explained their high arrest rate. Bordua (1967a) suggested that arrest rates reflect organizational pressures and procedures which vary not only between police forces but within them. The juvenile bureau was an important variable. Pepinsky (1976), found that patrolmen develop informal rules on the job to deal with ambiguities, and that these operate on a legal 'open or shut' basis to obtain convictions more easily. Cicourel (1968) in an important study showed that structure and ideology of particular organizations, such as the police force, probation service and social work agencies, are important in negotiating with offenders concerning their disposal, and that the seriousness of the offence is influenced by the class origins and home conditions of the offender. It was the organizational influences of day-to-day policy implementation which, Cicourel (1968, p. 329) considered,

> determine the nature of social control, the judicial procedures that are likely to follow, and the kinds of delinquent or non delinquent products officially recorded or not recorded.

Differential identification in the deprived neighbourhood

If, as is suggested above, cultural pluralism occurs in deprived neighbourhoods, it is important to consider the effects on the actor of this. In subcultural theory, Sutherland and Cressy (1966), postulate a learning theory model, based on operant conditioning in psychology, and extended to a wider sociological base. Briefly they argue that where there exists an excess of association with deviant actors, especially in conjunction with intimate positive reference groups, motives are learned which rationalize anti-social behaviour. This mixture of learning theory and symbolic interaction may explain how an ideology is brought into consciousness and even learned, but it fails to explain legitimacy of motives. Matza (1969b) has criticized it for its lack of humanistic purpose and meaning. Actors, he argues (Matza, 1969b, p. 107), 'intentionally move in search of meaning as well as nourishment', and what Sutherland has failed to appreciate is (Matza, *op. cit.*, p. 107), 'the interpenetration of cultural worlds – the symbolic availability of various ways of life everywhere'.

Glaser has made a more humanistic approach in his extension of differential association, as Sutherland called his theory, to incorporate symbolic interaction with cultural pluralism (Glaser, 1966). This indicates the use of imagery and role-taking in the construction of identity. Glaser suggests that during their lifetimes, most actors identify with both criminal and non criminal persons, and that this can be used to construct a theory of differential identification which Glaser (1966, p. 434), suggests is,

> In essence is that a person pursues criminal behaviour to the extent that he identifies with real or imaginary persons from whose perspectives his criminal behaviour seems acceptable. Such a theory focuses attention on the interaction in which choice models occur, including the individual's interaction with himself in rationalising his conduct.

Glaser has taken note of Shibutani's (1955), point that reference groups are not only real, but mythical or imaginary also. It is less what subcultures are which attracts adolescents, but what they fantasize them to be. This introduces also what Giddens (1976), calls 'slippage' into subcultures. Slippage occurs when (Giddens, 1976, p. 162), concepts are

> appropriated by those whose conduct they were originally coined to analyse, and hence to become integral features of that conduct.

The purpose and meaning of subcultures are important in the construction of an identity which is to evade the ascribed identity components in adolescence. Glaser (1966, p. 435), notes

> The image of behaviour as role-playing, borrowed from the theatre presents people as directing their actions on the basis of their conceptions of how others see them. The choice of another from whose perspective we view our own behaviour is the process of identification. It may be with immediate others, or with distant and perhaps abstractly generalised others of our reference groups.

Possible roles within the subculture, 'careers' on which to base the roles, and the meaning of the subculture are essential elements in constructing an identity. For example, the official school role of pupil may be rejected by an adolescent who has a semi-conscious recognition of a structural problem, the failure of school to meet the adolescent's needs due to contradictions in the actual purpose of education. This is experienced as school being perceived as meaningless. The deviant subculture appears as a positive reference group (just as the pupil subculture appears as a negative reference group), which offers symbolic and social support, with a counter-ideological stance to that of school. An achieved alternative identity can be constructed from subcultural elements which is an alternative to the ascribed school pupil role.

Plummer (1975), has noted important links between the construction of identity and subcultures. In the case of the homosexual subculture, there is a sensitization towards a future identity, heightened in the homosexual case of feeling different. This feeling develops a heightened self-awareness about subcultures which appears to offer a fit between one's desired identity and the present situation. This he calls signification, and it is followed by subculturization, the awareness of and entry into a specific subculture. Stabilization of identity follows supported by the normative system of the subculture. Stabilization is obviously more temporary in youth subcultures, but the model is useful. The contribution that subcultural theory has to symbolic interaction theory has developed beyond role theory and reference group theory, to considering the complicated links in the development of identity, and the important part various subcultures play in the construction of social reality.

Anomie theory and its influence on subcultural studies

Anomie is predominantly a Durkheimian concept which argues that a condition of normlessness arises when a disruption of the social order occurs (Durkheim, 1951). People's aspirations rise in this situation so that they are no longer controlled by the collective social order, and hence become aspirations beyond the possibility of fulfilment. The source of anomie is to be found in the strain arising between the collective moral authority ('collective conscience') and individual interests. Anomie arises where the 'collective conscience' fails to control individual aspirations. Horton (1964) suggests that this is radical conservatism. Durkheim argues that an equitable division of labour which permits meritocracy efficiently would create social altruism and disinterest, reducing institutionalized individual self-interest. Merton (1957), subtly changes Durkheim's meaning, implying a consensual notion of success. This is never defined beyond the crudely material. Merton sees anomie as endemic in American society, but moves away from Durkheim's radicalism about inequality and self-disinterest. Horton argues (1964, p. 284)

> Merton's anomie differs from that of Durkheim in one crucial respect – in its identification with the very groups and values which Durkheim saw as the prime source of anomie in industrial societies. Morality means to Durkheim . . . social goals obeyed out of disinterest and altruism, not self interest and egoism. To maximise opportunities for achieving success would in no way end anomie . . .

The roots of Merton's anomie lie in a structural strain, generated by differential access to opportunity structures. Such a strain is dangerous to society (Merton, 1938, p. 678):

> The consequences of such structural inconsistency are psychopathology of personality, and/or anti social conduct and/or revolutionary activities.

A major social danger is to posit the ideology of egalitarianism concerning internalized success goals, where there is no matching opportunity structures. Merton posits a model of adaptations (predominantly dysfunctional) as a response to the failure in society of both goals and means being acceptable to its inhabitants. This overlooks the complex diversity of values and actions in the modern industrial state, and is naïve about the relations between the state and the political economy. Anomie is a facet for Merton, of the built-in dissatisfactions due to the fostering of the need to consume, which entails ever-rising expectations which cannot be met. Merton's view that all members of a society have accepted material gain as a dominant value can be challenged. They may understand that money is essential to the maintenance of their life-style, but that it is not to argue that they have the same cultural goals.

Merton's influence on subcultural theory is however considerable. One notable response was the work of a major subcultural theorist, A. K. Cohen (1955). Whilst critical of Merton, Cohen remained outside the social ecology approach of the Chicago school. Cohen argues (1955), that Mertonian modes of adaptation to structural strain fail to account for 'non utilitarian, malicious and negativistic' behaviour in working-class delinquent subcultures. Delinquents steal, thus appreciating money, yet throw away what they steal, or concentrate on things of little value. Motivation of a delinquent nature is found not in anomie, but in adolescent status problems. Status occurs in a middle-class normative context. The paths to upward mobility are guarded by the educational system, which is apparently objective, but is dominated by the 'middle-class measuring rod'. The paradox for working-class youth is that, despite an adherence to working-class culture, they face 'middle-class criteria of status' which ensures they internalize middle-class values. Because they are excluded by limited opportunity structures from obtaining middle-class success, the delinquent subculture evolves as a 'collective solution'. This is particularly true for young working-class males, because their success depends more on achievement. For some working-class boys, there is the 'college boy' adaptation, the pursuit of middle-class education and life-style. There is also the 'corner boy' adaptation which allows a minimally criminal adaptation to working-class values but is not divorced from middle-class approval. The subculture for the young working-class male is 'a way of looking at the world'; it is 'a way of life that has become traditional', with the delinquent subculture developing behaviour which is 'negativistic, malicious and non-utilitarian', committed to 'short run hedonism'. By a process of 'reaction formation' the delinquent subculture inverts the middle-class value system, and offers a 'collective solution' in which, Cohen (1955, p. 28), considers that, 'the delinquent's conduct is right by the standards of his subculture, precisely because it is wrong by the norms of the larger culture.'

A social psychological process ('reaction formation') is used in response to a structural problem, which offers security 'against an inner threat to his defences'. The impossibility of avoiding the 'middle-class measuring rod' with its consequent threat to status and implied threats to working-class culture, cause delinquents to participate in a commonly experienced problem to evolve a collective solution.

Cohen was considerably criticized. Kitsuse and Dietrich (1959), argued that Cohen failed to demonstrate that working-class boys cared about evaluation, and that their delinquent instrumentality was underestimated. Bordua (1961), felt Cohen overestimated the non-utilitarian aspects, and underemphasized family dynamics. Miller (1958), argued that delinquent subcultures reflected less a reaction to loss of status than an extension of working-class 'focal concerns' which culturally differed from those of the middle class. For Miller delinquency was a product of lower-class culture, and it was lower-class culture which had an effect on delinquent subcultures rather than a reaction to middle-class culture. Miller suggested that 'focal concerns' were identifiable in working-class culture which he (1958, p. 7), defines as

> areas or issues which command widespread and persistent attention and a high degree of emotional involvement.

He identifies as focal concerns, trouble, toughness, smartness, excitement, fate, autonomy, and that the acting-out of these automatically violated dominant norms. He implies then that there is a close integration into the parent culture (working-class culture) of the delinquent subculture, with a focus on certain concerns, although Valentine (1968), suggests that his focal concerns can also be found in the middle class.

Cohen (Cohen and Short, 1958), replied to his critics by agreeing that there is more than one working-class delinquent subcultural type. A subcultural group of working-class delinquents ('parent male subculture') generates especially in schools, three types of subculture:

1 the conflict-oriented subculture, whose primary interest was violence.
2 the drug addict subculture, developed as a utilitarian means of obtaining access to drugs.
3 the semi-professional thief subculture, which in mid-adolescence provided a pathway into organized crime.

The emphasis remained on the parent male subculture defined

as (Cohen and Short, 1958, p. 22) 'probably the most common variety in this country – indeed it might be called the "garden variety" or delinquent subculture.'

Cohen's arguments are debatable. If working-class boys have internalized middle-class values (and the extent of this is an empirical question) they must also have internalized working-class values. It would seem that a delinquent subculture would not negate middle-class norms, but adapt them in some form, together with working-class norms. What does emerge is a central concern with masculinity, the ability to 'handle yourself' has a different meaning in working-class subcultures. It tends to emphasize fighting, whilst in middle-class cultures it emphasizes articulation, yet both can be central to masculine ways of relating to the world. It is true that Cohen is seminal to much subcultural theory, and he makes the connection between the neighbourhood and the subculture as a solution. His influence is distinct in later subcultural theory. He emphasizes (1965), that Merton's error was to conceptualize the solution to anomie as individual, whilst he, and Cloward and Ohlin, were to emphasize the collective solution.

Cloward and Ohlin are concerned with the problems of economic justice, rather than middle-class status, for working-class boys. They argue (1960, p. 62):

> It is our view that many discontented, lower-class youth do not wish to adopt a middle class way of life, or to disrupt their present associations and negotiate a passage into middle class groups. The solution they seek entails the acquisition of high position in terms of lower class rather than middle class criteria.

They combine elements of Mertonian anomie, and Sutherland's differential association. Working-class males are committed to success in mainly material terms, but in terms of working-class criteria. They have little access to institutionalized means, in terms of what they want, and what they realize they will get. Their response is not reaction formation, but a turning to illegitimate means, which includes both learning, and opportunity structures. Conventional goals are internalized, but legitimate means are perceived as blocked, so that strain occurs with consequent withdrawal of support for legitimate norms. Working-class neighbourhoods however possess access to illegitimate means, although these are admittedly differentially accessible. There is then, a local neighbourhood opportunity system which gives rise to

1 the criminal subculture, which offers an apprenticeship into adult crime.
2 the conflict subculture, which offers other adolescents rather than adults as peer models. This generates conflict gangs.
3 the retreatist subculture which offers a drug-using subculture for those who have failed both legitimate and illegitimate means. They are 'double failures'.

This typology is similar to Cohen and Short, and makes similar points about the social organization of a neighbourhood and the local opportunity system. A stable working-class district generates a criminal subculture, a disorganized district generates a conflict subculture, and a retreatist subculture develops where both legitimate and illegitimate opportunity structures are absent. Their solution, like Merton's, seems technocratic. Improve the opportunity structures and you eradicate inefficiency which causes strain in the system. They stress instrumental goals (concerned with deferred gratification, logic, planning and the seeking of status and income) rather than expressive goals (concerned with immediate gratification, hedonism, creativity and spontaneity) such as are found in bohemian subcultures. In his later work (Cloward and Fox Piven, 1974), however, Cloward takes a radical stance against countering anomie merely because it is technocratically inefficient, arguing instead for social justice, and criticizing the use of welfare for labour control reasons.

Young (1971), extends the concept of anomie as a result of a disjunction of instrumental means and ends to develop a theory of 'expressive anomie'. Once a culture becomes inadequate for solving a particular group's problems, the new cultural means are constructed. For him, cultures are transmitted intergenerationally, and hence class culture is important. These cultures become transformed to meet the exigencies of a new social situation, which the members find themselves in. Young (1971, p. 92), argues that, 'The old culture is the moral springboard for the emergence of the new'. For example, middle-class students, perceiving that the rewards of higher education are less fulfilling than they were led to believe, become disillusioned and drop out. They construct a bohemian subculture, related to their middle-class background, but structured to deal with their collective problem. Young (1971, p. 93), suggests that

> It will be like the culture of the working-class delinquent, in that it extols expressivity, hedonism and spontaneity, but will have a middle rather than a lower working-class orientation. Thus it will value expressivity through non violent

aesthetic pursuits and hedonism, through a cool (i.e. controlled) mode of enjoyment, rather than a frenzied pursuit of pleasure.

The availability of soft drugs in student bohemia means these are used to express culturally defined properties of the drug, aesthetic appreciation and bodily enjoyment. A new culture emerges, structuring and selecting the effects and use of a specific drug, which assists in solving the new problems. This can be contrasted for example, with the selection and use of alcohol in Irish, immigrant bachelor subcultures, which are used to solve the problems of homesickness, the absence of marriageable women and the alienation of the itinerant worker.

The influence of American naturalism, Matza and the drift into and from delinquency

Matza through the study of the delinquent subculture and deviancy has not only raised the level of debate in these fields to a high level but contributed considerably to phenomenological perspectives in sociology. Matza's framework is that of naturalism, that of being true to the phenomenon under study, and indeed his principle to subcultural theory is that it distorts what deviants would themselves recognize, the essence of their reality. In his earlier work (Matza and Sykes, 1957), he rejects the traditional model of subcultural theory, because of its claim that delinquents invert conventional values. Why then do delinquents defend their acts by a claim they were morally correct, and why do they show guilt? They are committed to wider values which do not reject conventional morality but which seek to neutralize its moral bind. Delinquents use 'techniques of neutralization', linguistic constructs which appeal to special mitigating circumstances. These act to neutralize pre-existing normative constraints, and five major types of neutralization are seen as operative. These are denial of responsibility ('I didn't mean it'), denial of injury ('I didn't really hurt him'), denial of the victim ('He was only some queer'), condemning the condemners ('Everyone picks on us') and appeals to higher loyalties ('You got to help your mates'). These techniques reflect the forces of social control. What Matza suggests is that delinquents are not really different, and he also introduces the ambiguous element of human will. However one can accuse Matza of naïvety. Accounts, especially by delinquents, are skewed to what the interrogated supposes the interrogator wants to hear. McIntyre (1967), has argued the fallacy of assuming how actors define situations as giving more than a part of the picture. Matza also ignores rationalization as a defence to self-esteem.

Matza argues that the subculture is a setting for the commission of delinquent acts commonly known to the group. It in no sense provides a frontal assault on conventional norms, but on the contrary indicates a moral bind to them. A 'comedy of errors' occurs with each group member mistakenly supposing the others to have a higher commitment to deviance than him. During periods of boredom, feelings of frustration lead adolescents to 'drift' into and out of delinquency. These are episodic moral holidays. Delinquents are ambivalent 'neither compelled nor committed to deeds, nor freely choosing them'. Hence they drift, as Matza (1964, p. 49), explains,

> Drift stands midway between freedom and control. Its basis is an area in the social structure in which control has been loosened, coupled with the abortiveness of adolescent endeavour to organise an autonomous subculture, and thus an important source of control, around illegal action. The delinquent transiently exists in a limbo between convention and crime, responding in turn to the demands of each, flirting now with one, now the other, but postponing commitment, evading decision.

The law is responded to, not as unjust, but as unevenly distributed. Matza argues against determinism, and attempts to restore humanism to subcultural theory. Delinquents feel themselves to be objects, pushed about by forces in society outside of their control. Their sense of desperation makes them (Matza, 1964, p. 49), 'attempt to restore the mood of humanism which the self makes things happen'. This can easily be an infraction of the law, as fatalism has neutralized its moral bind.

Matza's case is subject to criticism concerning his empirical evidence about delinquent accounts of their misdoings. Working-class adolescents are the least articulate about their relationship to the world, and whether they are committed to some form of central value system is an empirical question. They are unlikely to advocate counter-arguments to the dominant system, especially in court. Even if they understand the processes of the courtroom, they are too shrewd to address the bench on adolescent hedonism, or the nature of class-based law. Most youths perceive the law as an external unchanging force. Matza's evidence has been subject to much criticism. His data consists of a record of the attitudes of one hundred incarcerated adolescents about their reactions to a series of pictures of delinquent offences. Their responses led him to conclude (Matza, 1964, p. 49), 'and the adherents of the sub-culture of delinquency seem little committed to the misdeeds inherent in it'.

He does make a distinction, however, between the 'radical justification' of those convinced of the righteousness of their behaviour (for example, politically motivated criminals), and the 'apologetic justification' seen as typical of the delinquent. Hindelang (1970), criticized Matza's lack of a control group, and underestimation of how he would be perceived in the institution's staff hierarchy. He found in a similar study, that delinquents approved more than non-delinquents of delinquency. Spector (1977), argues that Hindelang's middle-class sample and relatively innocuous acts of delinquency limit its findings. Ball (1977), argues that Matza sees serious delinquents as the only unconventionally committed ones, but asks why then do they hold beliefs about neutralization. Austin (1977), found that Matza underestimated delinquents who are unconventionally committed to their misdeeds. Moral restraint, Austin argues, is neutralized, not just by techniques of neutralization, but by commitment to unconventional beliefs.

Matza in another paper (Matza and Sykes, 1961) suggests that delinquent values, the seeking of excitement, toughness, disdain for work, are in fact not so much deviant, as typical of swashbuckling leisure values held by us all. We indulge in them during competition in games, drunken orgies, gambling, cynicism and 'concealed deviance'. These are not counter-values, but values shared with the dominant culture which in fact binds the delinquent to it. The delinquent accentuates the 'subterranean values' of society, hedonism, disdain for work, aggression, violent masculinity, and excludes more official values, assisted in this by mass media mythical heroes. These are to be contrasted with the Protestant Ethic (Weber, 1930), summarized as ambition, individual responsibility, the cultivation of skills, worldly asceticism, rationality, manners, courtesy and personality, the control of aggression, 'wholesome' re-creation and the respect for property (Downes, 1966). Young (1971), feels these have been replaced by goal-oriented values necessary in modern industry. Unlike the Protestant Ethic which argued that man realized his true nature through hard work and duty, which established his position in the world, the formal values of production emphasize (Young, 1971, p. 127), that work is instrumental to gain money to

> spend in the pursuit of leisure, and it is in his 'free' time that a man really develops his sense of identity and purpose.

Work no longer expresses satisfaction in itself, in contemporary industrial society (Young, *op. cit.*, p. 127).

> It is during leisure and through the expression of subterranean values that modern man seeks his identity, whether it is in a 'home centred' family or an adolescent peer group. For leisure is at least purportedly non alienated activity.

Masculinity seems to be an important element of identity in these values.

Matza develops a much more mature and comprehensive theory of deviance, involving will (Matza, 1969b). He argues that deviants are not objects propelled by social forces, but subjects involved in meaningful action with their world. Naturalism is a major theme in this work. Social circumstances permit 'affinity' – a deviant has a pre-disposition towards deviancy because it has an 'attractive force'. An actor is attracted, and he chooses. This affinity, this choice to commit infractions, occurs in the context of 'affiliation', which is according to Matza (1969b, p. 169), 'the process by which the subject is converted to conduct novel for him, but already established for others'.

One is able to perceive oneself as someone who might commit a deviant act, one is predisposed, not yet committed, merely 'turned on'. One may be prevented by 'ban', socio-legal control creating secrecy. Because 'ban' makes a deviant act more secret than necessary, the deviant is sensitive to organized authority, especially the state. 'Ban compounds disaffiliation and thus contributes to the process of becoming deviant' (Matza, 1969b, p. 148). The secrecy of deviancy may make actors more deviant than they originally intended. Because any deviant act to be concealed makes an actor play at being ordinary, he glimpses himself playing which compounds deviation. Matza's sophisticated phenomenology is in direct contrast to the positivistic roots of traditional criminology. However, as Pearce (1976) suggests, his subjectivistic emphasis means that he loses the sense of the state as a concrete entity, which acts in specific ways at particular moments in history. Nevertheless Matza opens up the question of how actors choose deviancy, and why others do not, even in the same social situation. This is a useful counter-development to the danger of structural determinism.

British studies of working-class delinquent subcultures

American subcultural theory has been viewed as inappropriate to Britain by most British subcultural theorists. Downes (1966), argues that American theory is intrinsic to its own culture, whilst the British working classes have their highly developed, historical traditions. School has been seen as important in Britain, and also local working-class neighbourhoods and communities. The British social structure is more historically class-conscious, and does not share the neo-colonial immigrant past of the United States. Neither does it have a nationally born group of impoverished ethnic minorities who contribute to the popular myth that the poor are non-whites. British studies have concentrated on local neighbourhoods with local peer groups. However this has sometimes caused confusion. Whilst gangs tend to be near-groups, composed of a closely linked core with a looser network of peripheral members, subcultures are wider than this. They are constellations of actions, values, style, imagery and even life-styles, and through media reportage extend beyond a neighbourhood, possessing a complex relationship with other larger cultures. Gangs have often been confused with the symbolic pseudo-community of the subculture.

Subcultural theory has developed considerably since the mid-sixties. It can be divided into four approaches. First, there is the early social ecology of the working-class neighbourhood carried out in the late fifties and early sixties. Second, there is the relation of the delinquent subculture to the sociology of education, a tradition which is still continuing. This examines the relationship of leisure and youth culture as an alternative to achievement in the school. Third, there is the cultural emphasis of the Centre for Contemporary Cultural Studies at Birmingham University. This approach, which is influenced by the new criminology developed by the National Deviancy Conferences, uses a Marxist framework to consider youth cultures and their style, in terms of their relationship to class, dominant culture and ideology. Involved in this is the attempt to examine the ethnography of youth culture, their relation to popular culture and their moments in class history. Lastly there are the contemporary neighbourhood studies which look at local youth groups, not as the early social ecologists did, but in the light of influence by contemporary deviancy theory and social reaction. Both of these approaches consider the meaning that youth cultures and subcultures have for their members.

The social ecology of the British working-class neighbourhood

The clash between working-class and middle-class values, the different focal concerns, and the high rate of delinquency and crime meant that the theory of social disorganization was popular as an explanation in early subcultural theory. Differences in class values have deep historical roots. In the medieval London docks, stevedores were permitted by their guild to carry off part of a ship's cargo as a 'perk'. When this became disallowed by law, there were cases of stevedores suing shipowners for these traditional craft rights. It can be seen that in such a district as Dockland, traditions which permit theft from an employer, but not a work-mate, have roots which are now forgotten. Writers as varied as Mayhew, Engels and Steadman Jones have shown how hardship brutalizes the poor. Chevalier (1973), shows this effect on the high crime rate in early nineteenth-century Paris. Migration, fertility, mortality and disease all influenced everyday life with devastating effects on work, leisure and sleep. One hazard for the poor was a violent, criminal street life. Similar conditions occur in present-day New York and Detroit in the ghettos, with their violent street life and collapsing social services. One result in the nineteenth century was the fear of civil insurrection and rioting. The dangerous classes were closely surveilled by the police, and harsh penalties were not only applied to crime, but also to sexual morality, vagrancy and poverty. This meant that a different perception of and relation to the police developed in down-town neighbourhoods, with a consequent more ambivalent attitude to legality. Even today purchasing stolen goods 'off the back of a lorry' is seen as a sensible form of thrift.

Obviously the young are subject to a different socialization than their middle-class peers. They are not so much under-socialized (Eysenck, 1970; Trasler, 1962) so much as differentially socialized. In such neighbourhoods, Mays suggests (1967, p. 88), that

> a subculture may be said to exist in parts of the older and deteriorated urban centres . . . sometimes they correspond to areas of high crime and delinquency rates, and in such cases it is theoretically proposed that the residents of such districts share a number of attitudes and ways of behaving in common, which predisposes them to illegal conduct.

Mays subscribes to a model of cultural diversity. He continues (1967, p. 89):

> Working class ways of living are not so much a hostile, negativistic and resentful reaction against higher income group ways of life as the development of an indigenous culture, which met their own peculiar, personal and social needs in a fairly satisfactory way. Working class culture is not so much deviant as merely an alternative pattern.

Young (1971, p. 56) also stresses this cultural diversity:

> the apparent social disorganisation of slum areas is often merely organisation centring around different ends than those of respectable society . . . . To grow up as a mature adult in the East End demands the inculcation of different norms by different means than does that needed to produce a well balanced citizen of Knightsbridge.

Most adolescents grow up in these neighbourhoods without becoming a delinquent, although they are more likely to statistically. They develop a mix of values, and it is probably those for whom education and careers seem untenable, and who feel little investment in the educational process and career system who dissociate from respectability. They have problems whether caused by structural problems, status or identity which cause them to be attracted by subcultures which almost by definition have deviant values.

The idea of the delinquent neighbourhood is not a new one in British criminology. Buchanan in 1846, and Mayhew in 1864 both indicate that there are neighbourhoods where delinquency abounds, a fact also noted in the Select Committee Report on Criminal and Destitute Juveniles, 1852 (see Carson and Wiles, 1971). Bagot (1941), published one of the earliest ecological studies comparing data gathered in the 1930s on Liverpool, and the rest of England and Wales. It owes much to Burt, and indicates poverty as a major variable in delinquency, whose roots were in unemployment, bad housing, low incomes and overcrowding. A year later, Carr-Saunders, Mannheim and Rhodes (1942), published an important statistical survey of pre-war London and this assisted Mannheim (1948), in his research carried out now in Cambridge due to the evacuation there of the London School of Economics during war time. The data in these studies all emphasized poverty as being at the roots of delinquency, with the absence of a father figure (to be contrasted with the concern over the absence of the mother figure suggested by Bowlby in the fifties), usually serving in the war-time forces. Public guilt over the breaking-up of the family in a national crisis, and bewilderment at the continuance of crime and delinquency during a period of peace, prosperity and the welfare state led to a concern over youth. On the one hand the Welfare State was seen as making life too easy; on the other hand there was a concern that the poor were too concerned with materialism, with the consequence that women were neglecting their families to go out to work.

The fifties saw the advent of several community studies which included subcultural studies. Spinley's (1953), study compared working-class and middle-class families in Paddington, concentrating on differential socialization patterns, and suggesting that in the slum these were dominated by values relating to economic insecurity and immediate forms of gratification. In 1954, Mays published his study of Liverpool youth, and Sprott, Jephcott and Carter looked at a Midlands town 'Radby'. Both studied values and behaviour in English slum neighbourhoods. Sprott *et al.* compared streets with high and low delinquency rates, suggesting that delinquency was only one of several elements of a way of life among the 'unrespectable' or 'rough' poor, and that these patterns were carried on into adulthood. Mays found these juvenile patterns were not sustained in adult life. Sprott (1954) finds his areas reflect the 'rough' and 'respectable' divisions of working-class life. He suggests subcultural support for the delinquent in 'rough' working-class life, and indicates that disturbed delinquents will be found in the 'respectable' strata, rather than the 'rough' where such behaviour is normal. Mays' delinquents reported themselves as having passed through a delinquent phase between the ages of 11–15, but now felt they had grown out of it. The social structure of the Liverpool docks had a long social history of economic disadvantage, migrant labour, poor educational facilities and irregular work. The value system generated by this was partly fatalistic and depressed and partly aggressive and 'devil may care'. The young strongly desired a close asociation with their peers, and this led to an overtly delinquent tradition, which involves a tradition of risk-raking as proof of strength, courage and skill. The subcultural tradition emphasized toughness, daring and defiance to authority, and the reward it offered was emotional solidarity. Delinquency was in Liverpool for Mays (1954, p. 147)

> not so much a symptom of maladjustment as adjustment to a subculture which was in conflict with the culture of the city as a whole.

The social conditions for Mays predispose the young to delinquency, but whether they indulge or not, depends upon the companionship of the subcultural peer group. Mays underestimated the relationship to school, concentrating on those who continued delinquency after leaving school. Morris's Croydon study (1957) in one of the first essentially sociological studies of an area suggested that there was a confusion in the literature between territorial uniformity and cultural uniformity. He combined informal interviews with residential participation, statistics and case histories, mapping out areas of criminal offences, and residences. Delinquent and criminal residence was mainly in the deteriorating slums, or the new estates the slum dwellers had been rehoused in. The dumping of problem families on these estates contributed strongly to delinquent areas, as did child socialization techniques. Lax control of teenage leisure was for Morris a result of the only free areas for delinquents being the streets rather than an abdication of parental responsibility. Morris's view was that delinquency rates reflect socialization patterns in different classes, geographically distributed. Rather than social disorganization, the working class reject many middle-class norms, and the reality is an unambiguous subculture at variance with middle-class values. Kerr's Liverpool study (1958), confirms much of what the earlier studies suggested. Subcultural values exist which permit for example shoplifting, but not theft from your parents.

Also, this neighbourhood had a community which acted against 'getting above yourself'. Consequently scholarships were refused, as were jobs and houses in other districts. The rigidity of the local neighbourhood cultural patterns makes any alternative life-style impossible. The studies all suggest alternative working-class values, roughly based on a casual attitude to money, hardly surprising in poor neighbourhoods, an attitude to theft which does not discourage it, but may select the targets, a casual attitude to truancy because of the pointlessness of school and a cynical attitude to employers, and to the police. Willmott's study of adolescent boys in East London (1966), found these subcultural values, as did Downes (1966). Andry (1960), found two-thirds of his non-delinquent sample reported stealing, and theft from employers continuing into adulthood, supported by the view (Willmott, 1966, p. 143):

> No matter what you do, if you're making something on the side, the governor's making more.

Fiddling at work, stealing from wealthy institutions and shops is allowed, toughness and masculinity are central, and vandalism seen as attacks on property not particularly belonging to anyone. For Willmott the delinquent subculture arose because a rejected group of adolescent males rebelled against a vaguely conceived 'society' which prized achievement. Downes (1966), in what is still the best discussion of subcultural theory, argued against the American theories being applied to this country. In the two London boroughs in East London he investigated, he found that the first stage of delinquency was between the ages nine and fifteen, and involved larceny, followed by a second stage at fifteen to eighteen concerned with motor vehicles, rowdyism and some violence. He notes (Downes, 1966, p. 257),

> Their illegal behaviour seemed to be due not to 'alienation' or 'status frustration', but to a process of dissociation from middle class dominated contexts of school, work and recreation. This disenchantment provoked an over-emphasis on purely 'leisure' goals sedulously fostered by commercial 'teenage' cultures – rather than on other non-work areas.

The class position of an adolescent dominates his access not only at school and work, but also during leisure where autonomy, excitement and enjoyment are sought to escape the monotony of school or work. Lacking the means to achieve the glamorous elements of leisure consumption, the working-class boy reaffirms his working-class value system. He finds that working-class culture of a traditional form no longer satisfies him in leisure areas, so he reacts against both middle-class and working-class culture. What happens is (Downes, 1966, p. 136):

> differential response by social class to the newly emerging 'teenage' culture can lead the 'corner boy' to adopt a collective delinquent solution along 'contracultural' lines, although disdain for the limited job-opportunity market consequent upon educational 'failure' is a necessary basis for this sequency.

Downes sees teenage culture as largely synthetic, created for, rather than by teenagers. This raises an important question, that of the influence of mass media and marketing on youth cultures. A popular culture has a relationship with marketing forces, in that it is developed by them to become a commodity aimed at profit-making, but to what extent this can succeed depends to a degree to the extent to which it is produced by those whose needs and desires it stimulates.

The popular explanations of the fifties drew on a picture of a bored teenager, affluent, with excess leisure, time and money, against a classless background. The classlessness was emphasized by the growth of teenage synthetic culture, and this was emphasized by Abrams's (1959; 1969), suggestion that the affluent working-class young were the largest consumers in the economy. This reflected the general optimism about affluence and embourgeoisement among the working class during the fifties. Poverty studies of the period (Titmuss, 1962; Townsend and Abel Smith, 1965) revealed that the gap between the classes economically was relatively similar to pre-war divisions, and that 12 per cent of working-class people lived close to official subsistence levels.

At one level there was an argument that youth was a 'classless' group, a view often put forward by the proponents of youth culture (rather than class-based youth cultures). Another error was the suggestion that delinquency was related to the presence of dangerous youth gangs, rather than spin-offs of subcultural responses. Scott (1967) found no evidence of gangs in the London area, discovering instead groups of loosely-organized delinquents, short-lived, and not necessarily delinquent. They were more transitional shelters from the emotional dependence on home to a more self-determined existence, and indeed often provided a protection from close relationships with girls. Yablonsky (1967) notes that in New York gangs were neither as large or as well-organized as popular opinion supposed. He found a 'near group' composed of a central core of near-psychopathic members, with a largely illusory penumbra of subordinates. Downes found no evidence of this in Britain, although Patrick (1973), disputes this for Scotland which he finds uniquely different.

Subcultural studies of delinquency during the period up to the mid-sixties favoured either specific studies of delinquency, or community studies with youth as a subsection. Both approaches saw youth as a social problem, and because of this emphasized delinquency, with class a very latent factor. The popular concern with adolescence was the generational gap over issues of morality. Despite the fear that there was a discontinuity of values, in fact empirical evidence argued against this. Schofield (1965), found only one-third of his boys, and one-sixth of his girls were sexually experienced, most of these with regular partners. The Eppels (1966), found that most young people felt that they were stereotyped by the older generations, and unjustifiably criticized. They were conventional young people, humane, anti-authoritarian, socially concerned and valuing family life. Veness (1962), found similar values among her school-leavers, and Peck and Havighurst (1960), found agreement on morality between young people and adults in the United States. The delinquency studies of the sixties favoured delinquency as a result of disadvantages, in particular educational disadvantage, as well as other adverse social conditions. Indeed conditions reflect those described in the war-time studies. Wallis and Maliphant (1967), in their study of 29 London boroughs still found a relation between delinquency, class, education, employment and poor housing, despite considerable social change in some of the boroughs. It was not until the late sixties and early seventies that class was to become a major issue in subcultural theory.

Structural contradictions in the educational system, and the subculture as a 'solution'

An important and often overlooked factor in subcultures is the meaning of school. Even when the studies look at older age groups, education is an important variable, strongly influencing them. Downes not only drew attention to class-inequality, he also plainly saw the meaningless of school for most working-class youth as central to any analysis of delinquent subcultures. The child responds to the factory-like system of school preparing him for his factory-like work life with typical working-class fatalism (one of Miller's focal concerns). A meritocratic educational system forcibly recruits most working-class children into a system which is designed to exclude most of its recipients from higher educational success. Disenchantment results in 'dissociation' rather than a contracultural rebellion. What occurs is (Downes, 1966, p. 273),

> an opting out of the joint middle class and skilled working class values system, whereby the adolescent of semi and unskilled origins is enjoined either to 'better himself' or to 'accept his station in life'. To insulate themselves against the harsh implications of this creed, the adolescent in a 'dead end' job in a 'dead end' neighbourhood extricates himself from the belief in work as of any importance beyond the simple provision of income, and deflects what aspirations he has into areas of what has been termed 'non-work'.

Abrams (1959) found working-class boys and middle-class boys spent almost the same amount weekly on the same goods (£3.40:£3.50 per week respectively). Working-class girls (£2.40 per week) spent less than middle-class girls (£3.60) and boys. However there are important regional and age differences in wages, which have been overlooked by Abrams. Jephcott (1967), found five years later her average girl in the provinces earned only £3.50 during her first two years at work, and only 9 per cent earned over £9 per week, and in fact despite increases for age and bonuses, 41 per cent of 17-year-olds earned between £5 and £7 per week, with 15 per cent earning less than this. Smith's Bury sample (1966) found 90 per cent of 17–18 year-olds spending less than £2 per week on leisure, and 40 per cent of his 18-year-olds spending less than 75p per week on leisure. Despite this, the myth of teenage affluence (as part of the general myth concerning the affluence of the working class) persists. A fear of delinquency developed, and the Albermarle Report (1958) suggested the provision of youth work projects for unattached youth who rejected normal youth work provision. Despite the cultural diversity suggested by Willmott and Downes, the separation of youth as a class persisted. Musgrove (1964), argued that adults consigned youth to a self-contained world. The argument remained that whilst young people have economic independence and power, they have a subordinate relation to the adult world, and have developed as a separate class (Musgrove, 1969, p. 50), 'in effect a "social class", a class relatively independent of the stratification system of adults'. However as Murdock and McCron (1976, p. 18) argue, it is true that young people reside in

> age specific institutions, it does not follow that they are cut off from the wider system of class stratification. On the contrary through the insistent mediation of the family, the neighbourhood and the school class inequalities penetrate deeply into their everyday lives, structuring both their social experience, and their response to it.

Downes quotes Cotgrove and Parker (1963), who suggest

> For the less able child in the lower forms of the secondary modern school, the dominant picture that emerges is one of school as a source of boredom and frustration . . . Many expect little from work and are satisfied with what they find . . . The secondary modern boy leaving school at fifteen has received early training in dissociating himself from the demands which 'they' make upon him. He simply does not care . . . dissatisfaction is the measure of the gap between aspiration and achievement. For many no such gap exists – their expectations and aspirations are centred on the world outside the factory.

Hargreaves (1967), shows that during the last year at school two subcultures divide the school, which reflect streaming within the classroom. These are the higher educational streams, with pupils identifying with the pupil role, and the lower streams dissociating from school and forming a 'delinquescent' subculture potentially rather than actually delinquent. Labelling is of primary importance here, the response to the school means that 'careers' are created in achievement or in potential delinquency, and a self-fulfilling prophecy operates. These are the pupils about whom Holt (1969), writes:

> It has become clear over the years that these children see school almost entirely in terms of the day-to-day and hour-to-hour tasks that we impose upon them . . . they were in school because they had to be . . . it is a place where *they* make you go, where *they* tell you to do things and where *they* try to make their life unpleasant if you do not do them or do not do them right.

Feeling they have no control over their school life, seeing no relevance in the curriculum to their future occupations they do not invest themselves in school, but in the youth subcultures found outside of it. It is from these that they create some form of identity. Downes (1966, p. 274), reminds us,

> In the absence of work orientation and job satisfaction accruing from non-work . . . the 'corner-boy' attaches unusual importance to leisure. There is no reason to suppose that the delinquent 'corner-boy' does not share the more technically classless 'teenage culture', a culture whose active pursuit depends on freedom from the restraints of adult responsibility, but which reflects the subterranean values of the adult world.

Sugarman (1967), makes a similar point for his London schoolboys. Those dissociating from school, identify with a role drawn from the youth culture outside the school. He concludes (Sugarman, 1967, p. 154):

> This is the role of 'teenager' which is roughly an inversion of the official pupil role. In place of the officially expected deferred gratification, it puts an emphasis on spontaneous gratification . . . boys committed to the teenager role and to the youth culture . . . are on the whole rebelling against norms imposed by the school and performing academically below expectation . . . youth culture defined and measured in this sense is the culture of the mobile working class; the downwardly mobile, and those who cherish hopes of mobility along channels where the criteria do not apply.

This is reminiscent of Coleman's (1961), analysis in the United States which has a similarly functionalist approach. Sugarman's disapproval reveals itself in his over-simplification of class and education with the comments (Sugarman, *op. cit.*, p. 158):

> It is no accident that the heroes of youth culture, pop singers, song writers, clothes designers and others have mostly achieved their positions without long years of study, work or sacrifice . . . youth culture is the new opium of the teenage masses . . . it may not be true that all boys with bad conduct have long hair, at the same time it may also be true that all boys with long hair do have bad conduct.

This statement contains a dismissal of the technical difficulties of design and music, combined with philistinism and a reductionism to a form of hirsuite determinism. Surely all boys with long hair did not have bad conduct. Also overlooked is the fact that middle-class achievers dissociate from higher education, but that this may occur at a later age. I have reported elsewhere (Brake, 1977), of a high level of disenchantment with higher education among hippies, with a consequent dissociation. Boring curricula, decreased graduate employment, lower financial reward than expected after years of study all contributed to the drop-out culture of the student hippy. The relationship of school to youth cultures is of primary importance, and this theme is prevalent in the studies which posit a 'teenage subculture' or 'youth culture' of a general form, or where the subculture is presented as a solution to educational contradictions. This is implicit in several of the subcultural studies discussed in this book.

The New Wave of British subcultural theory

The 1970s saw the publication of several subcultural studies. These reflected important debates in the sociology of deviance during the sixties. The National Deviancy Conference was established in 1968 in response to the domination in criminology by establishment-based research. It was felt that a radical critique, involving the dynamic investigation of criminal and deviant 'careers' was a necessary starting-point for any understanding of deviancy. Labelling theory, in a symbolic interactionist framework concentrated on societal reaction as a major variable in deviant career-making. This approach itself became subject to criticism which in turn led to two debates (details of this can be overviewed in P. Wiles, 1976) – first, the importance of meaning examined both from a transactionalist and an ethnomethodological stance, and second, the political implications of deviancy from a more structural investigation. On the one hand is the pursual of the deviant as subject, including a study of a theory of action and a theory of social process. On the other hand there was a desire to develop a radical Marxist critique upon the political effects of state policy. This latter was developed as the New Criminology (Taylor *et al.*, 1973; 1975), which argued that a theory of criminology needs to be intrinsically related to a political analysis. But as knowledge is not neutral, criminology is related to a theory of knowledge which breaks with correctionalism and is committed to the abolition of wealth and power differentials. Their orientation is Marxist, and as such it differs from a radicalism rooted only in scepticism or located in empiricist epistemology. This has been subject to considerable criticism both within Marxism (Hirst, in Taylor *et al.*, 1975), as well as outside.

The radical stance of the new Deviancy Conference influenced studies of youth culture. The transactionalist analysis of societal reaction and its effects by S. Cohen (1972), was the first of these, followed by several other writers. Two major contributors were the Birmingham Centre for Contemporary Cultural Studies, and Murdock's research in mass communications at Leicester University. Briefly these studies can be differentiated into cultural analyses, especially of style, of the relations between dominant class cultures, hegemony and subcultural derivation, and ethnographic studies of careers in delinquent subcultures. These involve a theory of the meaning that youth cultures have, and a theory of process involving the ethnography of youth subcultures. The cultural dimension concentrates on the meaning of style, and the subcultural dimension involves behaviour and life-style and its relationship to wider social structures. Obviously several studies have both dimensions, with a different emphasis, but for the sake of clarity I will try to separate culture and ethnography.

Chronologically the first major study of this new approach was S. Cohen's (1972), work on 'mods' and 'rockers'. Cohen bases his approach in a transactionalist framework, which takes as problematic the transaction between judge and judged, concentrating less on why an actor is deviant, but why is there a rule against certain forms of deviance. Cohen's approach is definitional rather than behavioural, and outlines the importance of societal reaction to deviance as a major variable. It is based on

Lemert's (1967), distinction between primary and secondary deviance. Lemert (1967, p. 48), argues:

> Primary deviance is assumed to arise in a wide variety of social, cultural and psychological contexts, and at best has only marginal implications for the psychic structure of the individual; it does not lead to symbolic reorganisation at the level of self-regarding attitudes and social roles. Secondary deviation is deviant behaviour, or social roles based upon it, which becomes a means of defense, attack or adaptation to the overt and covert problems created by societal reaction to primary deviation.

It was secondary deviance which was important to sociological investigation because primary deviance was so diffuse in its causal motivation. Societal reaction launched actors on deviant careers. Actors once publicly labelled as deviant perceived themselves as cut off from major value systems, and consequently they develop counter-values which increase their deviancy. In this way deviancy amplifies (see Wilkins, 1964). Cohen accepts the tenets of the anomic perspective in subcultural theory, and argues that structural strain experienced by British adolescents in the mid-sixties led to two socially visible and publicly responded-to styles, Mods and Rockers. He compared the stereotypes of these 'folk devils', who had brought on a 'moral panic' in the mass media, and found the accusations of being affluent yobs, of violence, damage to property and consequent loss of trade, greatly exaggerated. Societal reaction, and attempts at controlling stereotyped notions of what was occurring, only made the situation worse. One magistrate referred to them as (S. Cohen, 1972, p. 109), 'mentally unstable, long haired, petty little sawdust Caesars who seem to find courage, like rats, by hunting only in packs'. This was due to indiscriminate prosecution, over-reaction locally, and a mass media reportage which suggested 'cabalism' or the solidifying of amorphous groups of teenagers into a conspiratorial collectivity. The study was a transactional analysis of a disaster theory model, which looked at moral panic as a result of mass media reaction, with a consideration of its effects on the dramaturgy played out on the East Coast beaches. It was a distinct break from the anomic strain of Downes, but used some of its tenets to fill out the process of becoming a subcultural role player, and the part societal reaction played in this.

Murdock's work (Murdock and Phelps, 1972; Murdock, 1973; Murdock and McCron, 1973; Murdock, 1974, and Murdock and McCron, 1976), follows the tradition of the relationship of the school and youth culture. It also considers the important theme of the role of commercial youth cultures. Murdock and the C.C.C.S. have influenced each other, and both show perspectives developed from the N.D.C. Murdock reintroduced the class dimension to subcultural theory, and emphasized the model of subcultures as 'solutions' to collectively experienced problems and contradictions. The latter occur when there are gaps between what is supposed to be happening, and what actually happens. Murdock explains subcultures thus (Murdock, 1974, p. 213):

> Subcultures are the meaning system and modes of expression developed by groups in particular parts of the social structure in the course of their collective attempts to come to terms with the contradictions of their shared social situation. More particularly subcultures represent the accumulated meanings and means of expression through which groups in subordinate structural positions have attempted to negotiate or oppose the dominant meaning system. They therefore provide a pool of available symbolic resources which particular individuals or groups can draw on in their attempt to make sense of their own specific situation and construct a viable identity.

Murdock (1973, p. 9), sees a relation between work and leisure thus:

> The attempt to resolve the contradictions contained in the work situation through the creation of meaningful styles of leisure, typically takes place within the context provided by a sub-culture . . . subcultures offer a collective solution to the problems posed by shared contradictions in the work situation and provide a social and symbolic context for the development and reinforcement of collective identity and individual self esteem.

There is a hint in this of A. Cohen's original notion of a collective solution arising as a result of status problems faced by working-class youth when compared against the 'middle-class measuring rod' of education. Youth faces several problems against which it attempts collective solutions, as I have suggested elsewhere (Brake, 1973b, p. 36):

> Subcultures arise as attempts to solve certain problems in the social structure, which are created by contradictions in the larger society.

Murdock argues against the concept of an overall youth culture, as suggested by Sugarman, and by the American theorists Parsons (1954), Polk (1957; 1966), and Coleman (1961), with the suggestion that youth is committed either to the culture of the school or the out-of-school youth culture. Murdock's research in ten widely different co-educational secondary schools found some pupils involved in both leisure and school activities. However the majority of pupils not involved in school activities were involved in a set of meanings which could be seen as a type of 'youth culture'. There were two major constellations attracting these young people – first 'street culture', characteristic of young working-class males, involving football, hanging about with mates, cafés, pubs and dancing; and second, 'pop media culture' based on activities, values and roles promulgated by sectors of the mass media for adolescent consumption. There was an overlap between the two, but the degree to which school rejectors used the 'pop media culture' varied according to sex and class. Working-class pupils with a low commitment to school were relatively uninvolved with 'pop media culture', and in the East End of London, where there was a vigorous 'street culture', the pop media was relatively unimportant. Middle-class grammar school pupils were particularly involved with 'progressive' music. This Murdock sees as an extension by successful pupils of individualistic values in the parent middle-class culture, emphasizing self-development and individual achievement ('doing your own thing'). For Murdock generational membership has in no sense replaced class membership as a key determinant of social experience, and he denies that generational consciousness has been sustained by the mass entertainment industry aimed at youth. Murdock sees youth located firmly within a framework of class relations which takes note of opportunity structures but which is quite different from the traditional model using that concept. This view was reflected also by Brake (1973b, p. 36):

> Youth is not itself a problem, but there are problems created for example by the conscription of the majority of the young into the lower strata of a meritocratic educational system, and then allowing them only to take up occupations which are meaningless, poorly paid and uncreative. Working class subcultures attempt to infuse into this bleak world excitement and colour, during the short respite between school and settling down into marriage and adulthood.

Both Murdock and Brake have been criticized by the C.C.C.S. (Clarke *et al.*, 1976), for too heavy a reliance upon subcultures as problem-solving. For them (Clarke *et al.*, 1976, p. 29),

> the young inherit a cultural orientation from their parents towards a 'problematic' common to the class as a whole, which is likely to weight, shape and signify the meanings they attach to different areas of their social life. In Murdock's and Brake's work, the situation of the subculture's members within an ongoing subordinate culture is ignored in terms of the specific development of the subculture. Thus a whole dimension of class socialisation is omitted and the elements of negotiation and displacement in the original situated class culture are given too little weight in the analysis.

The analysis of the C.C.C.S. stems from P. Cohen's (1972), seminal article. This exploratory article of working life in East London rests on the mutual articulation of three structures. The working-class community draws its strength from the extended kinship network which offers mutual aid and cultural continuity. This depends in turn on the local social ecology, the neighbourhood, a dense socio-cultural space which 'helps to shape and support the close textures of traditional working-class life, its sense of solidarity, its local loyalties and traditions'. The third structure is the local economy, tying the neighbourhood to the workplace. Post-war redevelopment broke up the traditional neighbourhood through rehousing, speculative development and the introduction of immigrant labour. The traditional extended family network became replaced by the privatized nuclear family, interacting only within its immediate kin structure and ceasing to be involved in neighbourhood life as was common in the old working-class communities. The extended kin network became replaced by an intense set of family relations. Cohen argues (1972, p. 17), that 'the working class family was not only isolated from outside but undermined from within.'

The social space of the pub, corner shops and the street had their communality destroyed by high rise flats. The decline of craft labour reduced entry into skilled trades with its accompanying craft pride. The work force polarized into routine low-paid industry, or rare specialized skills relating to the new technology, depending on qualifications and apprenticeship. This polarization extended into the respectable working-class community, now facing the problems of upward mobility into the new suburban working class, or downwards into unskilled routine labour. Cohen explores the complex ways different intra-class structures have their options determined by their relations to the means of production, with its effects on the family, and the physical relocation of the neighbourhood. He concentrates on the effects on the young. The local economy contracted, became less diverse, and the young travelled out of the community to work, or moved away. Those left were faced with problems of a material, cultural, social and economic nature. Cohen locates these problems to a class historically, and for him class does not disappear but becomes more complex because of socio-economic influence. For youth then, they have to attempt to 'resolve' shifts in these material, social, economic forms, and which are also experienced in the 'parent culture' (i.e. the dominant working-class culture in the neighbourhood). The differentiated working-class subcultures arise because (Cohen, 1972, p. 23),

> the latent function of subculture is this – to express and resolve albeit 'magically', the contradictions which appear in the parent culture. The succession of subcultures which this parent culture generated can thus all be considered as so many variations on a central theme – the contradiction at an ideological level, between traditional working class puritanism, and the new ideology of consumption; at an economic level between a part of the socially mobile elite, or a part of the new lumpen.

Subcultures try to retrieve lost socially cohesive elements destroyed in the parent culture, and to combine these with elements from other class fractions 'symbolising one or other of the options confronting it'. These problems are always experienced and 'resolved' at the ideological level, and this is why they are unreal, imaginary or 'magical' solutions. There are for Cohen (1972, p. 24)

> three levels in the analysis of subcultures: one is the historical . . . which isolates the specific problematic of a particular class fraction . . . secondly . . . the sub systems . . . and the actual transformations they undergo form one subcultural moment to another . . . thirdly . . . the way the subculture is actually lived out by those who are bearers and supports.

Cohen then places the subculture in its cultural context, raises the influence of material contradictions and their effects, and suggests a different form of problem solving from the anomic model, or the status dimension in its usual form, that of an ideological resolution of an experienced form arising from contradictions in the structure. Subcultures can never break out of these contradictions, they can only attempt to relocate 'in an imaginary relation' the real relations which the members cannot transcend.

The C.C.C.S. develop a sophisticated argument which attempts to consider the relationship between class and youth in a Marxist framework, and which involves the problem of ideology and culture. Class is itself a problematic area empirically (Reid, 1977), and theoretically (Poulantzas, 1973; Miliband, 1969; Westergaard and Resler, 1975). Parkin (1971), has suggested a useful typology of the relationship between working-class consciousness and social location. The normative order is best considered as a number of competing meaning systems. The dominant value system whose social source is the major institutional order provides a moral framework promoting existing inequality. Subordinate classes define the existing social system in deferential or aspirational terms. The subordinate value system has its social source in the local working-class community and promotes an accommodative response to the existing system. There is also a radical value system which draws upon working class political parties which promote oppositional interpretations of existing class inequality. The dominant value system, drawn from Marx's dictum 'the ideas of the ruling class are in every age, the ruling ideas' is middle-class culture, or the central value system, which is assumed to be the normative culture against which others are compared. Subordinate classes if they accept this culture, are either deferential (accept the world as it is) or aspirational (accept the world as it is, but not one's personal place in it). However there are also positions which are neither acquisitional nor oppositional totally. It is in this area that the C.C.C.S. place most forms of mediations between dominant and subordinate cultures. The legitimation of 'their' institutions is accepted (their firms, their education, their laws) but 'we' can negotiate a space within this.

An individual is born into a class location, involving him or her in a set of institutions and social relations, and also a configuration of meanings within that culture. Social groups develop distinct patterns of life, which involve giving expressive form to their social and material life. A social group then develops a particular way of life – meanings, values, life-style, and how it expresses relations both in material production and in leisure. The most important social group obviously is a class, sharing distinct historical and material conditions. Productive relations between classes are unequally ranked in terms of wealth and power, but cultures are also ranked along a scale of cultural domination and subordination. As was suggested, ruling class groups monopolize culture and ideology, popularized into a more diffuse 'middle-class culture'. This dominant culture has a monopoly legitimacy, reducing other values to reactions against or to it, subsuming a whole set of congruent theories involving notions such as under-socialization, deviance and so forth. Gramsci refers to this as 'hegemony' (1973), suggesting it occurs where a ruling class is able to exert total social authority over subordinate classes, so that alternatives and opportunities are contained such that the granting of legitimacy of dominant classes appears as spontaneous, natural and normal. There is not so much a lack of choice in a pluralist culture, but the preferences are shaped hegemonically. Power is then used 'to prevent conflict arising in the first place' (Lukes, 1974, p. 23). There is a hegemonic bloc of dominant class factions, supported by subordinate classes, with power legitimated through what Althusser calls 'ideological state apparatuses' (1971) – social, cultural, educational and legal institutions.

For Hall *et al.* (1978), the British working class have developed their own historical cultures, but the relations between these and the dominant culture is negotiable at certain historical moments. Working-class culture wins 'space' for the dominant culture is never total or homogeneous. Within the subordinate class cultures are the 'parent cultures' (the local version of the subordinate class culture) and subsets of these concerned with various 'focal concerns' – the subcultures. The 'focal concerns' are related both to the class culture and the parent culture. Hall *et al.* suggest that focal concerns are what is distinct generationally in youth cultures, which has been the main emphasis for subcultural study, whilst what has been neglected is what is shared with the parent culture. Class and generation act to produce style. Young people encounter the dominant culture not in an abstract distant form, but through institutions which mediate the dominant culture to subordinate cultures. They also experience the cultural milieu of their neighbourhood and (Hall *et al.*, p. 53)

> Many forms of adaptation, negotiation and resistance, elaborated by the 'parent culture' in its encounters with the dominant culture are borrowed and adapted by the young in their encounter with the mediating institutions of provision and control.

Clarke (1976a) uses Lévi-Strauss's concept 'bricolage', the re-ordering and re-contextualization of objects to communicate fresh meanings. Objects and meanings constitute a sign, and are assembled into meaningful patterns or messages. There is a transformation and rearrangement of what exists especially in fashion, which is translated and adapted into a new context. For example, Willis (1978), concerns himself with the relations of a homology or fit between certain types of style, artefacts and group identity. Subcultural style sets off certain members of a class from others, even though the subculture co-exists with a more inclusive class culture, to project an image which indicates a different cultural solution from their peers. The youthful version of the bohemian subculture of the *avant-garde*, the hippies, is related to its parent culture, the urban culture of the middle class intelligentsia, and is concerned with individualism, creativity and self-expression. However it also contains focal concerns of more working-class delinquent subcultures, hedonism, search for excitement and an anti-work ethic. There is for Willis a homology between the loose group affiliation, subjective orientation, immediacy and the selection of West Coast Rock music (acid rock) and drug use (especially hallucinogenics), and the hippy life-style. As Clarke (1975, p. 179), puts it,

> the eventually produced style is more than the simple amalgam of all the separate elements – it derives its specific symbolic quality from the arrangement of all the elements together in one whole ensemble, embodying and expressing the group's self consciousness.

When we consider different types of subcultural styles we will examine specific applications of the C.C.C.S. to particular subcultures. Woods (1977), has accused this approach of romanticization of working-class youth cultures. The problems of leisure apply to all, not just youth, and 'magical resolutions' must therefore apply beyond subcultural solutions. He also feels that focusing on a particular class or class fraction, can sentimentalize its virtues, and that problems such as queer-bashing, Paki-bashing and mugging are moved from being the personal responsibility of individuals concerned, to being fomented by ideologies or government in an abstract way. He suggests that where racialism is experienced by minorities in the same class position as those who attack them, it strains credulity to posit a class explanation. This is to overlook the divisionist consequences of a racialism (or a sexism) inherent in an ideology. One important aspect is the concept of masculinity which I shall discuss in the chapters on race and sex.

The ethnography and history of British working-class youth cultures and subcultures

The cultural analysis of the C.C.C.S. has influenced several subcultural theorists, Mungham and Pearson (1976), Willis (1978), Hebdige (1976a), Frith (1978), and this approach will be used to consider the history of subcultural themes in Britain. There have been other subcultural studies which have combined the social ecology of the local neighbourhood with elements of the new deviancy approach. Three important studies are Patrick's (1973), study of a violent Glasgow gang, Parker's (1974), study of down-town adolescents in Liverpool, and Plant's (1975), study of drug subcultures in a small British town. These reflect early neighbourhood studies, but make some interesting observations about contemporary youth. Patrick's gang had a deviant career structure built in through family associations and loose peer ties. The membership was age-stratified, each age group having its own gang. These possessed core members including leaders whose ruthless violence caused them to be labelled as 'psychies' by peripheral members. Glasgow violent gangs seem not to have a counterpart in England. The Glasgow gangs possess little camaraderie, mutual kindness or solidarity, with low cohesion and superficial personal relationships. As the Schwendingers (1967), remark of similar American gangs,

> It's fuck your buddy week, fifty two weeks a year.

Focal concerns were hardness or 'gemmie', drink, drugs, status, 'patter' or 'chat', clothes and sex. There was a fatalism towards their sense of educational, social and occupational failure, they called themselves 'slummies' (slumdwellers). They truanted from the hated school, but being too young to work had no money. Their behaviour only makes sense against the West of Scotland particularly the Glaswegian working class male culture. The heavy drinking and violence of this masculinist culture (the West of Scotland had a higher murder rate than Northern Ireland in 1977), all celebrate the 'hard man'. Parker's 'Roundhouse Boys' were in contrast a street corner peer group, closely knit, living in a down-town deteriorating neighbourhood. In reaction to the badly-paid, routine work available they hung around the street corners, reminiscent of Liebow's (1967), ghetto unemployed men. Demoralized by lack of money, they became skilful at stealing car radios, an activity thwarted by police surveillance and the re-opening of the job market. For a brief period they are able to reminisce about the 'good times' financed by the radio thefts, and their spontaneous enjoyment has to be understood in the context of the 'bad times' learnt from experience and cultural class traditions. There is a reflection of the C.C.C.S. analysis of generationally specific responses to common class problems. The socio-economic conditions create problems in down town areas which, because they are never basically altered at this level, re-occur generationally. Parker combines the Chicago tradition with Matza's naturalism. An important aspect is the threat perceived by the police concerning 'hanging around', a point well examined by Corrigan and Frith (1975). Plant's investigation was broader both geographically, it took in a whole town, and in scope, it considered 'drug users'. Two quite different drug-oriented subcultures emerged, seldom interacting. One group involved the part time 'head', who lived a conventional lower middle-class life, using hallucinogenics only in leisure periods, and the other involved working-class youths from the full-time 'junkie' subculture. The latter was a poly drug user, more delinquent, homeless, unemployed and drifting. The 'junkie' hierarchy was based on multi-drug abuse, and as such they were in danger from police surveillance. Their subculture offered a repository to those who felt incapable of dealing with their lives, either from personality problems or deprived social conditions. These studies reflect strongly subcultural solutions to wider contradictions. The working-class groups tend to share similar focal concerns, and face low prestige, poor employment prospects in a deteriorating district, which has a cultural emphasis on manhood and drink, or face these concerns combined with vagrancy.

A brief history of British working-class subcultures and styles

One problem as Murdock (1975), reminds us is that concentrating on subcultural members tends to ignore respectable youth in the same class location. This may be because where youth feels it has an investment in the social system as it stands, it can respond deferentially or aspirationally. Another problem is marginality, the extent to which actors are only marginally involved in subcultures. This seems to reflect a class difference concerning control of work and leisure. Another problem is overlap in membership in class terms. Certainly whilst subcultures seem to be class-based, this is not to argue there are not working-class members of middle-class subcultures and vice versa. However members tend to be from similar class backgrounds. As well as subcultures generated by groups, there is a relation to the manufactured or synthetic culture. Mercantile interests are always keen to exploit a marketable culture, and the 'bricolage' element indicates the confusion between the contribution of the marketed elements of fashion and the genuine innovation of style. The death knell of a style in youth culture is its appropriation by younger age groups, 'bubblegum' groups, or its mass production by chain stores. This popularization means that style has been robbed of its authenticity and its message. Another complication is separating the part-time and full-time adherents, separating the righteous from the poseurs. In a subculture with literary and artistic affiliations, there are core members at the centre of the culture, often creative artists, but followers and peripheral members who may adopt the lifestyle, or appearance, and who may or may not be perceived as 'real' members.

Teddy boys

There have been several delinquent subcultures since the end of the Second World War, with distinctive styles. In order to unravel subcultures' response to their own generational history it is necessary to describe some of the themes at this point. Societal reaction has often been quite severe, and the response certainly illustrates S. Cohen's 'folk devils' point. The first truly post-war working-class dandy was the Teddy boy. The post-war period of the late forties provided nothing exciting or specific for working-class youth. Fyvel (1963, p. 84), suggests they were rebellious youth drawn from a class of unskilled workers who were left after their more achieving peer groups had been creamed off into skilled apprenticeships, or grammar school upward mobility. The Ted was popularly supposed to earn compensatory high wages (non-deferred gratification), which compensated him for his exclusion from embourgeoisement. The style – drape jackets, velvet collars, drainpipe trousers, crêpe-soled shoes, bootlace ties – was developed from a brief flirtation with Edwardian dandyism by the upper middle classes. This was (Clarke *et al.*, 1976, p. 54), style in the classical sense in cultural studies.

> What makes a style is the activity of stylisation – the active organisation of objects with activities and outlooks, which produce an organised group activity in the form and shape of a coherent and distinctive way of 'being-in-the-world'.

Jefferson (in Hall and Jefferson, 1976), suggests that the Ted bought status, upper middle-class Savile Row suits, and then adapted an individual style. This symbolized a subculture which was in some way against the current mode of embourgeoisement and achievement, it celebrated the yob, the 'left-out' working-class youth. It also expressed a concern with dress which was unusually extrovert and which challenged what was a traditional female expression. This was why any insult to it, real or imagined, had to be met with toughness or violence. It had to deny any hint of effeminacy. The Mississippi gambler element of the image hinted at the outlaw, living on his wits with no real visible means of support. In addition Hall *et al*. (1976, p. 48), suggest

> (subcultures) 'solve' but in an imaginary way, problems which at the concrete material level remain unresolved. Thus the 'Teddy Boy' expropriation of an upper class style of dress 'covers' the gap between largely manual, unskilled, near-lumpen, real careers and life-chances, and the 'all dressed-up-and-nowhere-to-go' experience of Saturday evening.

Disparate groups involved in different events, owing to mass media coverage, became in the public mind a holistic structure, perpetuating myths which in time the subcultures began to believe and respond to. The cult heroes of the time, Dean, the sensitive, mixed-up kid, Brando, the menacing biker hipster, all gave specific interpretations of masculinity which found a parallel in the early rock and roll. Presley's deep voice and black gestures became exploited to fit the market demand, a black entertainer who was basic and raunchy, but who was white. The working-class Southerner from the wrong side of the tracks became an important influence in music.

Jefferson (Hall *et al*., 1976), suggests the Teds turned to the socially cohesive force of their peers in response to the post-war upheaval in the working-class community. Their butchness set off their dandyism and protected their masculinity. Societal reaction suggested another explanation (Article 'by a family doctor', *Evening News*, 12.5.54)

> Teddy boys . . . are all of unsound mind in the sense that they are all suffering from a form of psychosis. Apart from the birch or the rope, depending on the gravity of their crimes, what they need is rehabilitation in a psychopathic institution . . . . Because they have not the mental stamina to be individualists they had to huddle together in gangs.

> Not only have these rampageous youngsters developed a degree of paranoia with an inferiority complex, but they are also inferior apart from their disease . . . . It is the desire to do evil, not lack of comprehension which forces them into crime.

This reaction was widespread (Rock P. and Cohen S., 1970). Off-duty soldiers were forbidden to wear Teddy-boy suits, and a leading playwright was described as an intellectual Teddy boy. The folk devil image was launched, but Melly (1972, p. 38), reminds us:

> The fights and cinema riots, the gang-bangs and haphazard vandalism were produced by a claustrophobic situation. They were the result of a society which still held that the middle classes were entitled not only to impose moral standards on a class whose way of life was totally outside its experience; of an older generation who used the accident of war as their excuse to lay down the law on every front; of a system of education which denied any creative potential and led to dead-end jobs and obligatory conscription; of a grey colourless shabby world where good boys played ping pong.

Mods

A notable response in working-class youth culture is that of two reactions to working-class life. There is the celebration of machismo, of the heavy man and of conservative working-class values, and there is the attempt to abstract oneself from one's ascribed class location by a sophisticated distancing – the practice of cool. The heavy appearance of the Teddy boy, an example of the first response, was replaced by the second style in the mid-sixties. The Edwardian suit was replaced by a cooler, neater image, first by the Italian suit which gave rise to the 'modernist' (with its hint of progressive jazz) – the new hip youngster. Personal style was on its way to becoming a form of living performance art which was to reach its heights in the hippy and the punk. In the United States the new dandyism was to be found mainly among young ghetto blacks. Finestone's (1957), 'cats' combined a cool demeanour, elegant clothing as indicators of conspicuous consumption with esoteric jazz knowledge and heroin use, all paid for by mysteriously living on one's wits. The 'cat' set himself off from the square world, but the British mod's small, neat elegance set him off from his opposite, the clumsy, unfashionable, butch, class-bound rocker.

This dichotomy was how most people perceived mods and rockers as Nuttall (1969, p. 333), reminds us,

> 'Mod' meant effeminate, stuck up, emulating the middle classes, aspiring to be competitive, snobbish, phony. 'Rocker' meant hopelessly naïve, loutish, scruffy.

The division between the two occurred when some minor scuffles during August 1964 at East Coast seaside resorts became amplified by media coverage into a conspiratorial series of cultural battles. Suddenly everyone was a mod or a rocker. 'Mod' however, despite its use as an omnipresent neologism, had at least four subcultural streams.

1 The art school high camp version. This explored a new form of male imagery. Clumsiness was removed from masculinity, and the boys were elaborately dressed, often wearing make-up and carrying handbags. The descendants of these were the glamrock and glitter of the early seventies, the more outrageous hippies, and the New York 'camprock' scene, as well as the high camp of New Wave and punk. In many ways this was the beginning of the expression in art schools of the body as living art.

2 Mainstream mods. S. Cohen's (1972, p. 187) 'smooth mods', sharply dressed in suits, neat, narrow trousers, pointed shoes, accompanied by short-haired dead-panned girls, moved around the clubs displaying their clothes and presenting new dances. The rock and roll of the Teds, Melly's 'screw and smash' music, was replaced by rhythm and blues. Drink was accompanied by pills, uppers and downers, leapers and sleepers. For this group there was an attempt to fill a dreary work life with the memories of hedonistic consumption during the leisure hours, as Hall and Jefferson (1976, p. 48) put it,

> Thus in the expropriation and fetishisation of consumption and style itself the 'Mods' cover the gap between the never-ending-weekend and Monday's resumption of boring, dead-end work.

The insignificance of the work day was made up for in the glamour and fantasy of night life.

3 Scooter boys. The scooter, Italian in origin, became a working-class sports car. Covered in chrome accessories and several headlights (stolen from other scooters), they were ridden by young boys in anoraks, wide jeans and canvas shoes.These were replaced by suits and Crombie coats at night, when they could be afforded.

4 Hard mods. This harder, bottom strata sported jeans and industrial work boots. They earned too little to be part of the mainstream group involved in style as compensation. They were to develop into skinheads in the late sixties.

Mods for Hebdige (1976a, p. 91), were epitomized in their use of speed, both as movement, and as a drug. The solution subculturally was that

> the mod was determined to compensate for his relatively low position in the daytime status-stakes over which he had no control, by exercising complete dominion over his private estate – his appearance and choice of leisure pursuits.

Leisure replaced work as a major activity, status was from non-work, and city night life took on a major meaning. The clubs were a glamorous dream world where their elegance transcended the virtues of neatness prescribed by family, school and employers. Barker and Little's (1964) survey was less enchanting. Their Margate offenders mod sample were semi-skilled or clerical workers, who had left school early and earned £11 per week. They were in the lower echelons of white collar work, and wanted to indicate that the working class too could be neat, glamorous, expensively dressed trend setters. Indeed they were. Quant in her autobiography acknowledges the influence mod girls had on her fashion design. However their consumption was a gift to the market, and one result was Carnaby Street and 'swinging London', and the development of superstars such as the Rolling Stones and The Who. Mods were a symbol of affluent teenage consumption, and their neatness became transformed into a threat. Sexual boundaries were less distinct in the mod world, the girls with short hair, flat bodies and inexpressive faces, the boys elaborately smart and unbutch. There was a mid-point in the male–female polarity, unlike the hippies' move towards femininity and the skinheads' to masculinism. By the mid-sixties however, the cool, aloof mod girl had been replaced by the programmed girlishness of the long-haired, mini-skirted blonde 'dolly girl'.

Rockers

For most people, mods were unseparable from their youth cultural opposites, the rockers. According to Barker and Little, this group also had left school early, but were in more routinized unskilled work; they were left out of the mod new working-class teenage consumerism and fashion. Rockers can be seen as two groups, firstly the bikers, the 'Wild Ones' of Brando, the 'Hell's angels', hanging around transport caffs, in black leather and studs, performing ton-ups on the new motorways. They project an 'easy rider' nomadic romanticism, violent, loyal only to each other, anti-authority and anti-domesticity, the male free wanderer dream, living only for the present. The non-riders, 'greasers' had a similar image, but were less involved in the cult of the bike, sharing only the studied scruffiness and aggressively working class masculinity, bad boys against the mods' clean boy image. For them mods were contemptibly unmasculine. Their girls were like them, often aggressive, sexistly seen as property, and secondary to the male culture. Willis (1978), suggests a homology between the masculinism of the rocker, their rejection of the deferred future and the motor bike. The bike is not transport, but an object of intimidation and mastery, which projects the rider uneasily near to death. Dancing had also been transformed by them into a more individual style, away from the control of dance hall management to a more individual form. The early rock and roll of the 1950s was of a 'special resonance and relevance to their present lives'. The replacement of sheet music by singles meant the rockers could repeat records or create a repertoire both inexpensive, and individualized to specific tastes. The music of the golden age of Elvis, Gene Vincent, Eddie Cochran was physical and unchanging, making no demands on intellect or knowledge of melodic craft. It was related in a chain of events, music – dancing – motor bikes, with the additions of violence and sexuality. It was as Melly put it, 'screw and smash' music. The location in the golden age of rock ties it to a changeless moment in masculinist cultures. Men are men, aggressive, wild and protective, and women know their place. Rock is body music, simple and yet highly aggressive; death is ever present on the bike, and this threat is central to control, control over the machine, one's life, one's body, one's identity – one's manhood. Rockers were a kind of motorized cowboy, loners and outsiders, contemptuous of authority, and of women who were seen as the traditional ties of men to responsibility and respectability.

Skinheads

During the late sixties, the hard mods developed a new image, with jeans rolled high to reveal Doc Marten industrial boots, braces, hair cropped short (later known as suedeheads). All projected an aggression which was to gain for the skins a reputation as 'bovver boys' or 'boot boys', concerned with 'aggro'. They formed neighbourhood groups, sometimes taking a leader's name (e.g. Smithy's team) or a local area name (the Somers Town boys). They were ardent football supporters, and the terraces they dominated became a group name for skinhead supporters – Chelsea's Shed, Arsenal's North Bank, Liverpool's Kop. Their notoriety spread to their bigotry in support of traditional conservative working-class values. Their targets were immigrants, especially Asians, non-masculinity, and the work-shy (hippies). They indulged in Paki-, hippy- and queer-bashing. However as Pearce (1973b), argued, they merely reflected values about gays already held by respectable 'ordinary people', and I have discussed elsewhere (Brake, 1974), how in fact they became presented in the mass media as a deviant group, because of their racism. In fact this racism was endemic in British policy and politics (it was no accident that Paki-bashing skins chanted 'Enoch, Enoch'), and their racism was in no sense deviant, merely an extension of existing attitudes encouraged by British hostility to immigrants. Bigots were a lunatic fringe, skinheads, not ordinary people, and the racism of immigration and race relations legislation could be conveniently forgotten. Clarke (1976a), argues that skinheads used style to recreate the traditional working-class community, to magically recover it. They were preoccupied with territory, locally seen as threatened by immigrants, and often symbolically defended in football matches. They celebrated their working-class origins, their puritan work ethic, their maleness (Daniel and McGuire, 1972). An empirical study (Brake, 1977), found them to be drawn from groups of pupils who had been rejected by school, and who in unguarded moments revealed damaged self-esteem. Their response was to develop a strong working-class conservatism, and their work ethic was deliberately in opposition to the hippies' aristocratic disdain for work. They protected their world against pollution, the filth of hippies (unwashed and lazy), immigrants (dirty and lowering the respectability of the district) and homosexuals (corrupt and vicious). Again their ranks were mixed, not all were racist (some were West Indians), or anti-gay or anti-hippy, indeed ska and bluebeat were favourite music forms, as was reggae until the music took a distinctly pro-black political form. Nevertheless by 1970 they were the major folk devils. A quality newspaper describes them as (Fox, J., 1969),

> From London's Mile End, looking westward . . . you can see what a sociologist would call a phenomenon and what

> an authoritarian would class hooliganism. Young working class boys, average age 15 to 17 dressed in a sparse, inelegant way, but all dressed the same, out in the streets, looking for fights, playing pintables, dancing to Bluebeat music, causing 'aggro'. That's the skinhead term for aggravation, provocation, a state of mind, where it doesn't feel good to go to bed without having a good scrap . . . . What really maddens them and starts their shoulders rolling, and fists punching, shadow boxing style, is anything 'flash' . . . . Flowers, frills, colours are anathema. Hippy is a dirty word.

Local gangs fought Asians, hippies, gays and each other (Stimpson, 1969):

> Each gang seems perpetually on the alert for some trouble. Sometimes months will go by without a fight, then suddenly there'll be a fight every night. 'We are friends with no one – no joke. There was a time when we couldn't go out of our area like unless we was thirty handed. We hit every fucking crew from right round here, up that way, St John's Wood, the Edgware Road, Tufnell Park, Archway, Burnt Oak, Mile End, Kilburn, Highbury, Holloway, just sort of everywhere . . . . We wacked someone from nearly everyone of those areas, and they was all after us, there was a lot of aggro then . . .

The popular press put it more bluntly. An interview with 'a skinhead leader' (*Daily Express*, 31.1.70) comments,

> We are against everyone who screws (looks at) us, Pakis, students and queers.

Which would have been unfortunate for those who were all three. The attacks on Asians, led to Pakistani vigilante groups in East London, and in 1969 25 per cent of the Pakistani Student Federation reported being attacked in the London area. Their violence at football matches led to the police removing skinheads' braces, belts and bootlaces before the game, and warning local shopkeepers not to sell these to skins. Chief Constables admitted the illegality of this but the press praised it (see the *Sun*, 2.4.70), and a skinhead questioning its illegality was fined £50 for threatening behaviour. By 1971 however, longer hair was grown, and a smoother image adopted, and skinheads tired of being scapegoated by employers, teachers, the police and rival gangs, disappeared to reappear spasmodically in 1978.

Glamrock and glitter

By the early 1970s the new provincial city centres provided leisure areas, mostly owned by commercial managements but sometimes dominated by particular groups, as with Wigan's all-night Northern soul centres. This embourgeoisement of leisure, combined with the commercialization of football, Taylor and Wall (1976) argue, led to the development of a 'classless, universal manufactured culture'. In attempts to combine skinhead hardness and hippy progressiveness, glamrock, in particular Bowie, Lou Reed, Bolan and Gary Glitter, made a bid for support. It had an interesting effect. In a way reminiscent of mods, hard lads dressed up in extravagant clothes not unlike early hippies, and wore high heels, elaborate make-up, often set off with tattoos. This would have been unheard-of in the fifties amongst working-class hards. This decadent image, a sort of Thirties Berlin and New York gay combination was a masculinist version of camprock. It lasted a brief time and was replaced by the first working-class bohemian subculture – punks.

Punk

In the summer of 1976, after a dearth of youth culture in Britain, a new folk devil appeared in the media with a coverage reminiscent of the mods and rockers moral outrage of the sixties. This was the punk rocker. The name derived from punk rock, a form of New Wave music developed from music earlier in the decade in the United States. This was music based on the work of Lou Reed, John Cale and the New York Dolls whose imagery was outrageous and camp. The British trade papers had been trying to promote the sound from the early part of 1976 in opposition to reggae. Punk has been defined (*Melody Maker*, 28.5.77) as the less musically competent but more rebellious bands, and New Wave the same bands later in their careers, with a more sophisticated sound. This reflects British rock tradition which unlike American, uses amateur musicians with verve and rawness but little technique, whilst America has many excellent technical musicians to draw from but who lack the gut level of the amateur. The punk bands developed in pubs, and soon had a close following, with hair shaved close to the head, dyed vivid colours, and clothes based on bondage and sexual fetishism, made out of rejected items such as dustbin liners or old school clothes. In fact a genuine punk makes his/her own clothes, and integrity is valued in appearance. Punk band musicians base their stage appearance on characters developed from their own personal style and bizarre parts of their personality. They often take new names of a rebellious form – Poly Styrene, Sid Vicious, Johnny Rotten – and they owe much to the art school and conceptual art. In this sense they are in the tradition of art school high camp of the mods. In December 1976, a television interview with the anarchistic Sex Pistols, where their lead singer was invited to swear, led to a societal reaction which gave punk a boost into the public eye. It coincided with one of the biggest teenage unemployment rates since before the war in Britain. It has been described as 'dole queue rock' (Marsh, 1977) and bohemianism (Frith, 1978). In fact it is both, because it is a stratified subculture, drawn from lower middle-class art colleges attempting to '*épater* the bourgeoisie', and working-class kids rejecting the virtuosity of superstars, the wealth of successful musicians, and the hippies. Frith argues that punk has connections with the Surreal, hippies and the Situationists International. However the punk spectrum is wide: it covers many types of bands, nihilistic, anarchistic and political, and what it manages to do successfully is to upset everyone, left, right, centre, *avant-garde* and reactionary. The punk followers create an appearance of outrage which appeals to those who feel there is no future, no work and bleak prospects. The music not unlike reggae, has the beat emphasized, with the melody in the background, and this makes a connection with punk appearance and anarchy. The lyrics speaking of high rise flats, dole queues and white riots appealed to many working-class kids, and the Sex Pistols managed to get a hit single to number one, despite being banned on various airwaves because of its anti-Royal Family sentiments. The use of hints of perverse sexuality, sado-masochism, bondage and promiscuity was a deliberately anti-emotional element of their style.

Politics played an important part in this. The National Front, taking heart from the punks' wearing of the Iron Cross and the Swastika, approved the racist songs and comments of superstars Clapton and Stuart, and commended Bowie's praise of Hitler (see their publication, *British Patriot*, no. 47). However this caused several previously apolitical punk bands to take a stand against the Nazis, and at a Rock against Racism concert 80,000 people demonstrated against the National Front. The commercial potential of punk will undoubtedly destroy its vitality and verve, and the fanzines will become replaced by glossies, but it offers chaos, excitement and warmth. It is seldom violent despite a much-publicized 'war' in the summer of 1977 of teds *v.* punks in London's Chelsea. It shocks, either by fetishized costume, and ambisexuality uncovering desires we hide even from ourselves, or by its deliberate anti intellectual and anti-achievement statements. It is not surprising it came out against the National Front. This was not the Front's first sortie into the politics of rock. John Tyndall had written in the *National Socialist* in the early 1960s on another deviant rock group, the Beatles

> I had heard that their brand of music was thoroughly British . . . . But having sampled a few bars of it, I became convinced that this 'music' was certainly not native to Britain, nor to Europe nor to anywhere in the world where civilisation exists. As these effeminate oddities gyrated their underdeveloped bodies about the stage, looking for all the world like the members of a primitive African tribe . . . . Is this not the age of effeminacy and weirdness in the male type – as well as the age in which the cultural values of historic Europe have been relegated to the poorhouse to be replaced by the ravings of the new 'niggersymphony'. Is it not right that in order to be 'with it' our young manhood should ape the outer appearance of the queer and the musical incantations of the savage . . . . I could not help but recall the picture of another youth belonging to another age, and the standard bearers of another spirit, their bodies lithe and muscular as these were unmasculine and feeble, their faces as aglow with buoyant health as these were pale and dissipated, their voices echoing not the gruesome wailings of the African bush but the proud martial airs of their European fatherland.

This was hardly likely to appeal to the punks, and after all, as Mick Jagger puts it 'I know that it's only rock and roll, but I like it'.

From the analysis of working-class youth subcultures it can be seen that what emerges are several focal concerns which seem to be present in most of them. The most important is masculinity, and as I have suggested these are predominantly masculinist cultures, offering forms of masculine identity. In a study carried out amongst hippies and skinheads (Brake, 1977), a semantic differential revealed that both hippies and skinheads rated themselves similarly on a masculinity concept. This acts against the popular notion of hippies as feminized males. Similarly the imagery and style of these cultures explore different perspectives of machismo, relegating girls to appendages, and resisting their attempts at respectabilizing the male by marriage. Football is a second important focal concern both for the careers it offers and for its territorial symbolism. Taylor (1970), has suggested that the embourgeoisement of the game, the upward mobility of the players into the international superstar bracket has done much to preserve the player as the last working-class hero capable of making it into the big time. Clarke (1978), sees that football has moved from a pre-war event involving the whole ground, to a professionalization which makes the spectators passive. This may explain the reaction on the terraces to create some life. Marsh, Rosser and Harre (1978) suggest that football 'aggro' in fact has a set of orderly rituals. Terraces are converted into partisan home territories, and are peopled by hard-line supporters of youngsters who offer a deviant career structure and an identity. This is by an informal apprenticeship system based on age, tested by partisanship. A repertory grid analysis revealed the importance of style, showing that costume in fact signalled important cues about hardness and team loyalty. The fights were ritualized, turning a dull match into an exciting day out. Masculinity was important, and the demasculinizing insults jeered at opponents emphasize this. Marsh *et al.* found that injuries and arrests were less than 0.01 per cent of a season's attendance. There is a distinct social reality on the terraces, and this is an important element in constructing an identity outside of work and school. Ethnocentricism is a third important element. As youngsters have to deal with the contradiction of a push towards affluence, success and consumption, they also face the run-down of the local economy, and the increase of unemployment. The result of this is to blame deterioration of the community on the newcomers, immigrants. This has been discussed above and will be taken up in the section on black youth. This means a return to working-class conservatism.

Puritanism is another focal concern but usually in the work ethic. Puritan work ethics allow a dehumanization of those seen as wilfully idle. Skinheads (Brake, 1977), relegated their victims, hippies and immigrants to these categories. It is a spin-off from working-class realism, in the sense that everyone has to be made to work, and it makes no sense to speak of enjoying it. A cynical world view is another element which acts where the working class are not oppositional. The social structure is seen as run by employers and politicians who are seen as liars and exploiters. However because of a cynicism towards politicians, it is not felt that much can be done. This means that brutalized, they often fall back on masculinism and violence as a form of self-reliance.

Fatalism and realism are the final focal concerns. Most studies of young workers have shown a frightening degree of realism about their location in life, and their ability to do anything about it (see Veness, 1962; W. B. Miller, 1958; Downes, 1966; Hargreaves, 1967; Brake, 1977). The work world is accepted as dreary although shop-floor culture acts against this (Willis, 1978). Marriage and parenthood are seen as inevitable, especially for working-class girls, and as one respondent remarked to the author at the tender age of 15

> You have a good time until you're about twenty, and then it's all over, ain't it? You settle down like, get married.

These focal concerns of masculinity, football, puritan work ethic, fatalism and realism reveal what are genuine areas of concern for working-class youth. Aspirational and deferential youth will accept the situation and invest in it to gain the best returns. Delinquent and deviant youth however takes a rebellious fatalism as its stance. You may not agree with 'them' but you can hold out against 'them' for as long as possible. The solution often takes a conservative turn, although in moments, such as strikes, there is a heady sense of collective radicalism.

Willis (1978), has interestingly pursued the notion of the relations between class-room anti-school culture and shop-floor culture, which illuminates these focal concerns for us.

Willis sees deep disjunctions and contradictions in social and cultural reproduction. Class domination in capitalism is not simple and deterministic, but a constant struggle. Capitalism is never secure, what is accommodating in working-class culture is also resistant, and the modern, liberal, democratic form of capitalism contributes to this insecurity. What are possible freedoms for working-class kids, are used for self-domination: working-class people collude unintentionally in their own oppression. State institutions such as the school, are not intentionally run merely for the benefit of the ruling class, they are not simple unities with particular types of reproduction taking place within them. Indeed a major problem would arise if working-class kids absorbed 'the rubric of self development, satisfaction and interest in work' which the schools try to instil. Working-class kids take up working-class jobs because some of the 'real functions of institutions work counter to their stated aims'. The counter-school culture has to be seen outside its immediate institution, and located outside in the very nature of labouring in capitalism, in sexism, ideology and general abstract labour. The working-class lads' own culture, anti the school, prepares them for work, and is paradoxically experienced by them as true learning, and as resistance. There is a relation between the counter-school culture discussed in the literature (see Hargreaves, 1967; Shipman, 1968; King, 1973; Young, 1971; Lacey, 1970), regional working-class culture and the culture of the shop floor. It 'provides powerful informal criteria and binding experiential processes which lead working-class lads to make the "voluntary" choice to enter the factory' (Willis, 1978, p. 188), and reproduces the class structure of employment and shop-floor culture. The latter allows people to find meaning in their work despite hard conditions and external authority. Paradoxically the culture allows them to enjoy a basically alienating experience, already reflected in the anti-school culture, which has values refound in the actual physical work of heavy production. Opposition to official authority and norms at school is found in evading work ('skiving'), education is perceived as social control by the counter-school culture. At work this develops into coarse humour, sexism, rough horseplay, badinage and vandalism, developing a solidarity with workmates to resist the authority and meaninglessness of work. It is the antithesis of academically oriented pupils, and of white collar work. At school there is already a division which influences thoughts about work, and concepts about different futures. The anti-school 'lads' commit themselves not to particular jobs, or careers, but to a future of generalised, routinised labour. 'When the lad reaches the factory there is no shock only recognition', because he is familiar with defeating boredom, time-wasting, and with fiddling and 'handling himself' because he learned these as real experiences of mediating alienation, at school. The result is typical working-class fatalism ('Life's like that, it's nobody's fault'). This symbolic resistance to authority never develops into real power: on the contrary it reinforces real power relations. There is in both counter-school and shop-floor cultures, a rejection of officially approved roles, a mistrust of official values, a wish to be a non-conformist, but naturally one has to make a living. A distinction is made by the lads between the official view of how things work, how they really work, and being involved in survival. Willis sensitively explores these themes, and he is the only writer really to bridge with insight the gap between work and school for manual workers.

3 The trippers and the trashers – bohemian and radical traditions in youth culture

The cultural rebels – bohemian subcultures and middle-class delinquency

> They were . . . well Beautiful People . . . not 'students', 'clerks', 'salesgirls', 'executive trainee' – Christ, don't give me your occupation-game labels! we are the Beautiful People, ascendant from your robot junk-yard . . . (Wolfe T., *The electric cool-aid acid test,* Bantam, New York, 1969)

The concept of 'youth culture' has been applied popularly to bohemian subcultures. Although they have conceptualized themselves as being outside of class, they can be linked to middle-class intelligentsia in origin. Middle-class subcultures can be differentiated from working-class both in their formation and their organization. Working-class subcultures are clearly part-time, temporary episodes of shorter duration, and are neighbourhood-based with local peer group affiliations. As we have seen, the neighbourhood is an important element in the transmission and interpretation of working-class youth cultures. Working-class youth tends to be involved in leisure activities which are able to mediate the control of adult authority. Middle-class subcultures tend to be more diffuse, more conscious of an international cultural influence. Obviously this is nationally shaped, but there is a wider sphere of influence, for example, student cultures which may reflect political and cultural ideas articulated into a more distinct style and form. They have a longer influence over their members' life cycle, and have a distinct relation to the values of the dominant class, although they may be 'stretched'. ('Doing your own thing' is a hippy 'stretched value' of the middle-class evaluation of individualism and self-growth.) Explorations may also be made of alternative adaptations of middle-class forms of dominant institutions, for example 'alternative' life-styles, communal child care, 'free' schools, fringe medicine, self-awareness groups and so forth.

Often these involve a fusion of the distinctions between work and leisure – 'work and play', and a relationship to material production which involves a relation to surplus where welfare provision or the use of rejected consumer goods provides a modest minimal standard of living. A central economic element has been the provision of higher education grants, and indeed the very notion of 'dropping out' presupposes a location in the class structure from which to drop (and to return) as opposed to the harsh reality of working-class life, a flight from the 'never had'. The discipline of industrial life acts as a great socializer. After a week-end of 'Saturday Night Fever' the young worker has to face Monday morning. Work and leisure remain separated, work providing the means to enjoy leisure, and play which is involving enough to detract from the boredom of work has a luxurious element which is expensive for young industrial workers.

The diffuseness and articulation of middle class cultures means that when they are oppositional, they tend to be more overtly political and ideological in their critique of work. They have been assisted in this by the development of the underground press which presents a political and cultural critique of the establishment, and which also spreads the notion of an organised and coherent counter culture.

One problem in distinguishing working-class and middle-class youth subcultures is that of membership. The marginality of membership is a problem, and whilst youth subcultures tend to follow class traditions, individual members may be exceptions. Buff (1970), found in Chicago that his working-class boys tended to become 'greasers', but some took up hippy subcultures. However in the United States, some estimates have claimed something like a million teenage runaways are on the road. This means that there is a considerable working-class section to apparently middle-class subcultures such as student or freak cultures, usually known as 'street people' or young vagrants. Brake (1977), found a hard core of working-class 'drifters' in his hippy sample, rejected by the underground for many of the reasons wider society had rejected them, lack of skills, capital, education and prospects, combined with quasi-criminal interpretations about 'liberating' property and 'free love'. Punks have both working-class and middle-class groups, and these sometimes overlap. Class is also complicated by age, Monod's (1967), Parisian working-class youths adopting the 'snob' style (based on a Rolling Stones imagery) marked themselves off from the local gay community (who had a similar image) from the younger 'voyou' boys with their greaser style.

The emergence of youth culture in the United States

A complication in delinquency studies is the degree to which it can be found in the middle class. Its presence there has been attributed to several causes – unhappy broken homes and lack of parental concern and discipline (Nye, 1958), academic failure and absent fathers (Greely and Casey, 1963), downward mobility (Pine, 1965), and family conflict (Herskovitz, Murray and Spivak, 1959). Most studies concentrate on minor offences (Vaz, 1967a), and favour psychological explanations. They tend to overlook subcultural attachment, although England (1967), does suggest that adolescents do see themselves as a collectivity with similar interests, and therefore 'youth culture' does have an effect on middle-class delinquency. Youth culture has been used uncritically in post-war American literature, favouring a generational rather than a class membership. Parsons (1954), suggests that youth culture is a separate cultural system shared by the young. A 'more or less specifically irresponsible' youth culture exists in conflict with the adult world's sense of responsibility, conformity and productive work. It emphasizes hedonism, and 'its recalcitrance to the presence of adult expectations and discipline'. Smith (1962), notes a generational conflict in America, but mainly over sexual matters, although he takes note of subcultural features such as dress, language and appearance, strong peer loyalty and youth's own forms of conformity. He and also Hollingshead (1949), note class differences in youth culture, and Barnard in a monograph on youth as it once again became a burning social problem (1961), stresses class as pervading all parts of teenage culture, including political views. She notes also their use to the adult economy due to consumption, a point Friedenberg (1966, p. 102) makes:

> Only as a customer . . . are adolescents favourably received. Otherwise they are treated as a problem, and potentially as a threatening one . . . . Adults attribute to them a capacity for violence and lust, in this respect teenagers serve the rest of us as the occasion both for wish fulfilment and for self fulfilling prophecy.

On the whole, however, youth culture was explained in terms of the generation gap, rather than conflicts and divisions due to class. This approach was favoured in an influential study by Coleman (1961), who was distressed to discover that student and high school cultures favoured sociability, glamour, social status and athleticism, rather than academic orientation.

Murdock and McCron (in Mungham and Pearson, 1976) remind us that Coleman's original intention was to indicate that different status systems evolve from the pluralism of high school cultures. Coleman discovered that in some of his high schools, status was linked to class origin rather than to individual achievement. His intention of presenting a pluralistic analysis was undermined by these class-linked variables.

Polk and Halferty (1966) argued that where a lowering of the commitment to success was present, there was a move towards youth culture, with a stress on anti-achievement and delinquent behaviour, reflecting middle-class and working-class youth cultures respectively. Berger (1963b) notes that Coleman's youth culture reflects American values in the adult world closely. Youth culture, he reminds us, has often not much to do with youth; instead (Berger, 1965, p. 394), 'What we are in the habit of calling youth culture is a creature of some young and some not so young persons'. Instead the type of behaviour witnessed in youth culture is found also in bohemian cultures, and certain working-class occupations, rather than the young *per se*. The youthful, rather than the young, create youth culture. Berger challenges the overgeneralizations of explanations of youth culture. Its roots are to be found outside either the delinquent subculture, or the oppositional nature of some universalistic youth culture.

Youth culture was cited for what it was contrary to, rather than analysed as to what it was. Matza (1961), suggests that deviant patterns of adolescent behaviour are in fact unconventional versions of conventional traditions. Teenage culture may, in fact, prevent individual adolescents from adopting deviant behaviour patterns. There are three subterranean traditions of youth (Matza, 1962), springing from the mainstream of rebellion which has created a special appeal to youth, a rebelliousness which is frequently stigmatised as immaturity and irresponsibility. These traditions are

1 Delinquency, which whilst not denouncing property arrangements, yet violates them. It rejects methodism and routine especially within the school system.
2 Bohemianism, whilst actually indifferent to property, attacks puritanism and mechanised bureaucratic society.
3 Radicalism, which by focusing on economic and political exploitation, has a less generalized cultural attack, concentrating on specific areas of economic exploitation.

These traditions remain true of youth cultural analysis today, and form much of the body of analysis in this book. The delinquent tradition has already been discussed, but the consideration of middle-class youth cultures can be subdivided into political and bohemian formations of rebellion. Both groups may overtly use deviancy as a weapon against the prevailing hegemony and the dominant class formations. Certainly the late sixties saw interesting fusions of the radical and bohemian traditions which used forms of collective anarchism to develop new dimensions of consciousness. There developed the understanding that for the left, there had to be a cultural revolution as well as a material redistribution of resources. Certainly the particular moment in history (the late sixties) generated a spillover into extra parliamentary and extra trade union struggle involving issues over housing, community politics, feminism, (see Brook and Finn, 1977; Mayo, 1977; Wilson, 1977) and gay rights.

The Beat generation

In post-war Paris, there developed on the Left Bank, a traditional student area, a youthful subculture which was based on a literary and philosophical group of intellectuals – the 'existentialists'. Although existentialism has a long and honoured tradition in European philosophy, there grew up a bohemian subculture based around the Boulevard St Michel, and the congregations in cafés such as the Café des Deux Maggots. The intellectuals were headed by Sartre and de Beauvoir, but there were artists such as Cocteau and Picasso, and performers like Petit, Babilee, Jeanmaire and Greco. As with all bohemian subcultures these were the intellectual-artistic nucleus which was the centre of a far larger expressive social movement, which generated followers of a life-style symbolized by the philosophy of the leaders, in the intelligentsia and the arts. Existentialism became the basis of a life-style among students and bohemians, and its style of plaid shirts and blue jeans was spread by Parisian expatriates to other parts of Europe and North America, known in the latter country as 'boheys' (bohemians). The movement reflected the concern in the *avant-garde* at the time with the subjective and the interpersonal, and the growth of interest in psycho-analysis and surrealism. It was to predicate libertarian movements such as the Situationists International with their roots in Dadaism. The war had cruelly interrupted these factions. Hofstadter (1955), argues that during the 1920s 'bohemianism triumphed over radicalism', and the depression of the 1930s produced a 'lost generation', unemployed, drifting through a world where effort and reward had little relationship to each other (David, 1936). The 1940s were dominated by the war, but the 1950s saw the growth of Riesman's 'found generation', polite, conforming, suburban 'other directed' people lost in the 'lonely crowd'. Individualism was a major theme, with the solution to alienation sought in psycho-analysis. However existentialism was developing a bohemian movement which took in Eastern mysticism, jazz, poetry, literature and drugs. This area has been well documented (E. H. Powell, 1962; S. Krim, 1960; Kerouac, 1959; Feldman and Gartenburg, 1959), and became known as the beat generation. Beat, according to Holmes (1960), was 'emptied out . . . a state of mind from which all unessentials had been stripped, leaving it receptive to everything around it.'

From the literary-artistic movement there developed bohemian values – spontaneity, expressivity, creativity which were used not only in art, but through free form and improvisation, were used to develop life-styles. The beat was separated from the 'square', from the grey flannel mind in the grey flannel suit.

The beat writers had taken as folk hero the hipster. The hipster was working-class and often black, a cool cat operating by living on his wits. He was a violent extension of the beat, stripped, state of mind, who dissociated from his feelings and who felt (Powell, 1962, p. 367), 'violence jolts to jar him out of his lethargy'.

There were two models in beat life, the beatnik and the hipster. Both detested the straight world, yet each saw elements of the square in each other. Beats saw hipsters obsessed by expensive commodities, caught up in consumer production, and hipsters saw beats as failed middle-class retreatists. Class separated them further, the hipster working-class, and usually black, the beat white and middle-class, often an intellectual.

The cultural ambience of the beat world differed empirically from its sociological elements. Polsky (1971) in his empirical study, suggests that beats avoided interaction with squares. Two-thirds of his sample were middle class, but were highly antagonistic to the middle-class career system. Like many bohemians they developed a radical critique of what they saw as wrong with society, but not why, ignoring the role of the state in their analysis. Instead they voluntarily espoused poverty, dis-affiliated from family, career and prospects in any conventional sense, and withdrew from a society they detested. Being basically present-oriented, they concerned themselves with individual rather than collective solutions. They lived in a bohemian ghetto, and became involved with religion, drugs, and existential insecurity. Their subculture was distinguished by focal concerns of

Withdrawal – from all but the bare minimum contact necessary for survival, with the square world.
Disaffiliation – from traditional family life, society and career structures.
Existential solutions – to what was seen as basically existential problems.

The beats moved by the early 1960s from Venice West, California and Greenwich Village, New York to North Beach, San Francisco and finally to Haight Ashbury. This latter was to become a hippy epicentre, a cradle of the new bohemianism.

Hippies, freaks and heads

The term 'hippy' obviously covers a vast array of bohemian and student subcultures, and as with the beats there was a hard core of artistic-literary intelligentsia, with an aristocracy of rock musicians, and a vast following of life-style rebels. Hippies have been conceptualized as drop-outs from education (Geoffrey and Grafton, 1967), as antinomean personalities (Adler, 1968), seeking a return to an innocent childhood, and a romantic gnosticism. Westhues (1972), denies this, seeing them rather as possessing hang-loose transcendant ethics, seeking hedonism yet being anti-political. Their drug use has been scrutinized (Cavan, 1970; Davis, 1967; Davis and Munoz, 1968), their life-style and morality discussed in detail (Hinckle, 1967; Distler, 1970; Partridge, 1973; Berger, 1967; Willis, 1978). In much of the American literature hippies have been explained as a generational unit, seen as producing a counter-culture against what is defined as the main enemy, technocracy. Because age cohorts are seen as starting their life courses at unique points in time, they share a historical base, which can influence generational consciousness. It is argued that because of important changes in the economic and social institutions of American society, the vision and analysis of that society was distinctly different for middle-class youth by the 1960s, from that of their parents. The analysis favoured is that of Mannheim (1952), who narrows age cohorts to generational units, that is actively involved members of an age group, who influence social change. Laufer and Bengston (1974, p. 186), delineate this further,

> We would argue that generational analysis, as distinct from cohort lineage or maturational analysis, is concerned with age groups as agents of social change, with their intellectual and organizational alternatives to existing world views, values and life styles; with the sources of opposition within the existing society; and with the developing relationship between these agents of social change and others within their age strata.

These generationally based movements for social change occur when the criteria for social and economic patterns of leadership change. Changes in life style and values arise in response to these. These occur in upper-middle and middle-class groups, because subordination is largely a feature of age in these groups. This follows their hypothesis that (Laufer and Bengston, 1974, p. 188),

> The more intense the experience of subordination (racism, sexism, class exploitation, ethnic discrimination), the greater the continuity of experience across age boundaries.

The exclusion in the here and now of this age group from power, and their self-conscious development of the relation of self and society in higher education (see Keniston, 1972), develops an oppositional consciousness. Their distrust of the political establishment, and their critical awareness of inequality and affluence leads to generational identification as a process for social change. It is a concern for the quality of life, and a rejection of the 'system' although this opposition is often simplified to the 'people' versus the 'pigs'. This type of analysis accepts the subjectivity of age consciousness, but overlooks the objective element of class and its contradictions. Youth's response was to explore alternatives to the received traditions of career, life-style, and occupationally-linked identity. Obviously this disaffiliation takes different forms, for some militant and political, for others mystical and religious. Wieder and Zimmerman (1974) found in their research on hippy communities, that generational units exist which showed intense hostility to and alienation from conventional American society. Their freaks showed distinctly opposite values to the Protestant ethic, favouring immediacy, spontaneity, hedonism, rejecting property because it ascribed status, and having no qualms about welfare or 'pan handling'. They sought an identity outside occupational role or family, which I have suggested is a dominant feature of youth cultures. Youth seems to be for them a conscious political role (at a demonstration Abbie Hoffman suggested no one over thirty should be trusted). This self-consciousness of youth, with the dominant social force being technology, is to be found in Reich (1970), who sees the corporate state as usurping all values. He suggests that Consciousness I, the traditional values of rugged individualism and self-help found among the farmers, small businessmen and workers of the C19, were replaced by the values of organizational society, Consciousness II. The 'contradictions, failures and exigencies of the Corporate State' generated Consciousness III (not unlike Marcuse's new sensibility), which is non-violent, non-judgmental and honest, and which Reich (1970, p. 1) says 'has originated with the individual and with culture and if it succeeds it will change the political structure only as its final act'.

Consciousness III is against uncontrolled technology, the destruction of the environment, the decline of liberty, pointlessness of work, absence of community and loss of self, and will counteract these negations. Roszak (1970) also examines youthful opposition to technocracy, which he sees as based in the work of Marcuse, Brown, Ginsberg, Watts, Leary and Goodman. Visionary experience has been subordinated in our culture, and the counter-culture will present a new vision of how to live. This emphasis on idealism with its ignoring of the political economy and the state are at variance with more Marxist explanations. Flacks (1971, p. 129), argues,

> The culture that is needed to mesh with our state of technological development is one that is incompatible with capitalism. The culture that is struggling to be born stresses cooperation over competition, expression over success, communalism over individualism, being over doing, making art over making money and autonomy over obedience.

These values were made possible by a technology which eliminated much routinized work, allowing the development of a meaningful life, but they are blocked by corporate capitalism which reinforces the mode and relations of production, in turn generating class exploitation and material inequality. Meaningful and creative work experience remain the privilege of the few, and the hippies mistakenly thought it the right of all. Hall (1969), argues that the hippies constituted a distinct grouping at a particular historical 'moment', providing a sketch of future possibilities in terms of post-revolutionary society. Hippies have contributed style – they live their disaffiliation, they add new scripts to the dramaturgy of revolutionary movements, they develop a set of counter-values, and they are an attempt to prefigure a new kind of subjectivity. They represent the expressivist rather than the activist pole, stressing the personal, the private and the psychological – that is subjectivity. This indeed is their major contribution.

The structure of the counter-culture

Hippies gave bohemianism a new, immediate expressivity. They represent a counter culture rather than a politically active movement (Westhues, 1972). Distler (1970), sees this as a flight from a patristic, instrumental culture to a matristic, expressive one, which results in a cultural gap. This places hippy values rationally and emotionally outside the comprehension of most parents, a theme which is found in most commentators on hippy culture. A major variable was the use of drugs, especially hallucinogens such as L.S.D. Another influence, suggested by Davis (1967), was the lessening importance of academic qualifications in contemporary society, which has developed a movement best conceptualized as a social experiment in life-styles. He sees (Davis and Munoz, 1968), drug use as a natural extension of middle-class values such as individualism, symbolizing an attack on normal forms of consciousness, and a disregard of normal society. He goes on to differentiate different meanings that drug use has. LSD is seen as a negotiated version of the basic values of self-exploration and self-improvement found in middle-class life. Young (1971, p. 157), also stresses the social meaning of drug usage,

> The bohemian seeks his identity through the pursuit of subterranean values. He is intent on creating a culture which is short term, hedonistic, spontaneous, expressive, exciting and unalienated. Hallucinogen drugs facilitate such aims admirably.

Brake (1977), in an empirical study found the hippy culture in Britain to be relatively well-organized, peopled mainly by students and ex-students, who had suffered a dissociation from the goals of higher education. Membership was very important to its members. The possession of student grants, or welfare payments permitted them a period away from home where they could experiment with new life-styles and identities. This was a major difference from the part-time membership of working-class youth cultures. Working-class hippies had to make a severe adjustment, and were liable to be rejected if they failed to comprehend or reciprocate appropriately in the loose normative system of the counter culture. Hippies were relatively older, more educated, more middle-class (although they self-reported themselves as working-class) and with better work prospects than working-class youth culture members, and also saw themselves as probably permanently hippies. Willis found in his study of British hippies a homology between immediacy, drug use, an omniscient spirituality and a sense of identity found in the hippy community, symbolized by the style and appearance of hippies. Hippies had an uncertain grip on their own identities, but this was experienced as a source of richness rather than a cause for concern. Immediate subjective experience was important for them, and drugs in assisting this projected them beyond the coercion of the world. Experience showed that the world was coercive, and this knowledge was strangely liberating, but the hippy felt nothing could touch him again, even after he came down. Hippies were concerned with transcendance, and the fuller states of awareness, but this awareness was by its very nature unrealizable. The unending possibility of resolution meant that the starkness of failure need never be faced. The East was admired because it was anti-technocratic. There was an important interaction between progressive rock music and life-style, the music dialectically pursuing the drug experience. Progressive music matched in its complexity and rhythmical asymmetry the hippy life-style, setting the form which through hallucinogenic drug use could be used to undercut the linearity of the straight world. For the hippies their culture was a subversive force cutting away at society's roots, a lived-out critique of the materialism and philistinism of contemporary industrial society.

In order to make sense of an often contradictory mass of material, it is important to consider the contradictions within the hippy subculture, its relation to the wider society and the massive societal reaction it had to contend with. Obviously the underground, or counter-culture was a loose expressive social movement, and researchers looked at disparate elements of it. The subculture developed in a period of relative economic prosperity. Indeed if the estimated one and a half million drop-outs of the sixties in the United States had demanded jobs, the situation might have been quite different. The economy was able to carry a large amount of voluntarily unemployed, living on subsistence incomes. There had been a move from a consumption-oriented economy from a production-oriented one, which was accompanied by a shift in values among the consuming middle-class. The hippy subculture can be seen as fitting in at an overlap of values emphasizing leisure and consumption, but also autonomy and individualism. The counter-culture was created in an affluent society, with an advanced technology, and it was parasitic upon the surplus of the dominant society, and yet antagonistic to it. Hippies were unconcerned about materialism, yet lived on a welfare system which itself related to surplus value; they were disdainful of technology, yet listened to complex stereo systems, watched complicated light shows. They felt freedom was an individual element yet were controlled by a powerful state. Whilst the software came out of the hippy culture, music, lyrics and design, the hardware remained in the possession of the media entrepreneurs. The small businesses, craft shops, restaurants are a traditional solution for the marginal petty bourgeoisie, and they depend on wage labour. Contradictions soon showed. In 1969 Haight Ashbury found itself with 100,000 teenage runaways with no assistance from the Public Health Department. Rape, violence and exploitation increased, 'freak outs' were common, and the Manson family showed itself as the evil joker in the pack (Brake, 1973a; D. H. Smith, 1970; Smith and Luce, 1971; Smith and Gay, 1972). The poor elements of the counter-culture 'ripped off' their brothers and sisters by theft, or 'burning' them with bad dope deals, and the more enterprising organized open air rock concerts with expensive seats and inadequate services. There were also positive elements. Communes were a genuine attempt at alternative living (Abrams and McCulloch, 1976; Teselle S., 1972; Houriet R., 1973; Rigby A., 1973). A concern with ecology led to the development of pure food shops, preventive medicine, pollution politics and organic farming. The necessity to develop new alternative legal and social services led to a new interest in community politics. Techniques of consciousness raising and 'rap' groups developed a new consciousness of oppression outside of traditional class lines, which became essential in the development of feminism and gay politics in their struggle against patriarchy.

The hippy movement provided for its members a moratorium of about five years in which to consider one's identity and one's relation to the world. This luxury is noticeably lacking in working-class life and working-class youth cultures. There was also a blurred yet distinct social system. The top elite was the 'aristopopcracy' of high status and wealthy groups such as super stars. They were beyond the relationship to scarcity as Young

(1973), notes, and they possessed considerable, sometimes absolute, sexual power. Next was the 'alternative bourgeoise' who had specialist knowledge (such as electronics, or production) or else were bohemians symbiotic to the underground. The 'lower-middle-class drop-out' lacked the skills of the above, but was employed in a minor capacity by them. Finally there were the 'lumpenhippies', the 'street people', working-class and vagrant, living rough and 'street wise'. They had run away from home, and were attracted to the hippy life, but found they had no place in the alternative society for mostly the same reasons as they had no place in conventional life, lack of skills, inarticulation and no capital. Lacking any income, they lived on their wits, by welfare, pan-handling, petty theft, and street dope dealing (the least rewarding and most dangerous form of this activity).

Societal reaction to the hippy culture was considerable. British newspapers between 1965 and 1969 report the hippy as dirty, idle, promiscuous and drug-using. A typical report (the *People*, 30.7.67) shows a naked male longhair dancing at the Alexandra Palace 'love-in' with the caption

> If you disagree with this – then this paper gives you ten out of ten – the hippy cult is degrading, decadent and plain daft.

Considerable alarm was shown as the hippies took up residence in new epicentres. In the United States they moved from Venice West, California and New York City, to San Francisco, first to North Beach and then to Haight Ashbury – 'Hashbury'. In Britain, the Cornish village of St Ives, fearing for its tourist trade, in 1969, refused to serve or to house hippies. Weymouth, another resort, used dried blood sprays to prevent hippies sleeping in the open, and the London Street Commune made international headlines by squatting in an elegant, empty Georgian mansion in 144 Piccadilly. A much-quoted report (*News of the World*, 21.9.69), describes the squat 'lit only by the dim light of their drugged cigarettes' as

> Hippies – drugs – the sordid truth
> Drug taking, couples making love while others look on, a heavy mob armed with iron bars, filth and stench, foul language, that is the scene inside the hippies' fortress in London's Piccadilly. These are not rumours but facts, sordid facts which will shock ordinary decent living people. Drug taking and squalor, sex – and they'll get no state aid . . . .

Another report (*Daily Telegraph*, 19.9.69), notes that on the eviction of the squat a hospital governor vomited, a policewoman became ill, and a policeman refused to allow his dog into the squat, all 'because of the filth'. The island of Formantera off Spain also expelled its hippies from a fear they would affect tourism. An 'ex-Military Medallist' is quoted (*Daily Mail*, 2.8.69):

> It makes me ashamed to be British, they have ruined the island. They live around in filthy clothes, mauling each other in the streets. No wonder our country has gone to the dogs.

And another English tourist complained (*Daily Mail*, 4.8.69),

> One of the hippies came to my table, as my wife and I were having a drink. He was obviously drugged to the eyeballs and shouted, 'Life is beautiful, make love together'.

By this time billboards were appearing in the United States proclaiming 'Beautify America – cut your hair'. However one unique feature of the underground was that it had the skills to develop its own press. This meant it could present an articulate counter-ideology, it could give coverage to political and social events not reported in the 'overground' press, and it could present a counter-information service for its adherents (see Glessing, 1971; Lewis, 1972). This was an advantage its middle-class followers with their literacy skills and articulate vocabulary had over the working-class. They possessed the skill and confidence to present a counter-ideology.

Societal reaction and mass media coverage amplified the contradictions of the hippy subculture. In the Summer of Love in 1966, spontaneous friendship and generosity were common, and the music and dance in the streets of hippy districts lent it a fairy-tale romanticism. Health hazards, police harassment and exploitation by landlords resulted in advice centres and free clinics. Haight Ashbury became a teenage slum (Brake, 1973a), and the murder of a black student before 300,000 teenagers by the Hell's angels, appointed as a security force who became police, judge and executioners, during the Altamont rock festival summed up the contradictions. As Eisen (1970, p. 163), argued

> there occurred a strange kind of self-glorification on the part of drop-out society . . . so eventually there came about the idea that somehow there was an essential and fundamental break that had been made as a result of the drugs, the new vocabulary, the music and the new life-styles. An illusion of superiority had suffused itself through the hip

> world . . . It was as though identification with the new culture, with long hair and serious differences with your parents meant that somehow you possessed a superior way of life and a superior insight into the nature of the universe.

The hippy culture evaded rather than confronted the state, it overlooked that any political solution at a reformist or revolutionary level must involve a relationship to the political economy. Individualism and art were presented as solutions. Its politics were (Lydon M., 1971, p. 117),

> a sort of turned on liberalism, that thinks the Panthers are groovy but does not like to come to terms with the nasty American reality. The politics of the much touted rock revolution – they add up to a hazy belief in the power of art to change the world, presuming that the place for the revolution to begin and end is inside individual heads.

As the art and the music became commercial possibilities, then they were transformed into a commodity for the larger society. San Francisco rock was financed, as were the Beatles and the Rolling Stones, by clever financial backers, the Free Press was saved by pornographic film syndicates, head shops taken over by mass production.

By 1970 the hippy subculture had divided into mystics and politicos. The politicos had become involved in New Left politics, combining politics and life-style, and combating Old Left puritanism. Gradually they moved to the periphery of class politics, becoming involved with community politics, or patriarchy, or else retreating into various forms of what Tom Wolfe calls the 'me' generation, encounter groups, bio energetics, massage or diet. The mystics tended to a pastoral arcadism, retreating into the countryside and becoming involved in agrarian communardism with a supportive mysticism. The permissive response of the hippy subculture was a reaction to the small-town puritanism and the Protestant Ethic of contemporary society. However the permissive tolerance degenerated, which meant that any music sounded good if you were stoned enough, anyone should do their own thing, also generated a tyranny of amorality and of structurelessness. Escape was sought from a genuinely oppressive society, which refused to take the straights along with them. Contradictions and oppositions were clouded over by rhetoric, there was no facing up to the internal divisions in the hippy social structure over the relationship to scarcity, no confrontation over the reality of the dependence on and hence relationship to the larger socio-economic system. Gleason (1970, p. 219), shows this lack of analysis,

> We've all gone along with the illusion that Ginsberg and Dylan and Baez and the Beatles and the Stones were all part of the same thing. Well, they are part of one thing, in the sense that we're all human beings and we are all part of the world and each other. So is Lyndon Johnson, so is the Mafia head of Chicago, so are the Hell's Angels. We've tended to make the distinction between Us and Them. Now if we've got to recognise anything, there's not much difference between the Angels beating that kid over the head with a pool cue, and the Chicago cops beating you over the head because you've got long hair.

A full-time leisure expressive subculture can only develop in an economy with sufficient surplus and full employment, but as this changed, then so did Flower Power. The Flower Children faded and died in the desert of unemployment and economic crisis.

The focal concerns of the hippy subculture are difficult to assess because the term 'hippy' is used very loosely. Nevertheless, certain major concerns do show themselves.

1 Passive resistance

The political stances of domestic and foreign policy in the sixties, and in particular the Vietnam war led to a disenchantment with politics. Instead there was a romanticism which argued that if love prevailed everything would be all right. This apolitical ignoring of the functions of the state led the hippy subculture to take up expressive values and idealism as an alternative to rationality and activism. Power as a major variable in political struggle was ignored and mysticism and ritual magic appealed to.

2 Movement

There was a concern both with travelling, often to the East in Europe, and across the United States in America, or to South America. This was seen both as a geographical and a symbolic journey. It was also felt that one should move oneself, by drug use, mysticism, religion or by self-exploration. Any journey was then both physical and existential.

3 Dissociation

Dissatisfaction was felt with the formal education system, at a higher level for hippies, both with the content of the curriculum which was seen as non-humanistic, and with the post college career structure. Hippies came often from materially comfortable families and wanted something else of a vague spiritual satisfaction. Poverty then was voluntarily entered into.

4 Expressivity
A creative, rather than an affluent work situation was sought. Work should be joyous and creative. Expressivity was against thrift and deferred gratification, it was a protest against materialism.

5 Subjectivity
Subjectivity resisted the standards and intrusions of the objective world, which were seen as competitive. Subjectivity opened the self to experience, assisted by drugs, and by religious and mystical even magical explanation. Tomorrow is unimportant, and pleasure, excitement and fear are increased. This explains the lack of standards in hippy life – if you are stoned enough everything is fine – and their hostility to 'put downs' or personal attacks. The danger is that idealism becomes a prime unit of analysis with devastating effects on health, hygiene and exploitation.

6 Individualism
This was a reaction to the facelessness of mass society. It meant 'doing your own thing' and also evading the contradictions of this argument. It meant believing that freedom 'was in your head', not part of an objective oppressive social structure with attendant institutions. Politically it meant romantic anarchy, or apoliticism. Eisen (1970, p. 163), notes this means

> Straight equals bad, freak equals free, and therefore good. This in turn has led to a permissiveness, an encompassing tolerance that accepts that everything that puts straight society and the pigs uptight. Doing one's own thing is the real byword for the culture . . . . But what has resulted has been a relativism that refuses to judge because it has abandoned moral standards . . .

It was this lack of analysis and refusal to face up to the contradictions of the relation to the state and the political economy which led to retreatism in the counter culture. This means (Hinckle, W. 1967, p. 27),

> The hippies have shown that it can be pleasant to drop out of the arduous job of attempting to steer a difficult, unrewarding society. But when that is done, you leave the driving to the Hell's Angels.

The hippy world has developed its own social history, documented in its own media. It was highly socially visible, and unlike the beats who kept out of the limelight, it deliberately attacked the perception of the silent majority. Men were flowing-haired and bearded, and both sexes wore elaborate robes of a non-functional form. There had been use of marijuana and some mild hallucinogens by the beats up to the late fifties, but in 1958 mescalin was produced and added to peyote. The cheap manufacture of LSD began in 1962, and the proselytizing of Leary, and the illicit acid factory of Owsley led to San Francisco becoming the acid centre of the world. (Acid was only illegal after October 1966 in California.) The use of acid by musicians probably contributed considerably to new progressive rock forms. Kesey's 'magic bus' journeys, and the 1966 Trips Festival spread the use of acid. The 1966 Summer of Love was the peaking of the acid experience. After this there became a confusion of politics and youth culture. The Chicago Convention saw the growth of the Yippies, and the Diggers also became prominent as a community political force. The counter-culture then became subdivided into militants and mystics, a dichotomy which lasted until the seventies. The roots of the British underground grew out of the beatnik literary-artistic scene and the peace movement (CND). There were American overlaps such as Ginsberg's (an original beat poet turned hippy mystic and militant) presence at the Albert Hall International Poetry Incarnation in 1965. As English rock music developed with the Beatles and the Rolling Stones, there was also the development of the underground press, either of an early mystical form such as *International Times*, which later became political, or a purely political form such as *Ink*, a mixture such as *Oz* or merely informative like the American *Rolling Stone.* The pro-marijuana stance of *IT* (as *International Times* was known) spread its readership, and the trial of the 'Rolling Stones' in 1966 created the information centre and legal advice service, Release. In fact, the marijuana laws were an important variable in alienating many middle-class young people from the institution of law. Input of a cultural nature also occurred from the Arts Labs, multi media arts laboratories, and the Anti-University Hallucinogens had caused a massive paradigm shift for thousands of middle-class young people. The Wootton Report on marijuana in 1969 in fact recommended its decriminalization, but the government's rejection of this led to a cynicism by hippies of the straight world's understanding of them. By the early 1970s hippies had ceased to be a subculture for the young, although the youthful still remained within it.

The radical tradition – political militancy and protest movements

Obviously a symbiotic relationship exists between the culturally rebellious and the tradition of militant radicalism in the young middle class. The contribution of the culturally rebellious is that they raised issues left out of traditional analyses of class politics in the revolutionary left, that of the place of cultural revolution. The student movement has played an important role since the middle of the C19 in political struggle, but usually at times of transition in societies. In Britain an important movement was the Campaign for Nuclear Disarmament, who from 1958 organized massive protest marches. Writing of CND, Parkin has this to say of middle-class radicalism (Parkin, 1968, p. 2):

> Whereas working class radicalism could be said to be geared largely to reforms of an economic or material kind, the radicalism of the middle class is directed mainly to social reforms which are basically moral in content

The difference is that

> Whereas the former holds out the promise of benefits to one particular section of society (the working class) from which its own supporters are drawn, the latter envisages no rewards which will accrue to the middle class specifically, but only to society at large, or to some underprivileged groups . . . . It will be argued in fact that the main pay off for middle-class radicals is that of a psychological or emotional kind – in satisfactions derived from expressing personal values in action.

CND was more than an attitude to unilateral disarmament, it was a focus for a whole array of radical and humanitarian issues and a vehicle for symbolic acts about a distinctive moral-political outlook, combined with disenchantment with democratic politics in Britain. However Parkin argues that CND supporters were not alienated totally from British society, but from certain dominant values, and thus CND was an expressive activity politically, it expressed and pursued certain principles rather than expected to achieve specific goals. He states (Parkin, 1968, p. 39):

> CND thus provided the one single political movement in which 'progressive' values were fully represented in their pure form, and where they could remain untarnished by the demands of electoral expediency.

It was typical of movements which offered no particular benefits to those who supported them, and in that sense was not an instrumental movement. It was a vehicle for 'personal values in action'. The same could be said of the Anti-Apartheid movement, and the white student support for the American Civil Rights movement. These are radical movements outside of class organised politics, and middle-class involvement is of a deeply felt ethical commitment. It is a humanitarian rather than a class struggle, moral rather than economic reform is sought. Parkin argues (1968, p. 54),

> The approach of the middle class radical movement, unlike its working class counterpart, is to treat each evil *sui generis*, and as not reducible to some greater underlying malady which throws into question the legitimacy of the existing order.

Certainly British societal reaction to CND was extreme, its youthful members in particular were seen as long-haired, beatnik, immoral 'bearded weirdies'. The effect of this was to attract into its ranks youth who were critical of authoritarianism, the state, traditional politics, and paternalism, and it certainly in its four-day-and-night-long march offered an opportunity to meet like-minded young bohemian politicals. Its direct action offered an adventure against the police, and a genuine stance against authority. CND was definitely not respectable, and its culture of folk music, bohemian dress, and its 'permissive' reputation made it a symbol of disaffected youth. It had two important groups of intellectuals, the older generation such as Russell, Taylor, and Priestley who saw it as a chance for Britain to gain a moral leadership to replace her lost military and economic prestige. The other group were the Young Angries, dramatists and novelists of the late fifties, such as Braine and Osborne, marginal or transitional in their social position. They were mainly working class in origin, were not notably university products, and wrote of the problems of being working class in a middle-class social democracy. Many of these writers have now become reactionary pillars of the establishment or noisy celebrators of sexism. The Campaign for Nuclear Disarmament (CND) was an important political mentor. In Parkin's sample 62 per cent of his politically committed subjects joined political parties and movements after being in CND. They were higher-educated, middle-class professionals involved in teaching, welfare or creative work. CND expressed a pro-life humanistic active protest against the feeling of helplessness over nuclear war, and the seeming inability of the electorate to influence politicians during crises. It involved a considerable amount of young people in active protest politics, radicalizing them often for life.

The Hungarian uprising and Suez in 1956 had polarized discontent with the official party line of the Old Left. CND acted as a springboard, which owing to the splintering off of the Committee of 100 showed the influence of the British Anarchist movement. It was an *ad hoc* spontaneous movement, unhampered by an authoritarian hierarchy which applied a policy of direct action. It marked the beginnings of the move to create a New Left, based not on the Leninist model of centralized political parties, but with a new libertarian base involving Trotskyite principles. The New Left was to show conflicts between these features during the sixties and seventies. As the anti-bomb movement lost impetus after the Cuban missile crisis of 1962, and the Test Ban treaty of 1963, the disparate elements in CND became separate both in analysis and action. It was the Vietnam War which was to capture mass support from radicals, with its militarism, neo-colonial economic elements and its racism. It marked a distinct move from disillusion with passive resistance and the way the state had accommodated this, to a more violent, liberating revolutionary action, which certainly showed itself in the campus battles of the sixties.

In the United States, the first major radical cause for youth in the post war period was the Civil Rights Movement. American students began increasingly to reject the commercial and national levels of America, in a country which did nothing about the legal rights of its own minority groups, and which despite its great wealth, did little for the poor. It was felt that the labour movement had become integrated into the established political system, and certainly in America the radical movement has a more established history, than class politics. Students adopted populist, egalitarian generational rhetoric and style, which grew out of the Civil Rights Movement, focused on the Vietnam War, and saw action in campus demonstrations, draft resistance and the Chicago Convention. Race became a major issue with the lunch-counter sit-ins in the South in 1960 (although there had been demonstrations in the late fifties), leading to the Student Non-violent Co-ordinating Committee (SNCC). At the same time Berkeley was protesting about the San Francisco Un-American Activities Committee. As with CND in Britain, direct action of a non-violent form was used, one highlight being the Washington Peace March in 1962. The Civil Rights movement was a coalition of black and white focusing on the South and using the process of law as an ally. It was essentially middle-class, non-violent and reformist using Martin Luther King and the National Association for the Advancement of Colored People. Violent Southern resistance, particularly by law enforcement personnel increased student activist groups such as SNCC and Committee for Organising Racial Equality. The move from passive resistance to militant action was notable after the murder of King in April 1968. Urban riots significantly increased in the ghettos and white assistance was regarded with suspicion and hostility. The separatism of the Black Muslims gave a new pride in black identity. The anti-colonial political and cultural resurgence of black activism made race riots and civil insurrection a central issue. In 1966 the Black Panthers were the central focus of militant struggle and were systematically attacked by the police and the FBI. Threatened with destruction they focused on community action and local politics, but their analysis and their pride in blackness gave a dignity and inspiration to a militancy found in contemporary Britain, the West Indies and Southern Africa.

Focusing on the Civil Rights movement, the Students for a Democratic Society attempted to organize students for social change in society, using universities as arenas for activity, analysis and discussion to radicalize grass roots movements. The desire to change the wider society was often expressed in such campus issues as free political speech on campus, such as the Berkeley Free Speech issue 1964, which had wide publicity concerning direct action techniques and which was to become a model for future student strategies. This was a turning-point in white student activism. As white involvement in civil rights for blacks began to fade owing to the increase of the demand for Black Power, white students were called upon to demonstrate their radicalism. Up to 1965 students criticized the failure of the political system to carry out its avowed objectives, but after this there was a distinct disillusionment with the authority of the state and a cynicism which demanded a revolutionary alternative which lasted until Watergate. University involvement with the war economy came under heavy criticism. Research involvement, police on campus, the censorship of criticism of the war or of the government meant the university had ceased to be a bastion of liberal discussion. The draft, based on scholastic achievement also became an issue, as did the pointlessness of most academic curricula to contemporary problems. By the mid-sixties, the civil rights movement had taken a new militant phase, the federal government seemed to be a cooling-out agent rather than a facilitator of legally established rights. The War on Poverty, a response to civil insurrection, was seen as preserving rather than providing significant reforms, the university was seen as preventing criticism, and the war had escalated. Passive resistance and protest had no effect on the Johnson administration, the war was misrepresented by the establishment. Students placed in competition over the draft, resisted it. There was a spill-over from these issues into a concern with poverty, urban decline and oppression, spreading from pollution, to community control such as the People's Park in Berkeley, to urban guerillas. Police violence in the confrontation at Columbia University and at the Chicago Democratic National Convention in 1968 meant that violent over-reaction on the part of the police radicalized countless previously middle-of-the-road students. The politics of confrontation became a common political weapon in student militant protest.

Student protest was of course not confined to America. Students were involved in transitional changes in Latin America, in the Chinese cultural revolution, in Japan over the alliance with the USA, with the Vietnam War and with the use of land for commercial purposes. In Europe there were struggles over an antiquated educational system in Italy; over democracy in Spain and Portugal; and in Germany over the heritage of authoritarianism and Nazism. The conformity of West German education was challenged on several fronts: by the SDS, the socialist German students' revolutionary organization; by social experiments, such as Kommune I, and by a massive anti-Vietnam campaign. The main targets were police brutality, regulations preventing Marxists working in the public service and the Springer media campaign against the left. In Holland a series of demonstrations had led to violent police reaction. The Dutch anarchist group, the Provos, using a series of peaceful and imaginative tactics, gained considerable sympathy among the young. Out of the libertarian roots of this movement, aided by the Amsterdam youth culture, sprang the Kabouters, offering community politics and environmental protection. An alternative society was suggested, developed from the Provo 'white bicycles', free transport for everyone. Alternative services were suggested for the elderly, the young, for food distribution and child care. A similarity can be noted with the San Francisco Diggers. The major student uprising was in May 1968 in Paris. The French student movement had been active against the Algerian war at a time when the organized Left had remained silent. In 1967 French students at Lyons had begun to organize against sexual surveillance in the halls of residence. Nanterre was demonstrating against poor cultural facilities, and the attempts to control this started the Nanterre student movement. Arrests of anti-Vietnam organizers led to an occupation. Nanterre was closed and student organizers ordered to appear before the Sorbonne administration in May 1968. A protest by the student left led the Rector to ask the police to clear the buildings. The students put up barricades, the police attacked, and a mass confrontation with the state occurred. Workers joined in student demonstrations, factory occupations occurred and an interesting mixture of violent confrontation and imaginative street slogans, the latter inspired by the Situationist International, took place. We can see a link between the Situationist International and the 'enrages' who fused theory and practice in the present situation, that is that praxis creates its own theory, and the libertarianism of the Kabouters and the American Yippies who also seize the time to show up the contradictions, and to create the strategy. A general strike followed which turned into massive factory occupations involving nearly 10 million workers. De Gaulle called for support for his government, and playing on fears of a communist takeover, broke the strike. One contradiction was that the industrial workers wanted fuller participation in, rather than an overthrow of social democracy.

One extreme polarity of the student unrest was the growth of the urban guerilla movement. The Black Power movement threw up urban guerilla defence groups such as the Black Liberation Front, and the Black Panthers. However the group which attracted most attention because of their contradictory position was the group composed of middle-class white ex-students, the Weathermen, who had sprung from the youth culture and from the SDS. American society is racist and violent, it has no real history of class struggle based on socialism as Europe has, it also has the wealthiest working class in the world, and as such class boundaries are far from clear-cut. Impatient with populist traditions in the movement, the Weathermen saw the American working class as bourgeoisified. Seeing a 'white honky-tonk pig racist Amerika' they decided to escalate the struggle, even against the people, and seeing an economy eventually ruled by a world proletariat. They wished to stand up with black militants against a white society, and to escalate a reaction which would reveal the oppression of the state (Walton, 1973). The logic of this was carried through so that support was offered even for Charles Manson. The Weathermen saw all whites as counter-revolutionary, unless involved in struggle, and shortly after they went underground (refuting their original sexism by becoming Weather Underground). The same impatience was shown by the Red Army Fraction, organized by Baader and Meinhof, by similar Japanese groups, and to a lesser extent by the British Angry Brigade, although strategies differ on whether property or persons are the target. The full contradictions of this approach was shown in the 1974 activities of the Symbionese Liberation Army. Composed of black ex-convicts who had been politicized, and middle-class white radicals from the Venceremos group, the group killed Foster, the Oakland black schools Superintendent, and kidnapped Patty Hearst. They show many of the contradictions of the New Left of the time. They substituted the feelings of alienation and meaninglessness they experienced in their personal lives for a theoretical analysis which understood that social change for the dispossessed can only be obtained by working-class support, which may have to be worked for during decades. The working class cannot be expected to give up what little they have because of the fervour of a group they are suspicious of, and who may belong to a different class and culture from them. Basing their guerilla activities on Debray and Fanon, they failed to realize they were working not in an agrarian Third World setting, but in a Western, industrial, urban society which had little history of class-consciousness, and an economy which rewarded different strands in the same class. They romanticized violence, and the brutalized aggression of the ex-cons presumably escalated the fervour of white middle-class radicals in the group who feared to look squeamish or fearful. Unlike the Panthers they were not offering armed defence to the ghetto, and the killing of Foster meant that they could not hide in black 'safe houses'. Violence followed the worst sort of masculinist protest which believes that relieving one's personal pain may be useful to a whole class. It was a misapplication of the new sensitivity. Such adventurism is dangerous because it gives the forces of oppression new reasons for increased legislation, and the romanticized violence can turn dangerously against the class it is supposed to help. (See Bryan J., 1975; Belcher and West, 1975; Carney, 1975.)

In Britain, the CND campaigns were replaced by anti-Vietnam war demonstrations. There were student occupations in 1967, at the LSE, and then at Essex University and Hornsey College of Art in 1968. The authorities feared that LSE would be made the base for the Grosvenor Square anti-Vietnam war demonstrations, and indeed it was used for planning strategies, once it was occupied, and as a hospital for the demonstration. This militancy was occurring at a time when Flower Power was coming to the attention of the British public, so that often the militants and the hippies were confused in the public mind. In 1970, the sit-in at Warwick University led to the discovery of secret political files kept on staff and students, as well as a record of the influence that various industrial enterprises had on academic courses and on research. Occupations spread over the country, and the invasion of the Garden House Hotel at Cambridge led to a pitched battle with the police. This was the year that Germaine Greer published *The Female Eunuch*, feminists disrupted the 'Miss World' contest, and *IT* was charged with obscenity. The mid-seventies (although one cannot generalize about decades) began to show a change away from student power. The Vietnam War drew to a close, and Ireland became an important political issue for the English New Left. Neo-colonial warfare moved nearer home. In 1971 the trials of *Oz* for obscenity, and the Angry Brigade were the result of charges of conspiracy, to corrupt public morals for the former and to cause explosions for the latter. These cases shared an interesting point, that the life-style of the defendants was citable as evidence for the prosecution, and that this has become common in charges of conspiracy, where life-style is considered deviant. (See Bunyan, 1977; Chibnall, 1977; Griffiths, 1978; Robertson, 1974; Palmer, 1971.) The Angry Brigade were libertarian situationists, in a Marxist framework. They presented a particular bogey for the general public. On the one hand the underground was seen as publishing morally-corrupt obscenity, as in *Oz*, and on the other it was seen as escalating the struggle beyond mere street demonstrations, and this was by middle-class educated men and women. They were placed by a puzzled mass media into the conspiratorial lunacy thesis. They sparked off a moral indignation which supported the increase of legal and police powers which were being more and more commonly used in 'political' and ideological matters. By the mid-seventies, Ireland had come to the fore amongst radicals, the first demonstrator had been killed in modern times in Red Lion Square (1974), and feminism had become a serious issue, as had gay liberation. The activities of the Red Army Faction in Germany caused a reactionary backlash there, with strong support for law and order. In American the Vietnam war had ended, the black militants had rethought their strategy and for survival had proceeded with community action and formal politics, with the Symbionese Liberation Army being the last major shoot-out.

Watergate had revealed the corruption of the President and the United States could no longer believe the integrity of even the highest in office. The counter-culture had given way to an interest in ecology, alternative psychology especially sensitivity groups, and various types of therapy. Individual rather than collective action concerned young adults.

Looking back over the sixties and mid-seventies certain issues show themselves. In America, because of the lack of a hard class-consciousness, class-based politics were not a heritage and did not fit a collective solution as easily as in Europe. People began to explore their oppression outside of class lines. For blacks they had an economic oppression, but even for the middle-class black there was a clearly visible cultural oppression and because it was linked to an unalterable visible stigma, colour, there was some inter-class basis for solidarity. There was a development of black pride, a rewriting of black history, a call for black power and an appreciation of black beauty and identity. These were the beginnings of the politics of the personal. Values, culture and identity have a political force, not just a psychological dimension. The counter-culture, composed of middle-class radicals and bohemians, protested not out of poverty, but against an affluence which had no moral content. Admittedly, voluntary stigmata such as long hair, can be removed but the embracing of such visible symbols was a statement of protest. Poverty and oppression were redefined in the counter-culture. As capitalism developed into a fusion of production and consumption, it was necessary to develop an awareness which would assist this. Middle-class radicals come from a highly educated group, educated not just for increasingly complex skills, but educated for an expansion of comprehension (Nairn, 1968). Now people are not just educated in the complex skills of selling consumption, as Mitchell (1971), suggests, but also to consume and indeed understand what is being sold. Mitchell suggests that ideologies are cultivated in order to develop choice over a consumer market but this can boomerang (Mitchell, 1971, p. 31).

> The cult of 'being true to your own feelings' becomes dangerous when those feelings are no longer ones that the society would like you to feel. Testing the quality of your world on your own pulse can bring about some pretty strange heart-beats.

Contradictions arise then with the development of any kind of consciousness. Those educated to a critical awareness of society become aware of contradictions both within it, and in their relationship to it. When this occurs questions are asked about the institutions which produce values and emotions, and this involves a critical stance concerning the quality of life of the questioner. Middle-class women, for example, may well accept a social and economic place in the world, yet question the emptiness of their lives as women. This will provoke a reaction which may lead them to reconsider their relation to the world and which may (but not necessarily, of course) open their horizons to make links across institutions to other elements of their personal oppression and the oppression of other groups. Middle-class groups may well morally question cultural institutions, but it must be remembered cultural institutions are dominantly middle-class. A crisis in middle-class educated youth, means a critique of the structure and ideology of the apparatuses which produced it. This is especially true for the women of this class, and it is not an accident that initially the women's liberation movement was a middle-class movement spread through the universities. As a result many things have been questioned: the nature and value of domestic labour, sexuality, the privacy of the family, the ideal of domesticity and sexual property and in fact the very nature of heterosexuality not only in its institutionalized form, but also its construction.

The mode of production in contemporary capitalism requires expendable goods, style and debt, not thrift and sobriety and deferred gratification. New forms of escape from the old values were necessary, usually contained within Marcuse's (1964), 'repressive desublimation'. The contradictions within predominant values which were a necessary response to a changing mode of production were responded to by reactionaries as a collapse of, or a conspiracy against dominant values. Social changes in the family, for example, were seen in the early sixties as the breakdown of the family: in fact it was the arrival of serial monogamy and a necessity for wives to work. At present the educated middle class, who have no wish to alter the mode of production, but who have become sensitive for example to the psychological strain, contradictions and alienation of mass society (there are at present an exceptional number of single young adults), have prompted the growth of encounter groups in California. There is a recognition that affluence is not a solution to unhappiness, isolation and competition, and group dynamics offer a way of exploring these problems in the supportive structure of other like-minded individuals. Consciousness may be raised on a number of issues, but the direction it takes, and the critique it makes are eventually collective political struggles. We can see that middle-class subcultures, whether political, bohemian or militant are also the result of contradictions in the social structure. They are, because they are experienced in the middle class, more indicative of changes in the mode of production, and they reflect changes in the values necessary to support these changes. As such, as Hall and Jefferson (1976, p. 69), suggest

> they also prefigure, anticipate, foreshadow – though in truncated diagrammatic and 'Utopian' forms – emergent social forms. These new forms are rooted in the productive base of the system itself . . .

Middle-class radicalism among the young has been seen since the late fifties as subversive, especially when it publicized and criticized the contradictions in society such as racism. Working-class youthful protest was enmeshed always in socially disapproved acts such as hooliganism, vandalism and theft. It was easy to respond just to the disapproved behaviour indices. Middle-class youth with its pursuit of hedonism and its criticism of puritanism and hypocrisy was responded to with a mixture of disapproval and envy. Again transgressions of the criminal law were publicized, for example arrests of leading underground figures for drug possession, and pornography charges against critical underground magazines. When more political action was taken, legal control was increased, particular use being made of conspiracy charges allowing evidence of life style to be brought into court. The conspiracy thesis and the writing-off of militant action as 'mindless' came to a new level with the fear of urban guerillas or 'terrorists'. With black youth, the policing of the ghettos, and the poor relations of the police and the immigrant community were dealt with by conspiracy and the suspected persons legislation. Campaigns for law and order are an important issue in present electoral campaigns. The fear of society that it has lost the confidence of its young and hence social control is expressed (often ambivalently) over fears of sex and drugs and rock and roll, to unemployment, terrorism, mugging and urban insurrection amongst black youth.

4 Dread in Babylon. Black and brown youth

Black and brown youth in Britain

> You always get this thing like when I went for a job up the road and the man he says 'You don't mind if we call you a black bastard, or a wog or a nigger or anything because it's entirely a joke'. I told him to keep his job. Him say 'I'm not colour prejudiced' . . . I don't want to work for no white man. Black people have been working for them for a long time. I don't want to work for them. I never used to hate white people. I still don't hate all of them. But it's them who teach me how to hate. (Black teenagers at the Harambee Hostel, Holloway, from P. Gillman,'I blame England', *Sunday Times*, 30.10.73)

One myth which was quickly dispelled for black and brown youth in Britain was the view that racial integration would grow through the education system. Hiro (1973), quotes a report by the Midlands correspondent of *The Times*, as early as 1963 who at the end of a long inquiry noted black and white youth left school separately, and certainly did not continue their friendships after puberty. As children of black and brown parents saw no evidence of adult integration, it is hardly surprising that they also should withdraw to the protection of separatism. It seems obvious to say, but what many whites forget is that for black people their primary identity, the way in which they are reacted to, and the way in which they act upon the world is mediated by their colour, and the oppression that brings, structurally, politically, psychologically and economically. The parents of black and brown youth were immigrants, and as such prepared to put up with difficulties here helped as they were by a culture with its roots outside of Britain. Their children are second and third generation immigrants, members of the previous host population, yet they are still rejected by it. Immigrants, a self-selected group of ambitious people, are often sustained by the belief they will return home, even though this is a fantasy. For their children, the Indian sub-continent, Africa, the Caribbean are not places they have grown up in, and these become nostalgic fantasies, substitutes for the bleakness and racism of Britain. Young non-white Britons are British, but the rejection they suffer causes them in turn to reject the British, and the crisis of identity suffered is devastating. It is hardly surprising they politicise these problems instead of being deferential or accommodating. They are marginal, separated from their white peers, experiencing a different upbringing from their parents, brought up in educationally disadvantaged areas, in poor inner city areas, facing poor employment prospects. This is not new. A 1968 study (Wright, 1968), found 72 per cent of West Indian workers would prefer a different type of job, and Figueroa (1969) found that in North London, more than half of his West Indian boys wanted to leave their jobs as opposed to only one in eleven white boys.

The present problems facing non-white youth have to be seen in the context of the economy of slavery and colonialism. As a result of slavery, black people have been living in Britain since 1602 (Hiro, 1973) and prejudice is no new thing. One fear racists expound is that of being swamped, yet there were disturbances as early as 1919, in the dock areas of Cardiff, Bristol and Liverpool, when the black population was minute, ending in a rampage against blacks and a black seaman being killed. However only large communities of Asians and Afro-Caribbeans lived here from the end of the fifties. The increase of Afro-Caribbeans was related to the McCarren Walter Act 1952 reducing West Indian immigrants to 800 per year into America, and recruitment by the Health Service and service industries attracted badly-needed unskilled and semi-skilled labour. Asians were also employed in the textile industry in particular, and their emigration partly sprang from India's partition into India and Pakistan after 1947. Emigration out of India was controlled, until a 1960 Indian High Court ruled this unconstitutional, and from 1961 Indian immigration into Britain increased. The 1962 Commonwealth Immigration Act was set up to control this. After 1968 many Asians immigrated here from Africa as a result of national government acts there against them. The Commonwealth Immigrants Act 1968 was set up, restricting right of entry to holders of UK passports born here, or those whose parents were born here. The 1971 Immigration Act restricted entry to 'patrials' (those with at least one British-born grandparent) and this act closed the door to future immigration. West Germany admitted ten times as many migrant workers as Britain during the sixties, making up 11 per cent of the work force in 1974. These workers are not encouraged to settle, and are deported at the end of their contract, and this was the position for prospective immigrants to Britain after 1971. The prosperous Western European economies no longer need unskilled workers from the economies they colonized. By 1974, there were 1.6 million non-white people living in Britain (2.9 per cent of the population). They had always been a contentious issue in political policy, and the xenophobic attitude of the white population was revealed in a 1977 BBC survey which found that two-thirds of whites over-estimated the population size of non-whites, 14 per cent wildly, only 10 per cent getting it right. This population (Smith, 1977) is composed of 43 per cent West Indian (two-thirds Jamaican, the rest from islands hundreds of miles apart) and 57 per cent Asian. Of the Asians 26 per cent are Indian, 16 per cent Bangladeshi/Pakistani and 15 per cent African Asian. The Asians are 40 per cent Moslem (mainly Pakistanis), 29 per cent Hindu (mainly African Asians) and 25 per cent Sikhs (mainly Indian). The West Indian infrastructure produces few middle-class immigrants. Their prospects are not good – for example those who nurse tend to become SENs (a qualification not recognized outside Britain), whose promotion prospects are poor. Asians have more middle-class potential: 22 per cent of doctors are Asian (see Kohler, 1975), but these are in the lower ranks of medicine. Non-manual work figures reveal 40 per cent of whites, 8 per cent of Pakistanis, and West Indians, 20 per cent of Indians but 30 per cent of African Asians. Although the heritage of the West Indian slave economy is that most West Indians are unskilled, yet 59 per cent of West Indians are in skilled manual work (1970 census) as opposed to 42 per cent of whites. The lower ranks of manual work reveal 18 per cent are white, 32 per cent West Indian, 36 per cent Indian but 58 per cent are Pakistani. Despite the stereotype, only 5 per cent of Asians are shopkeepers. Black and brown people are not then uniformly at the bottom of the class hierarchy, although there is a distinct skew this way. They are relatively in different class locations, skewed towards the bottom of the hierarchies. Black and brown workers in Britain suffer from the oppression which affects all working-class people, poor housing, poverty, and poor education, but they suffer from these disproportionately, in addition to which they suffer the specific oppression of racism. Immigrants sought to escape the colonial or slave-based economy of their own countries, with its educational legacy grounded in imperial ideologies. They sought better conditions and higher education facilities, only too often to find only menial jobs in Britain with poor work conditions, and lived in badly deteriorating districts, exploited by property owners. Racialism was encountered in the form of the 1958 race riots, the support for Enoch Powell during the sixties, the resurgence of the National Front in the seventies, and with two race murders of young boys in 1978. Black and brown youth born in Britain faced an education system which operated against their social mobility. Little, Mabey and Whittaker (1968), found that immigrant educational achievement was related to knowledge of English, country of origin and length of education in Britain. This particularly affected immigrant children who were newly arrived in this country. Obviously children from the Indian sub-continent do not have English as a first language. Anwar (1976), reports 85 per cent of Asian youth reporting they spoke their mother tongue at home, but the same amount also felt they spoke English as well as their mother tongue. West Indian children have different linguistic constructions from English, speaking Creole or a patois. Consequently they perform badly in vocabulary and verbal reasoning and as a result mathematics. There is for West Indians, twice the possibility over other immigrants, of being designated ESN (Coard, 1971). West Indians do not speak standard English, and according to Hebdige (1976, p. 136), slavery forbade the teaching of English to the slaves, but it was illicitly combined with the linguistics of a defiant culture.

> Distortion was inevitable, perhaps even deliberate. Subsequently the language developed its own vocabulary, syntax and grammar, but it remained essentially a shadow-language fulfilling in a more exaggerated and dramatic way those requirements, which under normal circumstances are satisfied by working class accents and group argot . . . language is used as a particularly effective means of resisting assimilation and preventing infiltration . . . it becomes an aggressive assertion of racial and class identities. As a living index to the extent of the black's alienation from the cultural norms and goals of those who occupy higher positions in the social structure, the creole language is unique.

An interesting development in Afro-Caribbean youth culture in Britain has been the conscious re-adoption of Creole by black youth. The education of non-white youth has in fact depressed the general opportunities for employment and educational advancement; it reproduces the young non-white worker at the lower end of education and skill. The culture of the school, argues Hall *et al.* (1978), unwittingly in the curriculum, but consciously in its attitudes, attacks the culture of the black. Creole is consciously spoken so that a 'resistance through language marks out the school as quite literally, a cultural background'.

Another problem non-white youth faces, especially in adolescence, is that of police harassment. Young Afro-Caribbeans in particular are seen as excitable and arrogant by the police, who have a long history of poor community relations with immigrants. The police culture separates them from the community and young policemen follow the 'hard man' cult. There has always been a history of bad relations between immigrants and the police (see Humphrey and John, 1972) and this was officially recognized by the Deedes Select Committee on Police/Immigrant relations. Asians complain that when they summon the police because of attacks on their person or property, the police seem more interested in whether they themselves are illegal immigrants. The raids on the Mangrove restaurant in Notting Hill led to a demonstration which in turn led to arrests of demonstrators later either acquitted or having their charges reduced (Moore, 1975). The Metro youth club was raided in the same district and again after being accused of causing an affray the jury acquitted the defendants. In 1975 the 'mugging' scare developed. A special Scotland Yard Report (not made public) on South London street crime (mugging is not an official term, but seems to refer to theft from the person with actual or threatened violence) suggested that '80 per cent of the attackers are black and 85 per cent of the victims are white' (see Hall *et al.*, 1978), a statistic that revealed that the police now record the race of assailants and victims. The report suggested that this was not a police matter, but was a result of the widespread alienation of West Indian youth from white society. However this information escalated a moral panic which linked race, crime and the inner city. As Hall *et al.* (1978, p. 339) put it:

> 'Mugging' is now unquestioningly identified with a specific class fraction or category of labour (black youth) and with a specific kind of area; the inner ring zones of multiple deprivation.

Hall *et al.* place the reaction to mugging and the National Front's use of it to equate racism with crime by a Marxist analysis of race, class and the economic crisis. They suggest that during the early 1960s a series of 'discrete "moral panics"' occurred (as with mods and rockers) which had a social and moral form, mainly a concern with youth and permissiveness. By the late

1960s these discrete moral panics were mapped together in a speeded-up sequence, so it was implied that they were an increasingly amplified general 'threat to society' element. This in turn heightened sensitivity to social problems so that during the early 1970s a general panic about law and order emerged. There was an unease about the stability of the state, and a crisis within it of hegemony. There was at work the dynamic of what they call a 'signification spiral'. A specific issue causing concern is identified, and with it a subversive minority. This is then linked ('convergence') to other problems. Certain thresholds, such as sex, or in this case violence, which once crossed, lead to an escalation of moral panic calling for firm steps and law and order. There had been in Britain previously a concern with various issues as we have seen, such as drugs, permissiveness, sex and student revolt. This marked a genuine disruption between disparate but large groups of people, and the authority and the hegemony of the state. There was on one hand a questioning of basic institutions, social roles, life-styles and the relation of these to the political economy, and on the other hand there was a right-wing backlash. The law and order campaign, occurring as it did in a worsening economic crisis led to trade union legislation, a concern with immigration control, fear over the Northern Ireland situation which led to encroachments on civil liberties all of which had an effect on dissident groups. It is against this that the politics of mugging has to be seen. Enoch Powell's speech in Birmingham in 1968 had struck a chord with the silent majority when he expressed fear of the American Black Power movement. He said he could see the River Tiber 'foaming with much blood . . . . That tragic and intractable phenomenon which we watch with horror on the other side of the Atlantic is coming here by our own volition.' By the middle seventies this feeling had escalated, so that the anti-mugging campaign was an emotive issue. Relations between the black and brown communities became full of hostility and distrust. However as Hiro reminds us, Powell was certainly a catalyst, but prejudice was strong before his speeches. Even in 1965, it was very difficult to start leisure projects with a mixed race group. These groups even then, as they do today, quickly polarize into all-black or all-white clubs, or mixed clubs with all-white or all-black evenings.

One disturbing effect of racialism has been the exploitation of racist feeling among the young by the National Front. The general view has been that prejudice is strongest amongst older adults who have little first-hand knowledge of non-white people. Harrop and Zimmerman (1977), argued that the increase in National Front votes in the Greater London Council elections (April 1977) was drawn from the ranks of the 'young, white and ungifted'. Youthful racialism is not a new phenomenon, and acts of violence have been blamed on the Notting Hill teds in the fifties to the East London and Wolverhampton skinheads of the sixties. Weir (1978), found in a survey of young voters in an East London Front stronghold a mixed reaction, in that whilst 15 per cent of their sample of 16 to 20-year-olds were committed to the Front, nearly 30 per cent were very hostile. However in terms of racialism one third were prepared to express hostility to non whites, and only 53 per cent were against repatriation of immigrants and their families. The Labour Party was still the dominant party for these working-class youngsters, but NF support was found amongst male, unskilled workers who were early unqualified school-leavers. The committed NF young tend to be in manual work although NF sympathizers are 95 per cent in white collar or skilled work. The committed NF young tend to be younger (36 per cent were 16 years old). S. Taylor (1978), looked at an outer London borough, predominantly middle-class, affluent and suburban, to see if similar findings were true for areas outside the inner city zone. Just as in Weir's study, 13 per cent of youngsters identified with the NF (the number who felt closer to NF than any other party in Weir), and they tended to be male, very young and from manual working-class families. The Taylor study found them to come from Conservative families, whilst the Weir study found they tended to come from Labour families, and the Taylor study found more support among school attenders as opposed to Weir who found most NF supporters had left school, but the Taylor study included a 14- to 20-year-old sample. However there is an indication that racism and NF support is to be found not just in inner-city deprived areas, and is to be found most commonly among young, working-class males. What does show in the survey is that most young NF supporters believe that their neighbourhood is going to deteriorate in the near future because of immigrants. They reported hostility to immigrants, and so did nearly a third of the young who were neutral or hostile to the NF. This reflects Marsh (1977), who found a third of secondary-modern-educated youngsters aged 16 to 29 were hostile to immigrants, and were therefore more hostile than a similarly educated older group. At this stage the NF is not an electoral threat, but it has reinforced racism and divisions between the races.

Youth unemployment is higher among ethnic minorities than for young whites. Certainly many young Afro-Caribbeans and Asians have come to cease to expect to find work, and the position for girls from these groups has worsened. Total unemployment increased between 1974 and 1977 over 120 per cent, but for non-whites it increased by 350 per cent (Manpower Services Commission; Review and Plan, 1977). Unemployment increased for this period about two and a half times as much for non-whites as for whites. Hurstfield (*New Society*, 5.1.78) suggests that between February 1976 and February 1977 black male unemployment remained stable, but black female unemployment increased by 24 per cent. Particularly illuminating were the figures for the 18 to 24 age group – 0.6 per cent for males and 33.8 per cent for females. The same article suggests that only 48 per cent of West Indian and 39 per cent of Asian women register as unemployed, so that unemployment among them is underestimated (as indeed it is for young West Indian males). It is worth noting that the Council for European National Youth Committee report (November 1977) states that between 1974 and 1977 unemployment among ethnic minorities increased by 347 per cent for males and 533 per cent for females, and that in 1977 the national unemployment rate for males was 8.1 per cent and for West Indians was 16.2 per cent. These figures were for the 16 to 25 age group and the 16 to 20 age group respectively. The British Youth Council (March 1977, *Youth Unemployment*) found that West Indian youngsters made three times as many fruitless visits to careers offices, took twice as long to find a job, and were made redundant more frequently than their white counterparts. This occurs at a time when the Office of Population Surveys accepts that up to 50 per cent of West Indian youth are not registering as unemployed. This all occurs in a situation where more people (three-quarters of a million by 1981) are chasing fewer jobs (between 1966 and 1976 the labour force shrank from 26 million to 24.2 million according to Manpower Services Commission statistics). Obviously ethnic minorities will suffer most from this, concentrated as they are in dense urban areas with accompanying problems of housing, failure to develop industry, and poor educational qualifications.

Rude boys and Rastafarians: Afro-Caribbean youth subcultures

Against this background of racism, educational disadvantage, coupled often with educational ambition, police harassment and family tension over unemployment it is important to consider the subcultural solutions open to black youth. The actual prospects for young blacks are poor, and just as their parents idealized Britain, then the young black often idealises a mythical Africa. It is important to understand how this came about. Racism can be seen as a systematic feature of the housing and employment markets, and Hall *et al.* (1978, p. 346), argue

> these structures which, working within the dominant 'logic' of capital, produce and reproduce the social conditions of the black working class, shape the social universe and the productive world of that class, and assign its members and agents to positions of structured subordination within it.

Race mediates the experience and lives of black people, but also raises a consciousness of their structured subordination which white working-class youth lacks. This subsequently develops a resistance which occurs in the context of a created 'colony' culture. The colony is a defensive cohesion of the West Indian community against white society, which is a cultural space allowing an alternative black social life. As the black population grew, and developed a West Indian consciousness, Hall *et al.* (1978, p. 351) argue that:

> Here began the 'colonisation' of certain streets, neighbourhoods, cafes and pubs, the growth of revivalist churches, mid-day Sunday hymn-singing and mass baptisms in the local swimming baths, the spilling-out of Caribbean fruit and vegetables from Indian shops, the shebeen and the Saturday night blues party, the construction of the sound systems, the black record shops selling blues, ska and soul, the birth of the 'native quarter' at the heart of the English city.

There is of course an Asian equivalent, but they brought with them the languages, religion and culture of home, of an integrated and complex society, unlike the West Indian, they did not have to draw on the response of a quasi criminal cool subculture of the urban downtown slum hustler. Hustling is earning a living outside of wage labour, and by definition involves petty crime. It also provides the supply of services, goods and entertainments in a quasi-legal manner to the respectable element of the black colony. Hustlers are men on the street with style, like Finestone's 'cool cats' laid back, yet doing well. They are those who cannot get work, or will not subject themselves to routine labour for white society, preferring to hustle. As such the West Indian hustler in Britain draws upon the 'rude boy' subculture of West Kingston. 'Rudies' are the Jamaican hustlers operating in the downtown areas of the West

Indies, who live by dope dealing, pimping and gambling, who live in the shebeens and clubs and whose style of 'stingy brim' hats and dark shades were to be sported by Jamaicans in the early sixties. Violence and marijuana surrounded the 'rudie', a night cat, whose music was ska, blue beat, rock steady and reggae, and who followed the sporting life of horses, dominoes and women. The other major subcultural figure is the Rastafarian locksman, his religious fervour a striking contrast to the rude boy cool. The Rastafarian movement draws upon the deep religious feelings African people have, but which reverses Christianity to draw upon Biblical metaphors to make political points. It is based upon Marcus Garvey's 1929 prophecy, 'Look to Africa, where a black king shall be crowned, for the day of deliverance is near'. This was said to occur in Ethiopia (itself a Biblical reference for Africa), and Emperor Haile Selassie was declared Ras Tafari, the living God, Lion of Judah, King of Kings, sometimes simply 'Jah'. Thus the black messiah was born who would lead the Children of Israel out from Babylon (colonized ex-empires such as Jamaica) to Ethiopia, to Zion, the promised land, the black man's home – Africa. For the Rastaman black people are descended from Solomon and Sheba, the descendant of whom is Haile Selassie, he shall live with his black queen (marriage is sinful) and as a true Israelite resist the ways of the white man who holds him in slavery. Capitalism is the system of Babylon, property, alcohol and gambling are disdained, but the 'herb' or 'Ganja' (marijuana) is sacred. With its aid thought is transformed into feeling, and belief becomes knowledge. Black people are reincarnated slaves and as such brothers and sisters, hence the Rastaman refers to a collective 'I and I' rather than we, those who know they are brethren are one and immortal. Haile Selassie's death merely confirms God is in all men, and will be reincarnated elsewhere. The Rastaman promises the 'rod of correction' for Babylon. He is an important symbol for black youth with his uncut, long dreadlocks, his beard and woollen cap of the Ethiopian colours of red, green and gold. His patriarchy, his mysticism and poetry are as important as his belief that all black men are Rastafarians and need only to realize this. A basic cultural connection between British youth and Jamaica is the music and lyrics of reggae. Jamaican music is important in the colony, it is music for dancing and music with a political message, both essential elements of Jamaican style. American Rhythm and Blues greatly influenced Jamaican music in the fifties. Its soul connections spoke from one dispossessed black population to another. It became blended into Jamaican music first in ska and then bluebeat, followed by rock steady and reggae. Reggae has distinctly Rasta feeling, the music based on the rhythms of 'burra' drumming (used to welcome discharged prisoners back into the West Kingston slums). The lyrics praise Jah, preach of black brotherhood and threaten revolution in Babylon. By the late sixties, rudies were sporting a Rasta style. A form of soul consciousness had been raised, wedding Rasta brotherhood and rudie violence. The writings of the American Black Power movement also became important, and their political message spread a consciousness of class and race oppression. The basically peaceful attitude of the Rastas was fused with rudie militance. Reggae became a poetic manifesto, and spread a political message to the young blacks in Britain. Hebdige (1976b) argues that gradually the music of Jamaica spread to the white population through West Indian clubs such as Brixton's 'Ram Jam'. From about 1967, not only black youth, but also whites were influenced, mainly those boys in transition from the 'hard mod' to the skinhead – a form of white rude boys, familiar with Creole and at that stage not especially racist.

But as Frith (1978, p. 219) notes, the origins of reggae are from a politics and culture outside Britain, and the consciousness expressed is neither youthful nor British. The Rasta influence insisted on a basic pre-condition for acceptance into West Indian subcultures, being black and proud. Hebdige indicates that as the demand for unskilled labour diminished, black and white school leavers came into fiercer competition for work. The Africanization of Rasta, and the exhortation of peace and harmony, found only in white hippies, a group despised by the skinhead, confounded white youth. The black separatism and metaphor of Rastafarianism doubly locked out white youth, and as reggae's lyrics got more political, the contradiction became insurmountable. Hostility between black and white youth increased, although as we have noticed, it was always there in the background. The solidarity of the black community against police harassment and the mutual support young blacks gave each other in fights was something not found in the white community. Robins and Cohen (1978) argue that the breakdown of stable, subcultural identity among young working-class whites, combined with the erosion of the traditional supports of their parent culture, led to white youth feeling particularly threatened by the presence of any socio-cultural group cohesion. White groups are separated by neighbourhood, subcultural form and inter-group schisms, but the very element for which blacks are despised – race – unites them against a common threat, be it white gangs, the police or other authorities. Certainly this is not to argue a simple form of cohesion among black youth, but the impression is certainly that they adopt style rather than content in Rastafarianism. However they have a popular culture which stresses black pride, and which provides an alternative to routine labour for the white man. It strikes a note with what is happening to them, and provides a supportive ideology. Young West Indians are increasingly conscious of the fact that they are being schooled for low paid and low status work. The degree to which attachment to Rastafarianism extends beyond its style to its content is difficult to ascertain. It has a definite meaning for young Afro-Caribbeans expressing for them their rejection of the white state and their ascribed place within it. The features of the Caribbean social economy have been reproduced in Britain, and one result has been a distinctly West Indian delinquent subcultural response. Dodd (1978, p. 598), describes this as

> 'a new revolution of the mind' is taking place in the black neighbourhoods of South London. There are new images and a new aesthetic on display. The function of public space – like street corners – has visibly altered as those who derive identities from their behaviour in such places try to make it private. The police have increasingly taken on the guise of aliens confronted by a culture they do not understand and so for which they feel contempt.
>
> But the contempt is mutual. For the streets of Brixton, once paved with hope, are now filled with the frustration, hopelessness and desperate pride of rebels and gangsters. They are the streets too of Laventille in Trinidad, West Kingston in Jamaica and South Georgetown in Guyana. The culture and meaning of black poverty is now as much of a reality in the industrial slums and housing estates of Britain as it is in the decaying urban villages of the Caribbean. The slave legacy has finally come home to roost.

The first generation of immigrants were ambitious to escape their homeland and happy to accept conditions as they found them, comparing them to those they had left behind. Their children however have only their white contemporaries to compare their lot with, and they are not prepared to accept their stigmatized position in white society. They have developed an urban street culture, with roots in the 'rudie' hustler value system, with an overlay of Rastafarian style, politics and rhetoric. They are sustained by the music and politics of the Caribbean, and turn to Zion, a mythical Africa where merit and identity are not judged by pigmentation. Parents were ambitious for their children, and the British economy has neither met these needs nor created opportunities for advancement. Black youth have been caught in an economic crisis where black unemployment is common, and work badly paid and demeaning. Often, because their children have rejected what work is available, strain at home can be severe, sometimes leading to children being ejected, and living in squats or youth houses. Those who continue to live at home face different problems from their parents, mostly confronting the reality that the prosperity and opportunity their parents sought is a myth cruelly dispelled by recession. Rebellion has become a solution, a subcultural style stretching from reinterpretations of Rasta, to street crime and 'voluntary unemployment'. Dodd (1978, p. 600), argues:

> For many black adolescents growing up in the slums of Britain and the Caribbean, crime is about the only freedom they have left.

One result of this has been the rise in street robbery, argues Dodd. It acts to depersonalize the victim (usually white, unlike the United States), and the dynamics are first of all a self-hatred, in which blackness is intrinsically involved, then hating the group who made you hate yourself, on whom you finally turn in revenge. This Dodd sees as the background to the rise of a black street subculture in Britain. Obviously the problem of personalising this type of hatred, is that the wrong target is inevitably selected. The subculture functions because (Dodd, 1978, p. 600), 'it provides an appropriate social context within which males are free to engage in "character contests" to acquire a reputation and secure an identity.' However the degree to which black youth is involved in delinquent or criminal elements is an empirical question as yet systematically unanswered. The traditional ways out of the ghetto for black people, where education has been blocked, have been through sport or entertainment. Hustling in some ways reflects these worlds: it is exciting and dramatic, and it is outside the world of wage labour. However the extent to which young blacks are involved in it is unknown, but if the figures for white working-class youth are a guide it is highly probable that most of black youth is not involved in delinquent enterprises. Voluntary unemployment is another confusing term. It is practically impossible to measure, and whilst young people living at home are involved in temporary voluntary unemployment, that is, they register with private rather than public employment agencies, long-term voluntary unemployment is a matter of conjecture. A Commission for Racial Equality (1978) Report, 'Looking for work', which compared white and black school-leavers in Lewisham, finds no evidence of this, but found most black and white unemployed youth actively seeking work (only two of the black sample said they were not). Black youth however were less likely to have jobs fixed up when they left school, spent longer finding a job, and made more applications, and were less satisfied with the jobs they found. Discrimination, deliberate or unintentional, seemed to be a major factor in this.

Asian youth is not involved in the same type of alienating processes as Caribbean youth. It is not still suffering as black youth does from the effects of a slave economy on its psychology and on its everyday life. It can draw upon its own historical, cultural and religious traditions, and importantly, its own languages. It draws upon these rather than developing a distinct youth subculture. The Asian community is itself divided by geographical origin, caste and religion as well as by language. Asians are rarely found in youth culture (although Bradford did have Pakistani teddy boys) and indeed are often absent from formal youth organizations.

Asian youth

The Asian community is made up of three major religious groups from the Indian sub-continent – Muslims, Hindus and Sikhs and also three major communities from different areas. These are the Indians from the Punjabi and Gujerati regions, Pakistanis from West Pakistan and Bangladesh, and East African Asians. Pakistanis tend to originate from the poor rural areas, and Indians from urban areas and traditionally the latter is a more tightly organized group. The East African Asians are more middle-class and Europeanized. Asian parents expect and exercise considerable control over their children, and most adolescents expect to marry a partner chosen and approved by their parents. Girls are closely surveilled by the local community and an informal network controls against the possibilities of clandestine courtship. Sharpe (1976), notes however that despite this many of her Asian girls went out with boys secretly, but her sample was mainly Indian and East African Asian. Asian youth mixes very little with white or black youth out of school. Livingstone (1978), found that regardless of area of origin or religion, Asian boys were unlikely to join multi-racial youth organizations. Anwar (1976), reported that Asian parents were not interested in youth organizations and feared the effects these would have in terms of bad company and different religious and cultural traditions. Sources of conflict within the Asian communities can be traced to feelings of discrimination about employment.

Asians have high expectations of their children, who suffer police discrimination especially raids for illegal immigrants, and tension between elders and youth. Asian youth suffer very distinctly from inhabiting a different world at home from that at school. The problems of 'westernization' were mentioned by a fifth of Anwar's group, and there seems to be some indication that family solidarity may well weaken in the future. Marriage was a particular problem, and the choice of a partner from the sub-continent particularly disliked. Women differed from men on the work situation, and Muslim women in particular suffered from this. The lack of youth subcultures probably symbolizes the extent to which Asian youth draws on its own traditions at present, but as these fail to resolve contradictions youth sub-culture will probably arise as a symbol of emancipation from the older generation. The problems of racist division will compel Asian youth to seek new solutions, and at present their cultures continue to divide them from differing Asian communities and from Afro-Caribbeans. However as successive generations grow up, they will find their cultural roots insufficient to assist them with the problems of a racist society.

Black and brown girls

West Indian girls suffer, as do their white peers, from having their problems sexualized by official agencies. However the structure of the West Indian family, with its roots in slavery, needs to be understood. In the Caribbean the structure of the family is such that women, both in the immediate and the extended family take the major responsibility for the care of children. The high degree of poverty in Jamaica, and the family relations of slavery meant that common law marriage was a common bond. One consequence was that authority was shared and both partners worked, but the informal nature of common law relationships and the poverty which necessitated the man working away from home, weakened the paternal role. Hiro (1973, p. 20), argues that the maternal role became more important than the marital role, and

> The main reason for a matriarchal family system evolving in the Caribbean (and black America) was the fact that the woman, with her historical experience of being a productive slave in her own right was not economically dependent on the man.

A matriarchal structure arose from three features – informal marital relationships, mothers providing the security, stability and discipline in the family and men being often absent or changeable. Other traditions left by slavery were fertility being highly prized and maternity as a highly desirable state for women. During emigration families were split, and children arriving in Britain found sometimes a new father and perhaps new siblings to deal with, as well as the grief of leaving behind in the Caribbean the substitute mother. This helps explain the high proportion of single parent families amongst West Indians (Smith, 1977), calculated at thirteen per cent of West Indian families. However this figure is confusing because there may be a stable common law marriage, and the fertility rate has to be contrasted against the use of contraception and abortion among white women. As most formal marriages have been preceded by trial marriages (a middle-class phenomenon among whites) it is pointless to compare Caribbean marriage patterns with Asian or European. Most present-day adolescents have been born in Britain, but nevertheless there are reports of strain between children and step-parents, and over children's desire for more independence and better work prospects than their parents. This is interpreted by the parents as ingratitude. The tension between independence and control, the contradictions of family authority based on the Caribbean, and the specific generational problems of young black Britons means that there are often severe family difficulties. Sharpe (1976), found close control over daughters' social activities, especially over boy friends. Three-quarters of her West Indian schoolgirls reported that their parents seldom or never allowed them out with boys (although over half admitted to boy friends). This applied especially to those from religious families. Reaction to pregnancy varies, but can be severe, the mother feeling the daughter has had more opportunities to avoid becoming pregnant and better alternatives. However a girl may even be turned out of home, but on the other hand there is more likelihood of there being a support network for the child. However the girl is seen as having let the family down. Where a girl is turned out, the problem is that there is not the supportive kin she would have had in the Caribbean, and so she has only the social services or other homeless young people to turn to. Kitzinger (1978), suggests that the social services provide a help network which would have been met by the extended family in the Caribbean, or by a nexus of reciprocal relations between the mother and daughter generation, which has become lost with emigration. Interestingly, an area of dispute between mothers and daughters, the amount of housework expected, is a legacy from back home reciprocal relations. Girls are restricted because parents fear they will be led astray, and girls feel strongly that they are expected to do domestic labour their brothers can avoid. Sharpe notes that her West Indian girls in fact placed less emphasis on marriage and a family than English girls. Whilst they found school boring, they placed more emphasis on education and job prospects. There is a growing recognition among West Indian girls as well as boys, that they are being schooled for lower-paid, low status work. The Lewisham study (CRE, 1978), found however that 75 per cent of West Indian girls in the sample found white collar work, against 62 per cent of white girls, and interestingly 17 per cent of white girls found shop work (a public area) but only six per cent of black girls worked in shops. Overall figures however show an increasing unemployment among black girls, and the extent and duration of this has yet to be considered.

Asian girls are expected to have a highly deferential attitude to their parents, and after puberty, especially with Muslim girls, are closely guarded. Despite the restrictions on the lives of Asian women, they work in Britain to a degree which would be unusual in Asia. The 1971 census revealed that 40.8 per cent of Indian and 20.7 per cent of Pakistani women were at work. This had had an important effect on their lives in this country, but Anwar (1976), notes that 85 per cent of his Asian girls over 16 felt women should work, and 30 per cent of young Asian males were opposed to this. The figures reveal considerable resistance by Muslims to women working, only about one tenth of Hindus feeling this way, with the Sikhs in between. Asian women are very dependent on their men, and isolation is an important social problem. Wilson's (1978) moving account of Asian women stresses their homesickness and isolation after marriage. It is a particular problem for immigrant women who have fewer contacts in their community than girls born here. The companionship of work is important, but religion is still a severe hindrance to this. A major problem for Asian girls is the arranged marriage. It is true to say that the young couple now have the last say in the choice, but the selection is still made by the parents. Anwar also suggests that this is a potential source of conflict between generations, although it is surprising the degree to which parental authority is accepted by both girls and boys. Marriage between castes is rejected, and between religions or races is beyond the pale. A girl's reputation is still of primary importance, and *izzat*, the male pride of one's brothers and father, acts against friendships with either sex outside one's immediate religious community and caste. There is little doubt that Asian women and girls face three major problems. These are sexism, especially for Muslim women, which operates to isolate them and maintain their economic and social dependence on their menfolk and their families. The second is racism, which acts against their obtaining the type of work they would like and which can result in physical attacks on them or on their houses, and class. It is worth remembering that even middle-class Asian women become declassed when they immigrate to Britain. Obviously it is hard for women to organise resistance to their situation, divided as they are by caste, tradition and religion. However there are some small indications that changing attitudes within the Asian communities will lead women to reconsider their position and to organize. There are indications that an information network concerning abortion exists, an Asian women's refuge has been set up by Asian community workers, and resistance to dowries and arranged marriage has started. It is as yet much too early to see these as anything but small beginnings, but it is inevitable that as more generations grow up here, the oppression of Asian women will be resisted.

'Let the power fall' – racism and its effect on youth

The position of black and brown youth in terms of its relation to the political economy of Britain has been made clearer during the economic crisis. Non-white youths have seen the market closed against them in terms of their skills and ambitions, and see no signs of social integration. The situation at present differs in response between black and brown youth. However the attacks on brown youth, including two racist murders, has developed a militancy which acts against the stereotype of the Asian as conformist and submissive. East London has a history of organizing defence groups in the Asian, especially the Bengali community. What is important is that families remain in communities which can form defence groups. There is a distinct lack of confidence in the white police in these matters. Black youth, cut off from the supportive yet divisive roots of distinct national cultures, has adopted Africanisation as a defence. There has been a rejection of the 'shit end' of the labour market. They have discovered that the system which needed their parents does not need them. A conflict of generations means that for some black youth a situation arises where unable to find work of a nature they want, a situation arises at home which ends in their leaving. Homeless, suspended, between hustling and the labour market, once they are drifting and 'dossing' they have to survive unemployment and so they turn to petty crime. Hall *et al*. (1978) indicate that consciousness and motives do not work so that crime is chosen as a political revenge. Black youth drifts, then develops a collective definition of a collectively experienced situation which draws on their anger and hostility about racism. Crime becomes a simple survival strategy, and is not a real solution, but is brutalizing and destructive. The police surveillance of the black community takes on a deeper political significance. Hall *et al*. (1978, p. 332), links this to the relations of the state and the employment market.

> Policing the blacks threatened to mesh with the problem of policing the poor and policing the unemployed; all three were concentrated in precisely the same urban areas – a fate which of course provided the element of geographical homogeneity which facilitates the germination of a militant consciousness. The on-going problem of policing the blacks had become, for all practical purposes, synonymous with the wider problem of policing the crisis.

The roots of crime lie in the double exploitation of black youth, as a deskilled class in an economy that no longer has a place for them, and as black people who experience their lives through racism. Black youth can only be understood as a class fraction, defined by age, by generation and by its position in the history of black migrant labour and its development into a black metropolitanized working class. What crime conceals, argue Hall *et al*., is wagelessness and the relegation of black workers to the position of deskilled labour. *Race Today*, a theoretical journal put out by the Institute of Race Relations, argues that the segmentation of classes means that each sector of the working class must develop and make felt its own autonomous self-activity. The refusal to work of young blacks as such is supported as a significant development by a youthful membership of a class fraction in refusing the traditional role of the reserve army of labour. Police activity then is interpreted as an attempt by the state to bring the wageless back into wage labour. These are differentiated from the traditional Marxist lumpenproletariat. The wageless are developed from a colonial economy in the Caribbean, and are a cohesive social force. The wageless have reconstructed in the metropolitan 'colony' a supporting culture in which the youthful second generation blacks are representative of a qualitative change in the composition of that class. This position has been criticized, especially by Cambridge and Gutsmore of the *Black Liberator*. Briefly they see the youthful refusal to work as an ideological rather than a political struggle, which has little effect on exploitation in any concrete sense. Black workers are super-exploited, economically as a substratum of the working class, and racially as a minority group. For them blacks are part of a reserve army of labour, indeed a disproportionate section of it, to be used when the economy needs them. The reserve army can be transferred into and out of the labour market as production and consumption patterns change. Permanently below white working-class groups, the black labour force becomes a sub-proletariat. Both groups agree that the black labour force is super-exploited, economically and racially, and both differentiate their position from the traditional Marxist analysis of the lumpenproletariat. To survive by hustling is to survive in a wageless world. Howe (quoted in Hall *et al.*, 1978, p. 373), argues that hustling is a cultural response by a 'vibrant, powerful section of the (Caribbean) society'. In fact only a minority of hustlers are criminal, hustling should be seen as living on one's wits, of resisting the humiliation of work discipline, and of developing a form of political awareness. The unemployed in the Caribbean are not downtrodden, but have developed a tough-minded pragmatism, they are 'street wise', the ways in which they make a living develops a culture which is certainly politically aware, even though it may not be directly political.

It is in this context that the quasi-criminal activities and voluntary unemployment of a section of black youth make sense. Historically there is an important link with the political economy of the Caribbean and the culture it generates as a response to unemployment. This is transferred to the situation that Caribbean youth faces in the light of today's economic crisis. Their subcultures are areas of resistance to racism and poverty. With Asian youth the situation has developed differently at present, because of the contributions of their differing religious and cultural backgrounds. Their problems may objectively be similar to those of black youth, but they are subjectively experienced in a different cultural setting. Both groups however resent their limited opportunities for work prospects and advancement. (For example, see the discontent with work and opportunities on leaving school recorded in the CRE 1978 Report 'Looking for work', and its companion report 'Aspirations and opportunities – Asian and white school leavers'.) These dissatisfactions have been recorded ever since British schools have prepared immigrant youth for the labour market. Police relations in the black and brown communities have been bad ever since there has been any sizeable immigrant population. These exploded in the 1976 Carnival, and the attacks on Bengalis in the East End in the mid-seventies. The hostile propaganda of the National Front has also left its mark. There is a growing resistance to racism among black and brown youth. As Sivanandan argues (1976, p. 366):

> That is not to romanticize their futile ambition to lay siege to the state but to acknowledge, even while acknowledging the romanticism of the act the deep dark concern out of which their commitment springs.

British black and brown youth faces the problems of the racism endemic in the country they were born in. It also suffers a generationally distinct awareness of the failure of Britain to offer educational and occupational advancement. Class as well as race is central to their problems. Despite the attempts of race legislation to create what Sivanandan calls 'domestic neo-colonialism' it is obvious that youth, especially black youth, is impatient. In the government White Paper 1975, the Home Secretary had already pointed out that where job opportunities, educational facilities and environmental conditions continue to be poor, the second generation would find itself trapped in 'a vicious downward spiral of deprivation' which would be amplified by racial discrimination. The position of black and brown people in the present situation works through the medium of racism, and racism is the common experience they are subject to. It is race which defines them, which acts against them, and which could unite them. Their class position subscribes their economic position, but race is the subjectivity in which their class position is lived, and shapes their relation to the world. Obviously at the present time, brown and black are divided, and brown groups are further divided by caste, religion and culture. Black crime also, as Hall *et al*. note (1978, p. 395), acts in a dividing way. Ideologically

> it transforms the deprivation of the class out of which the crime arises into the all too intelligible syntax of race and fixes a false enemy; the black mugger.

When black organizations defend black youth they appear as defenders of black criminals, yet not to do so would be to abandon them to the ranks of the permanently criminalized. The important thing concerning crime and black youth is neither to romanticize it, nor to condemn it as simple-minded, but to see it in the context in which it has arisen. It is not work which is refused by black and brown youth, but the sort of work and working conditions it is offered. Like all youth it is vulnerable, and has no organized base from which to negotiate. Aware of how occupation defines identity, black and brown youth seek a dignified identity in a world which has shown oppression, rejection and humiliation.

The black community at present faces many contradictions. The extent to which its youth is involved in criminal as opposed to deviant enterprises is debatable. The experience of black youth has led to not only its disaffiliation from white society, but also to inter-generational strain. It has to find an identity concerning its position as black British youth. At present it draws on the politics and culture of Jamaica. There is a reference not only to peace and love, but also to the Rod of Correction. Materially black youth is like white youth, but its identity is more fragmented and problematic. It is highly ambitious, dissatisfied with its prospects, and so rejects not work *per se*, but the work it is offered. The extreme highly-publicized pole is that of the young black criminal, or the revolutionary. It would be a mistake to see this as the only response. However black youth culture contains an inflammable rebellious element, and draws upon a heady mixture of religion and politics, combined with a deviant and quasi-criminal hustling style which, fed as it is by a constant sense of oppression and rejection, could become a serious political response.

5 The invisible girl. The culture of femininity versus masculinism

In most subcultural studies, girls are either invisible, peripheral or stereotyped, and as Wilson (1978, p. 66) notes:

> The history of the sociology of deviance as far as women and girls are concerned, is a history of the uncritical adoption of conventional wisdom about the nature of women, namely that anatomy is destiny.

Subcultures are mainly discussed in relation to dominant value systems, but as I have noted they are also central to the structure of identity outside of class ascriptions. In the case where identity is dominated not just by occupation, age and class, but also by gender and race, then the importance of gender is overlooked. If subcultures are solutions to collectively experienced problems, then youth culture is highly concerned with the problems of masculinity. In fact where ethnic origin complicates subcultural membership, young black and brown males will turn to an emphasis on masculinity. It is for these reasons that most subcultures are male-dominated and masculinist in form. This is not to say that the presence or absence of girls in subcultures is only related to femininity but also to women's relationship to production. As the expansion in population reached work age, then economic expansion has slowed down. This has been experienced throughout the population. Graduate youth has found it increasingly difficult to find work, but what this means is the sort of work graduate youth has found acceptable is scarce, whilst for working-class youth work in general has been hard to find. Minorities in particular have found difficulties in obtaining work, and especially girls. Manpower Services Commission report a rise of 120 per cent in unemployment among young people for the five years up to 1977 as against 45 per cent among the working population as a whole, especially for black youth (350 per cent). Female unemployment rose fast for the 18 to 24 age group for both black and white, but there was an increase of 30 per cent for black females as opposed to 22 per cent for all females. Given these figures, one begins to see the importance that the cult of femininity (that is of non-work-dominated identity) has for girls.

For boys, then, subcultures allow an exploration and an investment in forms of masculinity. Men in routinized labour, particularly in heavy industrial work, pride themselves on their ability to perform arduous work (even though they may 'skive' off from work). It is a fitting test of their masculinity, and they will emphasize this in crude sexist discussion about women and sex, and also in their parody of homosexual men. Their contempt for what is deemed unmasculine also extends to white collar workers and as such is flavoured with a class dimension. Willis (1977), illustrates the link between sexism and shop-floor culture. Manual labour in particular is given masculine qualities – 'man's work'. Work may be divested of its intrinsic significance, but patriarchy has filled it with masculine emphasis. Even the gains of trade union conflict are part of a masculine pride in struggling with the employers. Thus, as Willis (1977, p. 150), suggests:

> The wage packet is the provider of freedom and independence: the particular prize of masculinity in work . . . . The male wage packet is held to be central, not simply because of its size, but because it is won in a masculine mode in confrontation with the 'real' world which is too tough for the woman. Thus the man in the domestic household is held to be the bread-winner, the worker, whilst the wife works for 'the extras'.

This is not just true for the working-class household, but is also reflected in middle-class families. We see then that women have reality mediated not just by class location interpretations, but also by patriarchy, the system of subordination in a world which is male-dominated in sexuality and procreative potential; a system where women's labour is organised economically, ideologically and politically by males. It is a world where sexism is the articulated, as well as the taken-for-granted, unquestioned superiority of men. In this sense women inhabit two locations: their role in their specific social class and their position in patriarchy.

This is at the basis of the construction of the psychology of femininity and the preparation for this dual role poses problems for women during their socialization and education. There is a considerable debate on the question of domestic labour (see Dalla Costa and James, 1972; Gardiner, 1976; Bland *et al.*, 1978; Himmelweit and Mohun, 1977). In brief, the class analysis of women has traditionally been based on their husband's occupation whatever 'cultural capital' they may bring to the marriage in the form of skills or money. Patriarchy recognizes men as breadwinners, and women as financially dependent on them; a position reflected in women's incomes. Women work in an unwaged capacity, servicing and sustaining the family; reproducing not only the work force, but themselves as sustainers. However, women are involved in the work force in a very central way. In the United States over the past ten years, the average male wage has not risen substantially but more women in families have gone out to work, thus increasing the income of the household. Land (1976), has argued a quarter of a million families would be below the official poverty 'line' if they were not supplemented by the earnings of the mother, and that one-sixth of households are substantially or completely dependent on women's earnings (this excludes pensioners) and most of these families have dependants. Women are involved in the economy as casualized temporary workers, a reserve army of labour which services the work force, works as unpaid domestic labourers, and are also consumers within the economic system. Women are judged, then, not on their occupational status but on their femininity. They are assessed in terms of their sexual desirability (described by Zetterberg, 1968, as the 'secret ranking of erotic (hierarchy'), and their femininity is defined by their relation to consumption (appearance, taste, fashion awareness, clothes, children's appearance, home). Work available to women in industry is de-skilled, and even in the professions tends to be of low status. Whilst their income may be essential, their work is delegated to being of minor importance, both in its organization and its form; it is 'women's work'. It often contains elements of domestic labour such as servicing men as bosses (the clerical worker as 'office wife') and at work their source of power may not be in their function as workers, but their rank in the erotic hierarchy ('feminine wiles'), that is their social source of power. This is illusory power in any material sense, but it is a definite source of alternative power in the personal sphere, as illustrated by the schoolgirl flirting with the male teacher; the typist with the executives, nurses with doctors, the shop-floor worker and the male overseer.

The contradictions of these roles are founded at school. Whatever the egalitarian ideology of the school, girls and boys are seldom given equal opportunities to study. There is always a schooling with marriage in mind, so that girls have an ambivalent attitude to their future, turning partially on the romanticism found in popular literature and magazines, but also on an interest in caring for people which, given women's historical alternatives, is comprehensible. Sue Sharpe (1976), reminds us that schools have a 'hidden curriculum' where work is preferred for form rather than content, and pupils are steered towards 'girls' subjects such as arts. Girls are taught to be unassertive. They tend to under-achieve at the age of puberty, a time when they become self-conscious about femininity. Sharpe notes that girls report that boys dislike cleverer girls, so that socially there is a fear of success as well as a fear of failure. Girls can resolve this by emphasizing the feminine role. There is some slight evidence that girls may do better in all-girls' schools, away from male competition.

Love and marriage; escape into romance

Girls receive from the mass media and from popular fiction distinct signals about the cult of femininity. Reading primers reinforce sexual roles, and comics are divided strictly along sex lines from the age of seven or eight. The themes in girls' comics are often related to isolation, competition, loneliness and emotional problems. The market aimed at the pubescent girl and the adolescent have a central theme of romanticism. Romantic attachment, and dependency on men is emphasized and advice on emotions, make-up and fashion is given as well as glamorous hints of the lives of pop stars. These are succeeded by glossy fashion magazines, aimed at specific age groups, again with advice about romance and sex, with more adult stories, but nevertheless presenting an escapist unproblematic world. Appearance is stressed, and fashion is used to construct a self which indicates to the world that the girl is from a world of fashionable femininity, where she has a relation not to class, but to a mythical world inhabited by a fashion hierarchy based on popular media figures. As girls grow older they seem to seek magazines which emphasize fashion rather than romantic stories. De Beauvoir has put this well (1972, p. 543):

> to care for her beauty, to dress up, is a kind of work that enables her to take possession of her person, as she takes possession of her home through housework, her ego then seems chosen and created by herself.

Girls then have two sources of socialization for their future, school and at home, backed up by a media interpretation of femininity which adds a sense of fatalism about marriage and motherhood. For many girls, in particular working-class girls, these are attractive and seemingly fulfilling goals. It is only after marriage that women realize its isolation and emptiness. The reality is that the average age of marriage for a woman is 22, and the woman's age at the birth of the last child is 26, and 42 per cent of all married women work. Schools, particularly in poorer areas where opportunities for women are restricted, prepare girls for the marriage market as much as for the job market. The future work prospects are belittled as temporary and unimportant. As Shaw (1976, p. 146), suggests:

> The meanings and consequences of sexual divisions in our society are translated into educational terms so that the different subcultures of boys' and girls' schools are but specialised versions of a wider culture, in which female futures are still defined in essentially domestic terms – a stereotyping which our educational system does little to undermine.

The organization and form of girls' subcultures remain very much a matter of empirical investigation. As has been suggested, a prominent feature of male-dominated subcultures has been its exploration of masculinity, and its imagery, whether it is the ambiguity of mods and freaks, or the heavy machismo of greasers. Girls are present in male subcultures, but are contained within them, rather than using them to explore actively forms of female identity. The subculture may be a social focus, something to dress up for, and an escape from the restraints of home, school and work, but as yet no distinct models of femininity, which have broken from tradition, have evolved, although this may well happen when female-dominated subcultures evolve. This is unlikely at present, especially among working-class girls, because of the demands of adolescent heterosexuality and the female role. For working-class women, marriage is a role of primary importance, and economically essential. Marriage mediates against the starkness and drabness of work, it provides acceptable evidence of maturity and adulthood, and it is an important investment for the future. Its attraction may fade away with familiarity, but it is still strong enough to structure girls' choices. Working-class respectability has to be paid attention to: a girl is permitted sexual relations with her steady boy friend, but she must guard against a reputation which will relegate her to the role of 'slag'. She develops a cynicism about boys who demand a sexual relationship without emotional commitment with a view to permanence. Girls are located in differing contradictions, as McRobbie and

Garber (1976), suggest. They may be peripheral in one sphere, such as work, but they can be central in another, such as the home. Consequently, when they are mentioned in subcultural theory, they are seen as peripheral to the boys:

> Women were usually accompanied by a man and they did not speak anything like as much as the men. There was a small group of unattached females, but they were allowed no real dignity or identity by the men. (Willis, 1978, p. 28)

This, however, is because the largely male investigators accepted the masculinist definition of the girls' roles in these subcultures.

McRobbie and Garber (1976) argue that girls are not marginal, but structurally different, pushed by male dominance to the periphery of social activity because they are centrally into a different set of activities. Girls spend more time at home, according to Barker (1972); Crichton *et al*. (1962); and McRobbie (1978). Frith (1978), suggests three reasons for girls' absence from subcultures – first, parents control girls' spare time much more closely. Second, girls have to assume an apprenticeship for domestic labour which begins at home. In fact, girls often have to earn their pocket money by helping in domestic tasks. And third, girls spend a lot of time in preparation for out-of-home leisure activities. Frith in fact argues that (1978, p. 66):

> marriage is a girl's career and the source of the constraints on her leisure. This argument can be pushed further: a girl's leisure is her work. It is leisure activities that are the setting for the start of her career, for the attraction of a man suitable for marriage.

Where low job aspirations exist, as they do for most girls, then there is a commitment to early marriage. It is a way out, and a socially acceptable one, from educational failure and work dissatisfaction, and girls' job decisions tend to be made in terms of a short-term commitment and secondary to the long-term commitment of marriage. Romance is certainly central to girls' perceptions of the future and it is seen as a precursor to marriage. Sarsby (1972) found for a sample of 15-year-olds that girls sought partners who would be sensitive to them, whilst boys stressed physical attraction. Her working-class girls stressed the importance of security and support in marriage. E. Figres (1972), quotes a batch of essays written by London grammar school girls which reveal their thoughts are very centrally on marriage, and Sharpe (1976), found 82 per cent of her sample wanted to marry – three-quarters of them by the age of 25. McRobbie and Garber (1976), suggest that one of the most important forms of subcultures amongst girls of the seventies was the Teeny Bopper (although this phenomenon was certainly present since the early sixties). However, it became a centre for market focus during the seventies for the 10- to 15-year-old girl. It requires only the use of a bedroom, a record player and a friend. There are no exclusion rules, entrance qualifications, no risk of sexual or social failure. Frith (1978, p. 66), agrees:

> girl culture becomes a culture of the bedroom, the place where girls meet, listen to music and teach each other make-up skills, practise their dancing, compare sexual notes, criticise each other's clothes and gossip.

This is the place that other girls are allowed to visit by their parents. Frith brings marketing evidence to show that the focus of this Teeny Bopper culture is usually a pop star, and what is purchased are magazines, then records and symbols such as T-shirts, posters and pictures. This fades as the girls go out and dance and date, but their magazines still feature pop stars rather than pop music. Attacks on Teeny Bopper idols are a cause of friction, and they are passionately defended. Robins and Cohen (1978, p. 52), note:

> Osmond baiting was, in fact, one of the most familiar weapons used by older brothers in their continuous bickering with their younger sisters. A fourteen year old boy told how 'we went by the Rainbow [Theatre] once and we started screaming out of the window "Osmonds are bent, all queers" and they were lobbing everything that come in sight. You should see one of them, she's in a state crying over the railing, going "You bastards" and the next minute she picked up a bottle and threw it at the bus'.

It is worth noting that many pop idols who are ambiguously male in this subculture are sexistly reduced to 'poofs' by males more involved in other elements of rock culture. The Teeny Bopper subculture is a retreat and a preparation for young girls. They can relate to their best friend (girls often emphasize the importance of their best friend, whose friendship they see as continuing after marriage) and together practise in the secrecy of girl culture for the rituals of courtship, away from the eye of male ridicule.

There is a not dissimilar pattern for boys outside of the more dramatic subcultures, and who have the luxury of their own or a friend's room. They are more focused on rock music, and other masculine pursuits. The emphasis on romance in the culture of femininity leads to courtship practices. Dancing is important in this, and Mungham (1976), describes well the dance-hall scenario, with its heavy heterosexual machismo masking the fear of the independent woman. Girls in this setting learn an important area of their lives: that of waiting. They cannot directly initiate social encounters, but can only reject or accept what is offered. This is sometimes crudely and effectively done. One respondent told me how he went down a line of waiting girls to be brushed off with a crude 'Piss off – Dracula!' Girls become obsessed with romance in this context, realising that the only exciting event in their bleak lives may be marriage, and they have no intention of blowing this by unseemly independence. They prepare carefully for dances and discos, arrive immaculately dressed with friends, and dance well. They then have to manage the courtship rituals, from boys trying to 'split a pair' of girls, to getting off, to going steady, which means being sexual with one boy, yet guarding one's reputation against boys who, it is accepted, are after only one thing.

Girls in male-dominated subcultures

In the more dramatic forms of male-dominated subcultures girls are in a structuredly passive situation, but this can be complicated. During the period of the Teds, girls would be present during the social activities but absent from the street corner culture. With the Mods, girls were subordinate but the mod 'cool' style allowed them to go out in groups or alone. With bikers, they never penetrated the central masculine core, riding or owning a bike: they were always a pillion rider. In the hippy subculture, they were still contained within the sphere of traditional femininity, even though it allowed a moratorium which suspended marriage (but not steady relationships). Hippy girls were long-haired, wanton, wild flower-children or, as McRobbie and Garber (1976, p. 219) suggest:

> The stereotypical images we associate most with hippy culture tend to be those of the Earth Mother, baby at breast, or the fragile Pre-Raphaelite lady.

As early as school subcultures, sexual exploitation and the subordination of women is stressed. The boys in Sarsby's study who mentioned personal qualities sought in a girl stressed obedience, respect and virginity. The relations with girls in school means they must be sexually inviting but not sexually experienced; sexually attractive enough to raise the boy's status, but not experienced so that there is no kudos in having a relationship with her. They are expected to service the boy domestically; to be a surrogate wife. They are reduced to being the receiving end of masculine desire, and so have to operate within a framework of passivity. Willis (1977, p. 44), sums this up:

> Although they are its objects, frank and explicit sexuality is actually denied to women. There is a complex of emotion here. On the one hand insofar as she is a sex object, a commodity, she is actually diminished by sex, she is literally worthless, she has been romantically and materially partly consumed.

There lies under this a fear that if a woman's desire is awakened then she may become independent, and the male himself reduced to an object of comparison. A loyal domestic partner is sought, the 'good woman' based on the boy's image of his own, or an idealized mother.

With girls involved in delinquent subcultures, Wilson (1978), suggests interestingly that they may be in rebellion against their traditional role. The deviant or delinquent behaviour of girls tends to be sexualized both in the literature and in the popular mind. Wilson's sample of 13- to 15-year-olds followed the cult of femininity in that they saw themselves as one-man girls, and for them love was essentially involved in a relationship before sex. Their future jobs were seen merely as a step towards marriage, and they regulated their behaviour so as to avoid contact with 'easy lays' who might contaminate their own reputations. The girls were able to be sexually active without defining themselves as 'bad'. Because girls who are deviant or delinquent tend to have their offences sexualized, a latent function of control, care and protection orders is to reinforce conventional sexual morality. L. S. Smith (1978) investigating a sample of girls aged 14 to 16 in the Bristol area including those involved with skinheads and greasers found that court records revealed that in no way was female delinquency restricted to sexual misconduct, but also included the usual delinquent acts of boys of a similar age cohort. Terry (1970), found in America that girls suspected of sexual offences are more likely than boys to be charged, and Chesney-Lind (1973), found three times as many girls as boys institutionalized for sexual offences, running away from home and incorrigibility (again the care, control and protection areas), even though these offences are committed more by boys. Interestingly enough, Smith's girls tended to react to being stigmatized as 'sluts' or 'common' by aggression rather than promiscuity. They suffered a double rejection: first as delinquents, secondly stigmatized as 'sluts'. The girls rejected this latter view, and indeed they condemned promiscuity. They developed self-images as tomboys: tough, dominant and willing to join in fights on equal terms with boys. Sharpe (1976), notes that in one London school it is common for girls to fight each other until they are 14 or 15, yet still remain fashion-conscious. Smith's girls found themselves isolated, as bad examples, from other neighbourhood girls, which pushed them into increased dependence upon the delinquent group. They became involved in more fighting, shop-lifting and drinking. The girls were seriously involved in the subculture, and showed group solidarity and active participation during group fights. Because of this they seemed to be treated as equals. This can be contrasted with reports from other sources about skinhead girls (*Schools Bulletin*, West Riding, July, 1970):

> Skinhead girls admire the way their boys treat them. They treat them as if they weren't there . . . . They never include them in their conversation, they have no manners and are disrespectful, but the girls respect them for being this way. It is all part of the understanding that goes with being a skinhead and being a true one . . . . All skinheads are big-headed . . . he will make a small fight sound like a massacre . . . before a skinhead can carry a tool, he must be able to fight with his fists. A tool is no good if someone can knock you out with one blow. The girls take as much part in the fighting as the boys and will be ready to have 'aggro' at any time.

These reports from two different essays by girls illustrate the varied response: firstly the collusion with male chauvinism, and secondly the involvement with fighting. These girls dissociated themselves from the respectable working-class image of femininity, yet remained contained within the ideology of male supremacy. They were still sexually 'respectable'. Their fights were with other girls, but their relation to the culture of femininity is complex. In biker groups there is a fetishized image, a feminized counterpart of the male, but again the girl is the property of the male. As with skinhead girls there is the drawing on of an image found in working-class lesbian cultures: that of the 'diesel dyke' or 'stomping dyke', not so much a development of possible new feminine imagery but feminised interpretations of working-class male imagery. These girls must be seen, as Smith (1978, p. 84), notes

> in contrast to the males whose delinquent behaviour is often seen as an extension of their role, they were seen to

have offended against their own sex role and the traditional, stereotyped conceptions of femininity.

It is very difficult for girls to draw on any alternative concepts of femininity, because of their intimate interaction, especially in working-class culture with traditional familial roles. Any homology sought in youth culture is ruled out because popular culture is itself sexist. Whilst the explicitness of rock and roll struck an important blow against small-town puritanism, from Presley's pelvis onwards, rock and roll nevertheless is a celebration of macho male sexuality which has a traditional notion of women's place, whether it is the sexuality of Rhythm and Blues, woman's need for a man in blues, or the ideology of country music. Rock and roll is still 'screw and smash', screw the girls and smash the opposition. Musicians are mainly men, except for esoteric exceptions like Alice Coltrane, and women are presented as lyricists, singers of sensitive work, or sex objects. Punk has at least attacked this image, although fetishization remains, at least it has elements of shock and self-satire. The sexism of popular culture, especially music, is that it is rooted in an industry which is correctly called show 'business'. Its aim is to make money, and not to criticize itself or society. Any woman's band which challenges programmed femininity usually works outside of the industry. Mass-produced popular culture is important because it reaches a very wide audience, but it is dominated by the ratings, airplay and output all open to commercial and often corrupt manipulation. Despite this, and perhaps because of it, women's rock has taken a firm stance against sexism, and involves a different relationship from the audience than the sexual domination of male 'cock rock' bands.

McRobbie (1978), has argued, as has Willis for boys, that their own culture is itself the most effective agent of social control for girls. Their anti-school subculture stresses having a good time, not academic achievement. They are like Nell Dunn's heroine in *Up the Junction* who says, 'Time enough for night school, and all that, when you're an old bag.' Marriage is a fascination for them which, given their alternatives, is hardly surprising. It continues to be a major economic and emotional goal despite their knowledge of its problems. School for working-class girls relates to them contradictions in their class position, but home offers a less competitive position. The traditional female role is problematic but concrete, and their knowledge of it is not abstracted theory but direct and experiential. Like her brother, the working-class girl moves from one family to another on marriage. There is no room for a working-class single woman in traditional working-class culture, except on the margins of sexual failure. One is not prepared in working class to live alone. There is an antidote to this in family life: a bad marriage is seen as preferable to loneliness (at least during the first marriage although work on women's aid centres suggests when alternatives are possible, the hold of marriage is considerably less strong). As Rowbotham reminds us, the drudgery of housework is lumped together with the more rewarding task of child care, although there is no reason why one person should do this all the time.

For middle-class girls, the problems of femininity are basically the same. However, whilst their education prepares them for the dual role, there may be a period between school and marriage which is a moratorium in the sense that they have some time for reflection. It is hardly surprising that the women's liberation movement originated amongst women in higher education. It is amongst these women that sexual politics has been considering relations to men and to other women, in the political, economic, ideological and sexual spheres. It is from this political context that a culture is developing which is examining the role and style of the new feminist woman. Important in this are the attitudes, behaviour and image involved in this. These are important if they are to have any effect on working-class girls. These is evidence from attempts by feminist teachers, social workers and youth workers to suggest that this can meet with considerable response amongst working-class youth. It is through these spheres that new concepts of femininity will percolate but it has to contend with the culture of traditional femininity, and its class reinforcements to succeed. It can expect little assistance at this stage from popular culture or from masculinist subcultures. Working-class girls may well rebel against male supremacy, but even the aggressive subcultures do not direct their toughness against their men; instead toughness is a move to get themselves accepted by macho men. The major problem is that the feminine role is at present a solution for working-class girls especially.

The celebration of masculinism

I have noted above the importance of masculinity to working-class life in terms of what one is manly enough to perform as work, or capable of earning. These two elements can balance each other, in the sense that if one is not doing a 'real' man's job, this is excused by one's earning capacity. In this sense, because the female wage is only 75 per cent of the male wage (but the male wage includes overtime and bonuses unlike the female), women never do men's work in either capacity. For adolescents life, especially cultural life, is spent indicating in concrete ways to one's self and others just how one is a mature example of one's age group or gender distinction. Girls make a detailed study of femininity. (The only group likely to accurately see through a transvestite's performance are pubescent girls. Any male trying to pass in street drag dreads meeting them.)

Working-class boys who are involved with specific youth subcultures are placed in the contradictory predicament of attracting attention, and having to deal with challenge. If they sport heavy macho clothes, as with Hell's angels or skinheads, they are a walking challenge, and they have to be hard enough to live up to this image. They have to indicate they deserve the uniform. If they take up a glamrock or feminized image, they have to be either especially hard and confident, or very quick-witted in repartee. They are caught up in a situation where they are wearing a costume which transgresses traditional concepts of masculine dress, hence when challenged over effeminacy, they have to prove their masculinity, or prove by flight that they are not masculine. This is why hard glamrock boys had the sinister image of feminized hair-styles, elaborate clothes and make-up set off by scars or tattoos. They are dissociating themselves from the despised non-familial, non-masculine males – homosexuals. Interestingly enough, in highly macho surroundings, for example, the military or prison, gay men who are 'out' will present themselves as outrageous queens, backing up their role play with wit and repartee, earning themselves acceptability by 'being a good laugh' and removing themselves to a non-threatening 'mascot' role. This occurs even within the gay subculture. For working-class youth, masculinity is a problem. It is the mark of one's independence, especially in a context such as school, where the dominant code is rational discussion. If one can handle oneself, then this means that all discussion can be settled as a direct challenge. This sets one's position in the local youth hierarchy, and makes one a valuable member of local teams or fighting crews. As I have noted, teams now contain girls who are prepared to fight other girls, although as Robins and Cohen (1978, p. 96), say:

> this aggro did nothing to alter the girls' fundamental one-down position in the local youth culture – as in other areas of their lives.

Middle-class youth subscribe to the cult of masculinity, but less directly. They do not have the neighbourhood traditions of well-known hard local families, or the mythical accounts of famous past fights. However, their competitiveness and masculinity take more subtle forms, and are institutionalized into their education and work situations. In an empirical study (Brake, 1977), comparing a semantic differential score for real, ideal and perceived concepts of self between middle-class hippies and working-class skinheads, both skinheads and hippies saw themselves as brave, strong and masculine. Indeed, both groups had assessed themselves equally on the bravery and masculinity scale. However, their interpretation of this and the acting out of it at the behavioural level was quite different. Basically the cult of masculinity is at the basis of relations with other men, and with women. Whitehead (1976), shows how in a rural setting, the pub is used to reinforce the cult of masculinity: women are used to maintain solidarity and ambivalent rivalry between men; jokes were used to stereotype women as contemptible and as sex objects to be controlled; prestige was related to an ability to control one's wife; and that these invariably influence marital relationships. She suggests that these are a normal feature of heterosexual men in groups. Certainly, these attitudes filter down to young males, and the sexist jokes and shouts that girls and women have to put up with daily is an indication of the complex desire and hatred of that desire that men have for women.

Zaretsky (1976), argues that as industrial society organized production around an increasingly alienated labour, then personal relations became pursued as ends in themselves. Bereft of a meaning and an authority at work, men sought these at home. Obviously, responses are more complicated than this, as studies of the family suggest (Willmott and Young, 1957; Rosser and Harris, 1965; Gavron, 1966; Ball, 1968; Young and Willmott, 1973), but the home has become the focus for expressive life, leisure and consumption. This is however true only for men; for women the experience of home is housework. Manual labour is organized around the work group, and as Tolson (1977, p. 59), reminds us:

> Thus a man's personal experience of work is expressed through an endless drama of group interaction, and his social acceptability is defined in terms of his dramatic self-preservation.

Masculinity is important, and as such, swearing, sexist talk, a banding together against women, unite the individual into the collectivity of the work group and the company of men. They gloss over the contradictions of male chauvinism, and laugh off the unease that men feel about their need for love and for the support of women. Unhappily, often this takes the form of needing women for sexual and domestic services, but saving their deeper feelings for other men, with whom there is no complication of sexual relations. This is reflected in the male bonding movies which hint at this contradiction. There is an assumption that men have true egalitarian relationships, but must assume a power relation over women. The conquest of women is in competition with other men, who are also competing for status. Stoltenberg (1975, p. 35), says:

> under patriarchy, the cultural norm of human identity is by definition – masculinity. And under patriarchy the cultural norm of male identity consists in power, prestige, privilege and prerogative as over and against the gender class women . . . . Male bonding is institutionalised learned behaviour whereby men recognize and reinforce one another's *bona fide* membership in the male gender class . . . male bonding is how men learn from each other that they are entitled under patriarchy to power in the culture. Male bonding is how men get that power and male bonding is how it is kept. Therefore men enforce a taboo against unbonding . . .

This illustrates the importance of peer groups for males in youth cultures, and work groups in shop-floor cultures. Men develop a conflicting attitude to a family: they are a sign of masculinity, of being able to support and control it, but they are also a recognized rationalization for failure. Domesticity is a valid tie, a valid restriction on what might have been. The material support for the family is also the condition for the recognition by the family of the male authority and influence lacking at work. Home is a retreat from work, and Tolson argues that the harmonious façade at home is important for the breadwinner to continue to work. Hence working-class men evade or deny marital tension, leaving the running of the family to the wife. This retreat to the patriarchal role, and its support in working-class male culture, means that feelings and sensitivity are not discussed. Depression, particularly for men, is explained away as 'sulking', and emotional life remains an unspoken-of area, as does sexuality.

Middle-class men have a more individualized work life. The rough machismo of working-class men, often structurally encouraged because of the necessity to preserve a patriotic militarism in the past, is replaced by a smoother but nevertheless entrenched male identity. Education and careers are both competitive structures requiring self-confidence and aggressive drive. He is often supported at work by women who are expected to combine a quasi-domestic servicing as well as clerical and administrative skills. Tolson argues that middle-class men use their careers as indicators of identity and status, and where confidence in this is shaken, the professional man focuses his attitudes of patriarchy on his family. Where the middle-class careerist becomes disillusioned, family domesticity becomes the focus of his concern, protection and authority, and family interaction can become a focus for tension. However, the home is still central to male authority; it is his career and income that is central. The wife, like housewives in all classes, can become lonely, isolated, often too lacking in confidence to work even though she wants to, and depressed. Sexuality is often a problem, because there is a distinct emphasis on sexual success, and the concept of sex as entertainment which has increased since the sixties has undermined male confidence, or else substituted a stud ideology of sexual domination by skill.

One effect of heterosexual male culture and the response by the feminists has been on the lives of gay people. Subcultural studies of youth never mention homosexuals, and this is hardly surprising given the masculinist emphasis of practically all youthful subcultures. Young gay people are swamped by the heterosexist emphasis they find in peer groups and subcultures. As far as popular culture is concerned they are invisible. Young people tend to be aware at the age of about ten that they are different, and by the time puberty arrives they are generally aware what this difference is. However, admitting this to themselves and especially to others is delayed usually until some supportive subculture has been found to 'come out' in. Given the obsession of most young people's subcultures, especially in the early teens, with heterosexual success and identity, it is hardly surprising that finding other homosexuals is a problem. This is the basis of differing views of feminists and gay radical men about paedophilia. For most gay men, a pubescent or adolescent seduction with a mature older man would have eased their problems considerably, whilst for most young girls a paedophiliac relationship is very likely to be exploitative. Young gay people usually do not find homosexual subcultures until they have left home. There is a subculture involving young boys in the gay world, known as 'chickens'. They can be heterosexual boys, using a sexual market-place for prostitution (see Reiss, A., 1961; Brake and Plummer, 1970;

Harris, 1973). Most community homes and borstals have an informal information system telling runaway boys where the sexual markets are, or else a list of 'phone numbers and addresses that will offer somewhere to stay and a few pounds in exchange for sexual services. They are also a haven for young homosexual boys who have run away from an unhappy home, and from a dreary heterosexually dominated life in the provinces. There is a high status position for attractive young boys in the youth-dominated gay world, and it provides an alternative form of social mobility.

Young gay girls find the situation more difficult. There is an organization which holds meetings and social events for homosexual teenagers, and various gay organizations offer telephone and befriending forms of counselling. Working-class lesbians, if they are aware of their homosexuality at an early age, find the pubs and clubs but because of the secrecy about homosexuality, combined with the secrecy about women's sexuality generally, young gay girls are less present on the gay scene. Middle-class gay women, like their male counterparts, can find an entry to gay subcultures through gay socs at college and university. Outside of this student group, gay women find the gay world through the feminist movements, although it is probably true to say that most homosexual people are introduced by a relationship to the gay world or, in particular men, gradually become involved through local gay pubs and clubs. In general, however, for men homosexual behaviour may take place in heterosexual peer groups in contexts which permit the disavowal of homosexual labelling. Because of the nature of casual sex in the male gay world, it is possible to find sexual outlets whilst denying any self-labelling of homosexual, or being involved with the gay community. Women, however, tend to seek deeply affectionate relationships and so tend to concentrate on establishing and maintaining a loving relationship in their early lesbian career.

We can see then that the 'absence' of girls from masculinist subcultures is not very surprising. These subcultures in some form or other explore and celebrate masculinity, and as such relegate girls to a subordinate place eventually, within them. They reflect the sexism of the outside world. A sexism which still accepts the sexual division of labour and women's traditional place in the modes of production and reproduction. In some subcultures girls have won themselves acceptance, as for example in fighting teams, but again these teams operate against other girls. The male attitude when it comes to sexual relations remains traditional. However there are the beginnings of a challenge to this, but until this finds a response in the larger, in particular the working-class community, it is unlikely to be reflected in working-class subcultures involving youth. In popular culture such as the rock industry, women are still relegated to the role of singer, usually performing sexist celebrations of sexual come-hither or sad ballads of woman's lot. The culture of femininity is reflected in the various youth subcultures involving girls. But nevertheless popular culture can hint at alternatives. Frith suggests (1978, p. 207):

> Female musicians, whether through implicit but disturbing images of what a woman could be or on the basis of an explicitly feminist culture, can challenge the safe solutions to the glamorous star-as-mum.

That is not to say that girl performers are not controlled by the sexism which is a dominant form in rock. There are exceptions as Burchill and Parsons (1978) indicate. They accurately describe rock (Burchill and Parsons, 1978, p. 86):

> Rock is a pedestal sport, as in being a monarch – whenever possible a boy inherits the throne – females are not thought to be the stuff worship/idols are made for/of. Girls are expected to grovel in the mezzanine while the stud struts his stuff up there, while a girl with the audacity to go on stage is always jeered, sneered and leered up to – rock and roll is very missionary, very religious, very repressive.
>
> A guitar in the hands of man boasts 'cock' – the same instrument in female hands therefore (to a warped male mind) screams 'castration'.

Despite this generalization, this does help to explain why changes in girls' attitudes will come from the influence of an older age group, and through the medium of feminism. Nevertheless the political thrust at the periphery of popular culture will at some time attack the notion of the programmed woman.

6 Subcultures, manufactured culture and the economy. Some considerations of the future

Subcultures and manufactured culture

One problem in the analysis of any youth culture is the extent to which it is a response to a culture deliberately manufactured for marketing and consumption. Rock music, as well as the artefacts manufactured to accompany it, is very big business. Frith (1978), reminds us that in 1974 over four million dollars was spent on musical products in America, and in Britain 160 million records were produced, with popular music making up between 85 and 90 per cent of the sales. This consumption is an important element of youth culture. Eighty per cent of buyers are under 30, and the 12- to 20-year-old age group buys over 75 per cent of popular music. This commercialization has led to a theory of mass culture which Frith calls the Leavisites approach. He bases this on the followers of the literary critic F. R. Leavis who sees mass culture as effortlessly consumed, escapist and standardised and art as unique, challenging and instructive. The Leavisites reject popular music because it is mass-produced, profit-oriented and unauthentic. He quotes Holbrook (1973), who argues that youth is exploited by a commercial youth culture which separates them from their parents and the community, depersonalizes love and promotes sex and violence. Frith also attacks a form of vulgar Marxism which argues that the commercial input of youth culture deradicalizes it. He favours Benjamin's (1970), argument that the technology of mass production contains a progressive force which broke the traditional authority and awe (the 'aura') of art. Artists could become democratic producers and their work can become open to the mass of the people each of whom can become an 'expert'. Creative work can be collectivized into a socialist aesthetics: Laing (1969), extends this to consider popular music. Capitalist cultural forms contain liberating as well as oppressive elements, and rock music results from the music industry's attempts to develop new markets, and its youthful audience's attempts to find a medium to express its own experience. Musicians can exploit this tension to find a creative space in which to develop their art. It is because marketing influences are not entirely deterministic that a cultural struggle occurs involving both audience and musicians in a struggle for cultural symbols. Frith argues against romanticizing rock music into a revolutionary symbol and suggests careful consideration of patterns of consumption among teenagers, and how they themselves see their culture. He finds, with Murdock, sharp class differences concerning youth's use of similar musical symbols. Frith argues that middle-class children are interested in alternative values, expressed in the lyrics of rock music, whilst working-class children are more concerned with the beat and dancing, drawing their alternative values from their street peer culture. Music for working-class children, he argues, is a background for other activities, although I would argue it is an intrinsic part of other activities and they certainly listen to the lyrics. Frith emphasizes age as a major variable in musical preference, and he quotes the statistics of the BBC Audience Research Unit, which finds Radio 1 has an audience which is more significant on age than class differences, a finding reflected in readership of the musical press. Music, Frith argues, is an activity enjoyed by a vast number of non-deviant kids, and whilst subcultures give meaning to music, subculturists freeze the adolescent world into subcultures and the rest. A visibly different leisure style is elevated above the less apparent sexual and occupational differences, in leisure activities. He accepts Young's thesis (1973) that the use of rock music in the hippy subculture is an expression to the 'ethos of productivity' but only because they have a definitive ideology of leisure. This he feels cannot be extended to all youth culture, and suggests that the teds' interest in rock and roll was an element of their dependence on teenage consumption.

Willis, however, has shown (1978) that this is too simple. His rockers selected a definite musical style which was homologous to their life-style and use of activity through fighting, motor cycles and dancing. Frith breaks down the meaning of rock music into a distinct sixth form subculture which prefers progressive albums, and a working-class preference for Top Twenty singles and discos. For both groups in his sample, music was a background rather than a focus for their lives, although there are groups as with Northern Soul, a working-class youth culture focused on music and all-night discos. These are the exception, and for most young people music is a background or an activity and not a symbol. It is for most groups a background rather than a focus, even though it may make a symbolic community out of disparate groups. What is involved, he argues, is (p. 205):

> not the autonomous expression of cultural or sub-cultural values but the different patterns of freedom and constraint experienced by young people in different relationships to production.

However it could be argued that adolescents select certain types of music and whilst the music plays an apparent accompanying role, it is nevertheless central to their lives. Different groups select specific types of music and whilst it may be present in the background, it articulates rather than reflects meanings. As Willis (1977), suggests, cultures relocate given aspects of commercial cultures, and music is important because it articulates aspects of kids' lives, at a real or fantasy level. They select specific kinds of music (this is not to say that they are not influenced by opinion leaders) and their understanding of music is quite sophisticated. Involved in this may be what being a rock star or a footballer means for a group, but because a group does not articulate a definitive ideological stance does not mean it does not have an articulated meaning and value system. It is important to understand what meanings are typical for that group.

Frith also considers the origins of popular music. Rather than being mindlessly fed commercial products, the audience's response is carefully monitored by the industry. Commercial failure and over-production are avoided by careful selection from the vast amount of records produced. The needs and tastes of the prospective audience are carefully researched and record production boosted by the ratings, the star system and a 'reserve army' of musicians. Creative breakthroughs come from a combination of artists, subcultures, localities and audiences. Rock music then for Frith is an expression of popular culture which reveals certain contradictions between freedom and constraint. Rock projects visions which could become critiques of reality, and record companies and mass media ideologists try to control this. The ideology of rock rests on the relationship between producers and consumers, on the tensions between the attempt to make rock acceptable and its critical, anarchistic edge. Most of all it is enjoyable, it is fun, and it persists despite attempts to restrict it to leisure moments, and to freeze the audience into a series of market tastes. Internally this is done by using the ambitions of performers to control their less socially acceptable ideas or life-styles. This explains punks' aggression and deliberate bad taste. Ultimately the industry has to respond to the emotions, hopes and anger of its audience, and these can be political critiques of their everyday life, admittedly contained in a musical form, but critical nevertheless. There is a battle between artistic control and market production with the kids' hopes, desires, dreams and fears in the middle. This is why it is disturbing, joyous and intoxicating.

Despite Frith's criticism which may be true for rock music, only one element of a subculture, and despite his view of class which in many ways seems to focus on life chances, subcultures do seem to arise out of a series of factors related to the collective experience of a group of young people. These can be traced to structural contradictions arising from their basic class position, and involving employment, education, the tension of freedom and constraint, and also the local neighbourhood. Subcultural response articulates something about a group of young people's general relationship to the class problems of a specific age cohort at a particular moment in class history. They can become a source of alternative values, or less distinctly, a translation of class values develop to meet a generationally specific form of a traditional class problem. As such they construct a vibrant montage, they 'win space' from dominant cultures, 'warrening from within' to form a minimal unity within the class configuration, and relating to and responding to the parent culture. Elements are drawn from the synthetic manufactured culture of popular music and artefacts, but these are relocated and transformed ('bricolage'). As such they reveal much of the interstices and hidden space of the 'underside' of youth and its problems. From this culture and its symbols, young people can work at creating a collective identity which articulates their problems, and their values and their sets of meanings. From this material they can construct a personal identity which for a brief moment celebrates their youth and symbolizes for them an achieved identity which stands temporarily outside of the ascribed identity given by class, education and occupation.

One problem which arises from subcultural studies, is that they are adaptations for a minority, who because of their dramatic style, are given vast media coverage and presented as 'typical' of wayward youth, or confused adolescence. Murdock and McCron (1976), note that in their study many respondents were not involved in local subcultures, but had taken over styles from official youth provision, or the teenage entertainment industry. They were expressions and extensions of the dominant meaning system, rather than deviant from or in opposition to it. They reflect Parkin's deferential working-class group. Most youth subcultures unless they have an articulated political element, are not in any simple sense oppositional. They may be rebellious, they may celebrate and dramatize specific styles and values, but their rebellion does not reach an articulated opposition. Even where they do, they may be accommodated and contained. It has been argued that this has happened for example to the hippy culture, to the extent that there appears to be a belief that nothing really happened in the 'sixties' (that is the period between 1964 and 1972). However, as we have seen, the counter-culture covered several different types of groups, some deferential and some highly political. Where centuries of ideological domination, as for example with challenges to the traditional family and traditional femininity, failed to be overthrown overnight, conservative cynicism set in. But given the power of the opposition, this is not surprising. The exception in contemporary society may be black and brown youth, which cannot have its obvious exploitation easily accommodated by white society. The situation is that most of the younger generation are not conservative in some simple way, but accept their situation with realistic fatalism. They feel that they have some sort of investment in society as it is, that a rapid change may make things much worse. There are powerful ideological forces acting to reinforce this, increasing this investment by exploiting romance into the institution of marriage, and using work as a strong socializing agent. They fear opposition to the existing political economy and social structure may lose them the little they have. Hall *et al.* (1978, p. 155), note Parkin's views of a subordinate value system which produces a culture which is both different and subordinate – a 'corporate' system.

> The difference between 'corporate' and 'hegemonic' cultures emerges most clearly in the contrast between general ideas (which the hegemonic culture defines) and more contextualised or situated judgements (which will continue to reflect their oppositional material and social base in the life of the subordinate classes). Thus it seems perfectly 'logical' for some workers to agree 'the nation is paying itself too much' (general) but are only too willing to go on strike for higher wages (situated).

Groups then hold, in relation to dominant values, values which appear logically inconsistent with their official view. In addition the strong sense of identification they have with their neighbourhood, peers, immediate circle of kin, community and locality acts as a divisive force from other groups. Given this, it is hardly surprising that those young people who identify some investment in the present social structure, and who are then reinforced in this investment materially by work, marriage, dependants and possession of a small amount of property, adopt a conservative stance, and an identification with respectability. Conventionality, rebellion or a rejection of some form of respectability (usually a different interpretation of specific aspects of respectability, rather than a wholesale rejection of it) is related to the actual age group of young people combined with their class position. Those who have realistically seen school as not related to their future life in routinized labour have different attitudes to those who see a link between education and their future careers. Work is responded to with enthusiasm at first, then disillusionment usually followed by subcultural work adaptations which help the worker to deal with the work situation. Similar changes can be noted in those who are unattached from emotional relationships, as distinct from those who are engaged, newly married and so forth. These relationships also reflect an investment in society as it is. The transition from school to work, from unattachment to commitment in emotional relationships, from work as peripheral to work as central to existence, and the influence these all have on identity are important in understanding the social relations young people have to production. The reality of violence which runs through young working-class male culture needs to be understood not just as the response to brutalizing circumstances, but both as a role and an identity in a masculine career structure, and a muffled and semi-articulate form of communication. These all reflect different relations at different 'moments' to the social structure. Close attention needs to be paid to groups of young people at different stages and at different ages. A start has been made with the links traced between girls and the culture of femininity at school, work and at home, and with connections between shop-floor culture and school-resisting culture among adolescent working-class males along the lines of Willis (1977).

Class inequalities are mediated through subcultures, and the degree of oppression involved is not just simply a matter of life chances, the possession of goods and opportunity systems as suggested in the Weberian and Mertonian models. Materially we can separate young people, but we need to observe also their class location, and their social relations to production. Students materially can be separated from other groups of young people. They are numerically small, 520,000 full-time students (about 14 per cent of the 18-year-old age group), a figure expected to fall sharply in the 1990s (Department of Education and Science,

February 1978). Their income is hard to assess, because it is based on their grants, rather than any supplementary sources, but it seems much less than the average wage for a comparative working age group, but it must be remembered students are often subsidized from home and pay neither tax nor National Insurance. Their cultural capital is considerably higher, and their opportunity to experiment with ideas and life-styles, their moratorium from wage labour all place them in a unique and privileged position. The values of certification from higher education fluctuate according to the market, but nevertheless even with graduate unemployment, the embourgoisement of minor professions such as social work, administration and nursing still give students a favourable weighting towards employment. They may not receive so easily the jobs they have come to expect but they still have a relative advantage over the rest of the population.

Unemployment and the local economy

One problem which has increased for youth, especially working-class youth, is that of unemployment. The Department of Employment Gazette (November 1977) reports that in January 1977, 14.1 per cent of girls in the under-18 age group were unemployed, as opposed to 12.8 per cent of boys. Despite the fluctuations of the school-leaving age (29.6 per cent of under 18-year-old girls were unemployed, in contrast to 28.6 per cent of boys in July 1977), unemployment is having a marked effect on the young female work market. Opportunities for girls lead to a situation where the average woman reaches her maximum earning capacity by her mid-twenties, and the trend in women's wages indicate they are much less than men's. At present the figure quoted is that a woman's wage is 75 per cent of a man's, but these are figures which include all male earnings including overtime. The situation is probably nearer the 1975 figure where a woman's wage averaged 57.4 per cent of a man's. (The Equal Pay Act 1970, was amended and supplemented by the Sex Discrimination Act 1975 and the Employment Protection Act 1975. The 1970 Act came into force on 29 December 1975.) Training is poor for women, who mostly work in clerical and distributive trades, whose professional training is still mainly nursing and as a Council of Europe National Youth Committee Report (November 1977, p. 22) notes,

> In the UK less than half of all school leavers in 1974 received any long term vocational training, only 6 per cent of these were girls and their training was mainly limited to hairdressing.

This means that virtually half of Britain's school-leavers are unqualified, and face a work life of general routinized or unskilled labour. The National Youth Employment Working Party (1974), who cite this figure, stress qualitative factors they feel are as important as structural economic factors. The 'majority experience' of employers notes changes in the attitude of the present generation. Young people are now 'more questioning', 'less likely to respect authority', and 'tend to resent guidance about their appearance' (p. 74). Only a third of applicants possessed the 'smart appearance' and 'mental alertness' specified by the jobs. The report asks not only for training schemes but suggests attitudes should be affected, and motivation assessed. It seems that not only black school-leavers question employers' requirements outside specific job skills. Youth unemployment is not a temporary fluctuation. It trebled for the under-20-year-olds during July 1974 to July 1975, and for the period 1976–8 summer and winter unemployment rates had increased for this age group. The Department of Employment Gazette (March 1978) indicates 142,000 boys and 132,000 girls unemployed in this group. For the first time there were more under-18-year-old girls (67,900) out of work than boys (67,000), and this group make up one-sixth of unemployed women and 6.3 per cent of unemployed men. Youth is increasingly in competition for jobs, and the economic rivalry has increased between males and females, white and non-white. As Dean (1976), notes, that whilst there are a large amount of unemployed school-leavers, there are an equal number of unemployed other teenagers, and that this latter is not a temporary phenomenon as the former often is. Whilst the government has instigated schemes to combat unemployment (recruitment subsidies, job creation projects, community industry and similar schemes) are in no sense creating new permanent employment. These short-term measures in no sense relieve the unemployment situation, but merely shift it on to an older age group.

Several features have added to the present problems concerning the inner city and its effect on the young. Since the war, state involvement has increased in those areas which whilst necessary in providing materials and services for the economy, were themselves unprofitable. These were the older heavy industry sectors (mining, iron and steel), and services in the public sector (railways, health, education and the social services). The economy is serviced by these sectors, and allow it to concentrate on more profitable areas. State services grew at a time when capital began to experience problems of productivity and profitability. As a result, since the seventies, successive governments cut back on the non-productive sectors, the public services in particular. This was at a time when distinct effects were felt in the local economies of particular districts. Areas involved with the less profitable, older industries have usually had little reinvestment since the early part of this century. Where the local economy was based on coal, steel, shipbuilding or the docks there grew depressed areas, designated as 'development areas'. The worst hit were the large 'inner city' urban areas, as found in Glasgow, the North-East, Birmingham, Liverpool and East London. These areas are inhabited by the more depressed groups of the work force, the old, the unskilled and immigrants. There is a move away from a large skilled work force to servicing, distribution and warehousing needing smaller and less skilled labour. The reports of the Community Development Projects, set up in these areas, reflect these sorts of changes in the local economy. To take one area of East London, a traditional riverside area with the main industries of docking and sugar refinement, built up during the colonial expansion of the last century, several changes occurred. As docking declined, the dockers accepted a severance scheme which compensated them for their trade, and for their strong union protection. The docks became warehouse and storage units, requiring only maintenance staff, so that between 1965 and 1976, 25,000 permanent jobs were lost. Profits were never put back into the local plant, so that profits made in the area were taken out of it, and lack of plant, the expense of maintenance and replacement was avoided by the introduction of automatized or maintenance industries. In a situation, where at the start of the century industry was showing 25 per cent profit, as the area was allowed to deteriorate, the companies reinvested in other industries or, due to the transportable nature of contemporary light industrial plant, moved from the area when it faced deterioration of the area or militant union action. By 1976, the area had a 9 per cent unemployment rate, with the skilled workers and professionals leaving, so that only the unskilled and the young were left. Council house expansion coincided with deterioration of the housing units (by the 1940s) and because the area was scheduled for redevelopment, little was done to improve existing housing stock. The area had one of the highest perinatal mortality rates, a high respiratory death rate and a poor general health record. The older schools were kept for the less able children (70 per cent of schoolchildren in the borough) and there were no facilities for children after the compulsory age of attendance. (See C. Tyrell, 1975; Newham Community Development Project, 1976; Joint Docks Action Group Resource Team, 1976; Joint Docklands Action Group Resource Team, 1977; CIS/CDP Report 13, 1975; CDP/IP 1977, February.) This is a typical situation, and one which generates delinquent subcultures at a time when youth unemployment is the worst in the post-war period. It is however, part of a general unemployment crisis.

The response of the successive governments of the 1960s and 1970s was to make British capitalism profitable again. A concern was certainly shown for the depressed inner city area, but the paradigm used to explain it tended to be that of the 'culture of poverty' and the 'cycle of deprivation'. Briefly this argues that people inherit poverty, not due to poor economic planning, or industrial decline, but because their life-style and value system entraps them. The state's failure to deal with poverty is usually conceived by the government as primarily an administrative or managerial problem at the local level. What is overlooked is the local political economy. Areas need massive public investment, and the ending of cuts in the public sector. What in fact has happened is that there has been an attempt to involve community organizations, and to develop community projects rather than providing massive inputs of investment. The result has been in the words of the CDP/IP Team 'gilding the ghetto'. The Urban Aid projects, the Educational Priority Areas, Community Development Projects and the Comprehensive Community Programmes as well as schemes of area management have foundered on the economic crisis. The result has been to pressurize local authority management to redirect their priorities, and to finance them out of local decisions concerning cuts in the public sector. Cuts in, for example, the Rate Support Grant, means that local authorities are forced to bring their spending into line with central government policy. As a result there has been an increase in what Cockburn (1977) calls the 'local state', and decisions pass from the elected officers into the expertise of corporate management on the grounds of technocratic efficiency. Profitability in British industry seems to be founded on a reduction in wages, low employment and cuts in public health, housing, educational and social services. This has led to a situation where some observers see the entire Poverty Programme of the sixties as the management of poor people, and increasing community care to make local areas deal with problems traditionally dealt with by the public services. For the young unemployed even with cash injections, as with the Youth Opportunities Programme (based on the Holland Report, 1977, Manpower Services Commission), private industry has not responded greatly to the suggestion they should offer Work Experience Programmes to young people. As for the young people themselves, all that happens is that they are paid, instead of social security, £18 per week, which places them in the low-paid work force bracket, and provides them with temporary job schemes rather than permanent employment with some form of prospects.

Youth culture and identity

What can be seen from the above, is that a quasi-delinquent male-dominated subculture in a district as described above, perhaps with a high immigrant population, has its origins in structural contradictions, and is mediated by class, race and gender, and further modified by the local working-class community, and the local political economy. As such it is a far cry from a quasi-bohemian sixth form culture, whose roots are in the progressive middle-class intelligentsia, and whose concern is with liberal or radical criticism, and motivated by self-growth and individuality. Prospects for this group are not only different in terms of opportunities and alternatives, but also at the level of personal life, emotions and social relationships. Youth culture links and explores young people's relations to material production, and also the social relations that the ideological superstructure mediates to them. This is felt deeply at the level of the personal. A major attraction of subculture is its rebellion, its hedonism and its alternatives to the restrictions of home, school and work – it is fun. It offers a space to celebrate rebelliousness and hedonism. It also explores heterosexuality, masculinity and by definition femininity. It has an important socializing element for the continuation of society. Dominant ideology has managed to accommodate any attack on traditional notions and roles concerning sexuality and family life. Even when these have been articulated, as with part of the hippy culture, the changes have been more apparent than actual. Despite adults' fears of promiscuity, respectability, albeit redefined, has not been destroyed, and most subcultures reinforce traditional sexual roles. The only subcultures which have developed a critique of traditional heterosexuality and roles have been those which have developed out of being oppressed by traditional sexuality, that of radical homosexual and feminist subcultures. These have been more in the form of social and political movements, but they have developed subcultures within these. These subcultures have gained a space in traditional sexuality to develop an arena for struggle. Some middle-class groups such as 'swingers' or 'mate swappers' have used this to develop a strategy to combat sexual boredom, where permissive adultery is practised and carefully scripted to avoid an emotional entanglement which might threaten the marriage, described by Gagnon (1977), as 'formal rewriting' of the sexual 'script'. Such experimentation belongs to middle-class post-adolescent sexuality, and certainly the sexual behaviour (Schofield, 1965; 1973), remains monogamous and romantic. The area where sexual behaviour has increased is between couples having a steady relationship: indeed, the adoption of the contraceptive pill is a form of commitment ritual. In working-class groups traditional roles remain, but that is not to say there is no consideration of alternatives. Working-class women are very conscious about the restrictions of marriage, but they are also very realistic about their lives, economically and emotionally, should they reject it. It is not surprising that the cult of romance has such a strong grip on teenage working-class girls.

Youth culture also offers a collective identity, a reference group, from which to develop an individual identity, 'magically' freed from the ascribed roles of home, school and work. It provides cognitive material from which to develop an alternative career, kept secret from, and in rebellion with, the adult world. It is a free area between the control and authority of the adult world and freedom amongst one's peers. For a temporary period during youth, an alternative script can be performed, outside of the socializing forces of work, and before those of marriage become important. Young people need an identity which separates them from the expectations and roles imposed upon them by family, school and work. Once they have made this separation, which makes a dramaturgical statement about their difference from those expectations imposed upon them by others, they feel free to explore and develop what they are. They will create an image, often of a quasi-delinquent, or rebellious style, which marks them apart from the expectations in particular of their family and other adults. Once this separation has been made from the identity imposed by the family in particular, they are liberated to develop another identity. This helps explain why they often then give up this identity of transformation. They reject it as 'adolescent', in a very real sense it is no longer them. In this sense the material of youth culture is of considerable existential importance. It has a particular appeal to those young people who feel little commitment to or investment in the present state of affairs. It attracts those who feel they do not somehow fit, or feel rejected, where the life of the young person reinforces this isolation or alienation, where he/she feels a misfit, then the scripts being composed in subcultures are highly attractive. For working-class youth the subculture is usually a local variation of a nation-wide theme, where the neighbourhood mediates the form and style of the subculture. Middle-class youth is attracted to a subculture which usually is class-based, but not neighbourhood-based, particularly where it is influenced by sixth form or student culture. Minority groups are caught in a situation where their national cultures support and sustain them, but also constrain them and keep them separate from other subcultures. This can be a conscious espousal of a particular form of rebellion against a neo-colonial political economy, as with black youth's rejection of Britain and adoption of Caribbean accents, argot and style. This has its roots in the Afro-Caribbean slave economy, and the situation is different from that of Asians. Wilson (1978) describes Asian schoolgirls who seek support from their homeland culture and language, only to find that their retreat to this culture is the very reason they are disliked and discriminated against. Unlike Afro-Caribbean girls and boys who offer solidarity to each other and who will aggressively defend themselves, Asian girls find their different cultures, religions and geographical areas of origins divisive, and their upbringing as Asian women preventing them asserting themselves. Asians have not as yet found a subcultural identity between two cultures, as have West Indians, whose original national culture and language was destroyed by slavery.

Youth as a social problem

Youth, its cultures and subcultures, have always been seen as a social problem in the minds of general public and policy-makers. A failure to socialize adequately into its place in the work force presents serious consequences. The present situation of youth unemployment causes concern because one unintended consequence is the loss of work habits and work discipline. The young unemployed who have become disaffiliated from labour attempt to make a living from hustling, or criminal or quasi-criminal means. This has added to a general moral panic about lawlessness in the inner city which has been escalated by the National Front. A major function of job creation schemes has been to keep youth involved with work discipline. It is too early to say to what extent these will be useful, but they provide no real substitute for permanent employment. Delinquency prevention programmes have failed in the past because essentially they are piecemeal attempts to deal with structural problems, and as such offer no real structural alternative. Basically they have been composed of counselling methods based on individual maladaptation, group work, behaviour modification, residential programmes and community approaches. There seems little evidence that any form of counselling from an agency has much effect on delinquency. There is certainly scope for individual counselling and group work, but it needs to be in a community setting, on the kids' terms rather than with agency work on the organisation's terms.

Community programmes have been popular in the United States such as the Provo experiment and the California Community Treatment Project, which use a situation of boys living in the community, who spend some time at the project centre with group work programmes. These projects have had some success with adolescents identified as neurotic, but less effect on those committed to a deviant value system. The Chicago Area Project was based not on concentrating on individuals within groups, but on the ecological model of the early Chicago school, and as such focused on the neighbourhood in which delinquency took place. Basically the project attempted to develop local welfare organization among the community using local key figures. From this local neighbourhood groups were built up. The success of the project is hard to ascertain, and the conclusions reached are that the programme probably helped reduce delinquency 'because any substantial improvement in the social climate of a community must' (Kobrin, 1967, p. 330). (For fuller details of these studies see La Mar T. Empey and J. Rabow, 1961; M. Q. Warren, 1970; Kobrin, 1967.) Various other projects seem to have little lasting effect. The Cambridge-Somerville project (Powers and Wilmer, 1950; McCord J. and McCord W., 1959), had no significant effect on adult criminality, and other programmes using group work techniques in the mid-sixties met with little success. Reckless and Dinitz (1972), used a three-year programme based on fifteen years research, trying to resocialize delinquents by exposing them to socially approved models with little success, probably because the models and the assessment were respectable and middle class.

Other projects have used detached workers to work on the street with gangs (Yablonsky, 1967; Klein, 1971; Miller, 1962), seem to have a mixed effect. The street worker acts as a 'role model' and whilst this may be constructive it does not seem to have reduced delinquency rates. The orientation of these approaches are rehabilitative and by definition reformist. Schur (1973), takes a more critical stance, seeking radical social change rather than a reformed penal system, and rather than use the courts to any great degree 'leave the kids alone whenever possible' (Schur, 1973, p. 155). The emphasis is less on the individual approach, but rather on voluntary involvement in collective action programmes. Voluntary involvement reduces criminalization through the breaking of laws which in America only apply to children and juveniles (such as truancy, curfews, and smoking laws). Schur argues (1973, p. 155):

> Piecemeal socioeconomic reform will not greatly affect delinquency; there must be thoroughgoing changes in the structure and the values of our society. If the choice is between changing youth and changing the society (including some of its laws), the radical noninterventionist opts for changing the society.

He is less specific on actual applications of this principle, and can be accused of a form of idealism which suggests humanistic ideas on their own will alter the concepts of justice and the rule of law without being part of a wider class analysis, and related to working-class struggle. There is no pursuit of the problem of differentiating between actions which are the result of brutalizing and oppressive forces, and which raise serious questions of personal responsibility, such as violence, and those which are cultural expressions and adaptations as with theft from work, or informal receiving systems found in working-class districts. Ultimately criminal and delinquent enterprises are not solutions for adolescents caught up in the results of an economic recession. Ultimately it brutalizes and degrades them, creating a situation which makes it difficult for them to escape. But this behaviour has to be traced to what it is a consequence of. It has to be dealt with at the individual level, and this means working closely with individuals, but it also will not cease as a phenomenon unless its structural roots are altered. As Dean (1976) argues, there is no public consensus about legality, and because rehabilitationists have failed to see that groups inhabit different moral worlds, they fail to see that law is an expression of power of certain groups, and not some consensual, democratically reached legal system. As a result rehabilitative measures have made an assumption of individual maladjustment or social pathology. At present only official agencies offer assistance which is bound by statutory duties, but it is not hard to see that it would be possible to construct solutions which are built into a neighbourhood and which work at a grass roots level with particular groups. This has of course already occurred with particular groups which are problem-based, such as alcoholics, addicts, vagrants and so forth. For young people, the neighbourhood can be used and has been, as a considerable resource. There is some evidence to indicate that money spent on youth work provision, even where that provision is traditional club work, has lowered delinquency rates (Bagley, 1965).

There are obviously macro and micro levels to the problems of the inner city. More resources are needed in depressed neighbourhoods. The macro level problems of poverty, education, and unemployment are felt at the micro level of the neighbourhood. The valuable research of the Community Development Projects has traced problems which manifest themselves as delinquency, poor health, racism and lack of work, to the combined forces of the collapse of the local economy, and the reduction of public services. In the case of education, the results may be even more specific manifesting in particular local schools. Power *et al.* (1967) and Phillipson (1971), suggest there is evidence that it is specific schools which have high rates of delinquency and truancy. Power and Sirey (1972), found that two-thirds of their delinquent sample came from intact, concerned families, and that the important variable was the effect of the school. In the same school, a quarter of boys from a high delinquency area were delinquent, but so were a quarter of boys from a low delinquency area. West and Farrington (1973), argue that schools with a high delinquency rate were receiving pupils with a high 'delinquency prone' intake at the age of commencing secondary education. Schools are seen in a local neighbourhood as being for the delinquent and the scholastically poor, and the results are the internalization by pupils of being difficult and unteachable. Reynolds (1976), suggests that specific schools use techniques which individualize problems such as truancy. One problem with any organization such as a school, or social work agency, is that an individual, who is not catered for by the programme of the organization becomes a problem for that organization, but the problem is individualized. It is that individual who is 'difficult', not the fact that for various administrative reasons the organization cannot cater for him or her.

The deepening of the economic crisis and the overt racism of working-class inner city life, combined with its traditional sexism, create major problems for radical youth workers. Robins and Cohen (1978), suggest that where there are community demands from the local youth population for, say, a disco, this can be developed into an exercise in political power and strategy. In this way they follow community action tactics. However, whilst their disco contained local juvenile crime and neighbourhood vandalism, this only neutralized the local kids' bargaining power. Instead they suggest a form of social and political education, but not in a traditional sense, which would assist kids to become the teachers and spokespersons of their peers. However, the concrete way of doing this seems to be a snowballing technique of teaching individuals among the local youth community, who then set up teaching groups of their own. Such ideas may seem to kids very close to school, and may work in the area of black politics, but it is hard to envisage them developing among disaffected white youth. They are also male-oriented. Another suggestion the writers have is Young Tenants' Associations which serve 'the political, cultural and educational needs of the mass of working class youth in its vicinities'. Again, the technique of community work is used to develop core members from the 'young, about to be marrieds looking for respectability and status in this rough neighbourhood and tearaways wishing to reform'. The YTA acts as an advice group, defence group and also a communication centre. Again this depends on the local neighbourhood being stable, and would only develop in specific types of neighbourhood. These models drawn from community action and community organization could with some adaptation be used in certain neighbourhoods. Certainly middle-class youth cultures managed to develop several interesting forms of legal, clinical, advisory and housing centres which have been used in community projects in Britain and the United States. However, one model which seems to be of use in working with young people is a community-based project which takes up and defends the place of young people in the local community. Obviously one main aim will be to assist the jobless.

Future prospects

There are obviously different problems in different neighbourhoods. Those with racially mixed communities are in a potentially explosive situation. Many young black kids are homeless, and this has been tackled in some neighbourhoods by local community houses. This is part of the black communities' determined political efforts to offset locally the results of racism. There is an equal determination to defend black youth against police harassment through neighbourhood law centres which take up the cases of young blacks, and fight the present 'sus laws' which state someone may be apprehended by the police if they suspect he is about to commit a crime. Racism in local neighbourhoods has also managed to keep black and white youth separate, and this is probably one of the most worrying problems involving race and youth in Britain today. Cottle (1978), describes the bitterness felt by young blacks sensitive to the fact that white adults will not physically come in contact with them. White teachers often do not touch them during physical education, or even shake them during a school row. Youth workers worried by the National Front's attempts to gain places on the management groups of tenants' associations and youth clubs have formed a Workers with Youth against Fascism Group, which also tries to counteract racist propaganda. This is similar to the women youth workers who have formed a feminist pressure group to combat sexism in male youth club members and leaders.

One thing that seems to be constantly mentioned by working-class young people is the uselessness of school curricula in terms of their future lives. We should consider whether full-time schooling needs to be continued to the age of 16. Obviously there are reactionary dangers in a scheme of this type and this needs to be guarded against. I am not proposing that adolescents should be exploited as cheap wage labour. Wright (1977), has suggested decentralizing school authority between teachers, parents, pupils and the local authority so that no one group has control, and that compulsory education should end at 11 years of age. It would seem sensible not to force young people to learn things they reject, when they would prefer to work. The actual age of school-leaving is a matter for consideration but, perhaps from 13 years old, adolescents could start part-time work with a generalized apprenticeship scheme which would be occupation-specific later. They could then leave full-time education at 14 or 15, with an option to return in later life with up to four years' full-time education on a grant or on full pay. Bazalgette (1978), also considers that the experience of school is rarely examined or drawn upon by young workers, who perceive school as failing to provide them with anything which helps the difficult transition from school to work. School, they see, as preparing pupils for the public examination system, rather than for work life. Because young people are badly prepared for work, and because of the restrictions of the local economy, they either constantly move jobs, or find themselves in a stable situation, which only after a year or two at work, they recognize as a dead end. This is why some direct experience of differing jobs, realistic and precise information about the job market, and more discussions about careers would assist. The actual experience of working would be a valuable step, and an earlier start at full-time work, which did not close the door finally on full-time further and higher education would be preferable to the present system. It would also assist the projected crisis in higher education foretold for the 1990s.

A combination of these factors could alter the structure of schools as they are at present, so that instead of being age linked they become community colleges for the entire population. At present adolescents enter occupations which are either specific and tie them to a particular type of job, or general labouring. Even students preparing for a professional life undertake to study subjects which are offered at school, rather than considering a wider choice of curriculum. If adolescents are unhappy at school they may as well leave and work, with an option to return later to full-time education. Given the reduction in the birth rate it is fairly certain there will be many vacancies in higher education. What needs to be guarded against is the exploitation of this by employers, and here youth trade unions will be important. These must not be male-dominated, otherwise they will reinforce the career of housewife for girls. I am proposing that children and adolescents participate in the world around them, and receive reimbursement for this, from an early age. The exploitation of working-class children in Victorian industrial society must not be repeated, but its grim warning need not prevent experimentation. This means a form of partial deschooling, but not deskilling. Young people would be exposed at an earlier age to cultural and productive activities outside the formal educational setting. This would help them to select the work and training they experientially prefer. It would also provide a way out for those caught up in general labour.

It is, as I have suggested, important to involve girls and young women in this so that the career of housewife as an alternative to work is broken. The traditional female role in family life and reproduction has allowed women a temporary and false escape from work into domestic labour. What is important is that young women are exposed to wider opportunities and alternatives to their traditional roles. Our present social organization and work production is sexist, and obviously there are many complex factors of a concrete and ideological nature contributing to this. This means exposing women to opportunities to earn decent wages, and to occupations outside the casualized and sweated industries which have been traditionally open to them. They need to be aware of their work potential and power through trade union activities, and they need to be made confident enough to return to a full-time educational programme which would prepare them for alternative occupational opportunities.

Obviously this is only possible if there is sufficient work for adolescents to be integrated into. The economic crisis with its emphasis on cutting back in the state sector means that a large number of jobs has been permanently lost. There is a deep social and cultural crisis in society and there are dangers of a reactionary backlash not only amongst adults but also young people. Race, law and order, control of the trade unions, are central political issues in British contemporary politics. The brunt of 'policing the crisis' is felt by immigrants and their children at present. The development of policy concerning Educational Priority Areas, Urban Aid Grants, Community Development Projects are all part of a poverty programme which has, after ten years, had little lasting effect. It has been described by a group of community workers working inside these projects as 'gilding the ghetto' (Community Development Project, 1977). Home Office investment in the Urban Deprivation Programme was partially a concern with the welfare of the poor in deteriorating neighbourhoods, but also meant a 'soft' approach to social control. Urban poverty led to crime, delinquency and, in racially mixed districts, race riots. However, it would be a mistake to refuse such aid because of its social control components; what is important is to develop the community's ability to defend itself against unemployment, poverty, poor health and educational facilities. The crisis has given the state *carte blanche* in cutting back essential services and investment in deprived areas. This means that any such plan as that outlined above for schools means that it is essential that any money saved is not hived off from the educational sphere, but is kept as a mandatory duty for the Department of Education and Science to fulfil. It is important for local communities to resist the cutting-back of public expenditure and lack of investment under the ideology of 'the common good' and 'tightening one's belt'. Certainly at present there has been a return to community aid, which means utilizing local voluntary workers (i.e., women) to deal with problems usually managed by local social services. Community action often, as Cockburn (1977) suggests, points to deficiencies in the services provided by the 'local state', the local authority. It focuses on participation of small groups in a pluralist society, completely overlooking the reality of historical class struggle, which is powerful forces ranged against each other over centuries. Any struggle over services is a struggle over the forces of reproduction. Any struggle over youth and its cultures, over provisions for youth, youth employment, and schools, is part of this struggle. It is necessary to persuade youth to accept the relations of production and reproduction. Leisure is an area of social control, which is part of 'policing the crisis' in a very real sense. It reflects and reinforces the fundamental class relations of industrial society, and any analysis of it needs to consider these relations, and their position in the reproduction of ideology, and the reproduction of wage labour. It is part of monitoring a whole class to its historical destination. It is important to emphasize that any area of social control by ideology is never static. Because it is a process, there are shifting oppositions and resistances to ideological domination, although these need not be overtly political or even radical. The tensions between class interpretations generate tensions which in turn affect process, but the direction of this process remains an area of constraint and struggle. This is why cultural rebellion is so often quickly depoliticised, and relegated to areas perceived as trivial, such as bohemian baiting of the bourgeoisie, wayward youth or hooliganism.

That there is a struggle in the subcultural resistance to constraint by dominant cultures is felt by youth, and forms part of its attraction. Its symbolization of this through style is responded to emotionally rather than rationally. There is no logical comprehension of its meaning, and its appeal is because of its emotionality, and its perceived effect on the adult world. It is 'felt' rather than articulated. It has a particular dramatic form, symbolizing the relations of young males who feel in some way in disjunction with their world experience. It also reinforces traditional relations between the sexes at present. It explores, re-interprets and celebrates masculinism, and whilst the style of traditional sexual roles are re-interpreted, the context remains the same. The material offered by subcultures can be used to build identity, but the identity, way of acting upon the world is only revolutionary when the context and ideologies containing the traditional roles are attacked. Only then has a subculture any real potential to alter concepts of identity. Even then it must be recognized that a cultural attack is insufficient in itself, because it does not alter the relations of production which are part of the economic structure of society. At best subcultures are dramaturgical guerilla forays on the main body of a culture. Their importance is that they are rallying points and symbols of solidarity, and possible points for further analysis. Outside of subcultures with a political element, the analysis is not articulated beyond a form of a discourse of style.

Considerable work has been carried out empirically on subcultures, and on youth culture. The abstracted empiricism of the thirties, forties and fifties has been filled out with theoretical debates concerning the nature of culture and ideology in contemporary capitalism. There has been a recognition that links have to be made between a sociology of youth and the relations of class in an industrial society, and this means the relations with adults, and the total relations of these groups to the means of production. Many studies explore the impact of societal reaction, or the meaning of style, or the effects of neighbourhood, of immigrant culture, of femininity or of popular manufactured culture, and these are now being related to the struggle for space within dominant ideologies. Policy has tended to ignore the needs of youth exploited by their location in class, and has at best developed containment strategies which may in the light of the present economic crisis be inadequate. There is still a great need to examine and analyse subcultures as a key to comprehending any life-style or ways of relating to and acting upon the world outside of one's own parochial location within one's own parochial culture. There are considerable explorations to be made of subcultures, and these can be cultural, existential, structural or economic. One result of the cultural rebellions between 1964 and 1972 (loosely called the sixties) was that new forms of institutions and social relations have begun to be explored by an articulate minority. It is important that these are not lost in the conservative backlash of the economic crisis. They must not however become a substitute for political action *per se*. We need to hold firmly to the notion that society produces individuals, but that only collective action will act to change that society and its consequent social relations. Cultures and subcultures are not merely conveyers of alternative phenomenological forms of social reality, but indicators of material power and ideological domination. Some are trivial, some are hedonistic and joyous, some are expressions of the brutalizing effects of class oppression. Often they are all of these, but a few do contain the radical kernel of a revolutionary and liberated culture. Youth cultures are a response to the combined experience of primarily a location in the labour force and in social class, and the experience of a reality mediated by education, neighbourhood, generation, leisure, social control and dominant values. Youth culture is an essay in the mini-politics of rebellion against obscure social forces. From this is created a collective symbolic identity which for a brief time during youth steps outside the stark reality of industrial society to explore the excitement and vitality of being young, optimistic and joyous, a moment all too brief in personal biography.

Bibliography

Abbreviations used in bibliography

A.J.S.	*American Journal of Sociology*
Annals	*Annals of the American Academy of Political and Social Science*
A.S.R.	*American Sociological Review*
B.J.C.	*British Journal of Criminology*
B.J.S.	*British Journal of Sociology*

AARONSEN, B. and OSMOND, H. (1971), *Psychedelics – the uses and implications of hallucinogenic drugs*, Schenkman, Cambridge, Mass.

ABRAMS, M. (1959), *The teenage consumer*, L.P.E. Paper 5, Routledge & Kegan Paul, London.

ABRAMS, P. and MCCULLOCH, A. (1976), 'Men, women and communes', in Allen, S. and Barker, D. (eds), *op. cit.*

ADAMS, R. L. and FOX, R. J. (1972), 'Mainlining Jesus – the new trip', *Transaction and Society*, spring.

ADLER, N. (1968), 'The antinomian personality – the hippy character type', *Psychiatry*, 31.

ALBERONI, F. (1964), *Consumi e Società*, Il Mulino, Bologna, Italy.

ANDRY, R. (1960), *Delinquency and parental pathology*, Methuen, London.

ANWAR, M. (1976), *Between two cultures*, Community Relations Commission, London.

ARMSTRONG, G. and WILSON, M. (1973), in L. & I. Taylor, *Politics and Deviance*, Penguin, Harmondsworth.

ATKINSON, A. R. (1975), *The economics of inequality*, Oxford University Press, London.

AUSTIN, R. L. (1977), 'Commitment, neutralization and delinquency' in Ferdinand, T. N. (ed.), *Juvenile delinquency – little brother grows up*, Sage, Beverly Hills.

BAGLEY, C. (1965), 'Juvenile delinquency in Exeter', *Urban Studies 2*, no. 1, pp. 35–9. Reprinted in Mays, J. B. (1972), *op. cit.*

BALDWIN, J. (1972), 'Delinquent schools in Tower Hamlets – a critique', *B.J.C.*, 12, pp. 399–401.

BALL, M. (1977), 'Emergent delinquency in a urban area' in Ferdinand, T. N. (ed.), *Juvenile delinquency – little brother grows up*, Sage, Beverly Hills.

BALL, R. H. (1968), 'An empirical investigation of neutralisation theory', in Lefton, M., *Approaches to deviance*, Appleton Century Crofts, pp. 255–65.

BANDURA, A. and WALTERS, R. H. (1959), *Adolescent aggression*, Ronal Press, New York.

BARKER, D. (1972) '"Spoiling and keeping close" in a South Wales town', *Sociological Review*, 20.

BARKER, D. and ALLEN, S. (1976), *Dependence and exploitation in work and marriage*, Longman, London.

BARKER, P. and LITTLE, A. (1964), 'The Margate offenders – a survey' *New Society* vol. 4 no. 96, July, pp. 6–10.

BARNARD, J. (1961), 'Teen-age culture – an overview', *Annals*, special edition, teenage culture, vol. 338, November, pp. 1–12.

BARRIGAR, R. H. (1964), 'The regulation of psychedelic drugs', *Psychedelic Review* 1, 9, pp. 394–441.

BARTHES, R. (1967), *Elements of semiology*, Jonathan Cape, London.

BARTHES, R. (1970), *Mythologies*, Jonathan Cape, London.

BAYLEY, D. H. and MENDLESCHOHN, H. (1969), *Minorities and the police force*, Free Press of Glencoe, New York.

BAZALGETTE, J. (1978), *School life, work life*, Hutchinson, London.

BEALER, R. C., WILLITS, F. K. and MAIDS, P. R. (1965), 'The myth of a rebellious adolescent subculture', in Burchinal, L. G. (ed.), *Rural youth in crisis, op. cit.*

BECKER, E. (1964), *The psychiatric revolution – a new understanding of man*, Free Press, New York.

BECKER, H. (1963), *Outsiders – studies in the sociology of deviance*, Free Press, New York.

BEGGS, L. (1969), *Huckleberry for runaways*, Ballantine, New York.

BELCHER, J. and WEST, D. (1975), *Patty/Tania*, Pyramid, New York.

BELL, D. (1953), 'The end of ideology', *Antioch Review*, June, 12, 3, pp. 132–54.

BELL, D. (1957), *The end of ideology*, Free Press of Chicago.

BELSON, W. A. (1975), *Juvenile theft – the causal factors*, Harper & Row, London.

BENJAMIN, W. (1970), 'The work of art in the age of mechanical reproduction', *Illuminations*, Jonathan Cape, London.

BERG, L. (1968), *Risinghill – death of a comprehensive school*, Penguin, Harmondsworth.

BERGER, B. (1963a), 'Adolescence and beyond', *Social Problems* vol. 10, spring, pp. 294–408.

BERGER, B. (1963b), 'On the youthfulness of youth culture', *Social Research* vol. 30, no. 3, autumn, pp. 319–432.

BERGER, B. (1967), 'Hippy morality – more old than new', *Transaction*, vol. 5, December.

BERGER, P. and LUCKMAN, H. (1966), *The social construction of reality – a treatise in the sociology of knowledge*, Doubleday, New York.

BERSANI, C. A. (1970), *Crime and delinquency, a reader*, Collier-Macmillan, New York.

BLAND, L., HARRISON, R., MORT, F. and WEEDON, C. (1978), 'Relations through reproduction' in *Women's studies group, op. cit.*

BODINE, G. E. (1964), 'Factors related to police disposition of juvenile offenders', Youth Development Centre, Syracuse, mimeo.

BORDUA, D. (1959), 'Juvenile delinquency and anomie', *Social Problems*, vi, winter pp. 230–8.

BORDUA, D. (1961), 'Delinquent subcultures – sociological interpretations of gang delinquency', *Annals*, cccxxxviii, pp. 119–36.

BORDUA, D. (1967a), 'Recent trends; deviant behaviour and social control', *Annals*, January, vol. 57, no. 4, pp. 114–63.

BORDUA, D. (1967b), *The police*, John Wiley, New York.

BORGETTA, E. F. and JONES, W. C. (1965), *Girls at vocational high*, Russell Sage Foundation, New York.

BOX, S. (1971), *Deviance, reality and society*, Holt, Rinehart & Winston, London.

BRAKE, M. (1973a), 'How the hash turned to hate – intervention in a crisis area', *Drugs and Society*, vol. 2, January, no. 4.

BRAKE, M. (1973b), 'Cultural revolution or alternative delinquency – an examination of deviant youth as a social problem', in Bailey, R. and Young, J. (eds), *Contemporary social problems in Britain*, D. C. Heath, London.

BRAKE, M. (1974), 'The skinheads – an English working class subculture', *Youth and Society*, vol. 6, no. 2, December.

BRAKE, M. (1976), 'I may be queer, but at least I am a man – male hegemony and ascribed versus achieved gender', in Allen, S. and Barker, D., *op. cit*.

BRAKE, M. (1977), 'Hippies and Skinheads – sociological aspects of subcultures', Ph.D. Thesis, London School of Economics.

BRAKE, M. (1978), 'The homosexual in contemporary English and American novels', British Sociological Association, Monograph on *The Sociology of Literature, Applied Studies*.

BRAKE, M. and BAILEY, R. (1975), *Radical social work*, Edward Arnold, London.

BRAKE, M. and PLUMMER, K. (1970), 'Bent boys and rent boys', Paper to York Deviancy Symposium, 1.1.70. Unpublished.

BRAKE, M. and POLISH, P. (1969), 'Arts Labs and subcultures', Report to the Young Volunteer Force and the Arts Council. Unpublished.

BROOK, E. and FINN, D. (1977), 'Working Class images of Society', in *Working Papers in Cultural Studies*, 10, University of Birmingham.

BROWN, C. (1967), *Manchild in the promised land*, Jonathan Cape, London.

BRYAN, J. (1975), *The soldier still at work*, Harcourt Brace, New York.

BUFF, S. (1970), 'Greasers, dupies and hippies – three responses to the adult world' in Howe, L. K. (ed.), *The white majority – between poverty and affluence*, Vintage Books, New York.

BUGLER, J. (1969), 'Puritans in boots', *New Society*, 19 November.

BUNYAN, T. (1977), *The political police in Britain*, Quartet, London.

BURCHAL, J. and PARSONS, T. (1978), *The boy looked at Johnny: The Obituary of Rock and Roll*, Pluto Press, London.

BURCHINAL, L. G. (ed.) (1965), *Rural youth in crisis*, U.S. Department of Health, Education and Welfare, Washington.

BURNS, T. (1967), 'A meaning in everyday life', *New Society*, 25 May.

BURT, C. (1925), *The young delinquent*, University of London Press.

CARNEY, F. (1975), 'An American army', *New York Review of Books*, pp. 8–12, 26.6.75.

CARR-SAUNDERS, A. M., MANNHEIM, H. and RHODES, E. G. (1942), *Young Offenders*, Cambridge University Press, Cambridge.

CARSON, W. G. and WILES, P. (1971), *Crime and delinquency in Britain*, M. Robertson, London.

CARTER, A. (1967), 'Notes for a theory of sixties style', *New Society*, 14, December.

CAVAN, S. (1970), 'The hippy ethic and the spirit of drug use', in Douglas, J. D. (ed.), 1970, *op. cit.*

CENTRE FOR CONTEMPORARY CULTURAL STUDIES (1976), Mugging Group. 'Some notes on the relationship between societal control culture and the news media', in Hall, S. and Jefferson, T. *op. cit.*

CHESNEY-LIND, M. (1973), 'Judicial reinforcement of the female role – the family court and the female delinquent', *Issues in criminology*, vol. 8, no. 2.

CHEVALIER, L. (1973), *Labouring classes and dangerous classes in Paris during the first half of the nineteenth century*, Routledge & Kegan Paul, London.

CHIBNALL, S. (1977), *Law and order news*, Social Science Paperbacks, London.

CHRISTOFFEL, T., FINKELHORD, D. and GILBERG, D. (1970), *Up against the American myth*, Holt, Rinehart & Winston, New York.

CICOUREL, A. V. (1968), *The social organisation of juvenile justice*, John Wiley, New York.

CLARKE, J. (1976a), 'The skinheads and the magical recovery of community' in Hall, S. and Jefferson, T. (eds), *op. cit.*

CLARKE, J. (1976b), 'Style', in Hall, S. and Jefferson, T. (eds), *op. cit.*

CLARKE, J., HALL, S., JEFFERSON, T., and ROBERTS, B. (1976), 'Subcultures, cultures and class – a theoretical overview' in Hall, S. and Jefferson, T. (eds), *op. cit.*

CLARKE, J. and JEFFERSON, T. (1976), 'Working class youth cultures', in Mungham, G. and Pearson, G. (eds), *op. cit.*

CLARKE, M. (1974), 'On the concept of subculture', *B.J.S.* vol. xxv, no. 4, December, pp. 428–41.

CLINARD, M. (1964), *Anomie and deviant behaviour*, Free Press, New York.

CLOWARD, R. and FOX PIVEN, F. (1974), *Regulating the Poor*, Tavistock, London.

CLOWARD, R. and OHLIN, L. E. (1960), *Delinquency and opportunity*, Free Press.

COARD, B. (1971), 'How the West Indian child is made E.S.N. in the British School system', New Beacon Books, London.

COCKBURN, C. (1977), *The local state*, Pluto Press, London.

COCKBURN, R. and BLACKBURN, R. (1969), *Student power*, Penguin, Harmondsworth.

COHEN, A. K. (1955), *Delinquent boys – the subculture of the gang*, Collier-Macmillan, London.

COHEN, A. K. (1965), 'The sociology of the deviant act; anomie theory and beyond', *A.S.R.* 30, pp. 1–14.

COHEN, A. K. (1967), 'Middle class delinquency and the social structure', in Vaz, E. W. (ed.), *op. cit.*

COHEN, A. K. and SHORT, J. (1958), 'Research on delinquent subcultures', *Journal of Social Issues*, xiv, 3, pp. 20–37.

COHEN, P. (1972), 'Subcultural conflict and working class community' in *Working Papers in Cultural Studies 2*, spring, University of Birmingham, Centre for Contemporary Cultural Studies.

COHEN, S. (1972), *Moral panics and folk devils*, MacGibbon & Kee, London.

COHEN, S. (1975), 'It's all right for you to talk – political and sociological manifestoes for social work action', in Brake, M. and Bailey, R., *op. cit.*

COHEN, S. and YOUNG, J. (1973), *Mass media and social problems*, MacGibbon & Kee, London.

COHN, N. (1970), *Awopbopaloobopalopbamboom – Pop from the beginning*, Paladin, London.

COLEMAN, J. S. (1961), *The adolescent society*, Free Press, New York.

COMMUNITY DEVELOPMENT PROJECT (CDP) (1974), *Inter-project report*, CDP Information Unit, Home Office, London.

COMMUNITY DEVELOPMENT PROJECT (1975), C. Tyrell, *Rates of Decline*, January.

COMMUNITY DEVELOPMENT PROJECT (1975), July, *Poverty of the improvement progamme*, CDP Information Unit, Home Office, London.

COMMUNITY DEVELOPMENT PROJECT (1975), September, *Local government becomes big business*, CDP Information Unit, Home Office, London.

COMMUNITY DEVELOPMENT PROJECT (1976), April, *Whatever happened to council housing?*, CDP Information Unit, Home Office, London.

COMMUNITY DEVELOPMENT PROJECT (1976), *Profits against houses*, September, CDP Information Unit, Home Office, London.

COMMUNITY DEVELOPMENT PROJECT (1977), *Gilding the ghetto*, Mary Ward House, London.

COMMISSION FOR RACIAL EQUALITY (CRE) (1977), *Aspirations versus opportunities – Asian and white school leavers in the Midlands*, CRE, London.

COMMISSION FOR RACIAL EQUALITY (1978), *Looking for work – black and white school leavers in Lewisham*, CRE, London.

COOPER, C. N. (1967), 'The Chicago detached workers – current status of an action programme', in Klein, M. (ed.), *op. cit.*

CORRIGAN, P. (1976), 'Doing nothing', in Hall, S. and Jefferson, T., *op. cit.*

CORRIGAN, P. (1979), *The Smash Street kids*, Paladin, London.

CORRIGAN, P. and FRITH, S. (1976), 'The politics of youth culture', in Hall, S. and Jefferson, T., *op. cit.*

COTGROVE, S. and PARKER, S. (1963), 'Work and non work', *New Society*, vol. xli, July.

COTTLE, T. J. (1978), *Black testimony – voices of Britain's West Indians*, Wildwood House, London.

COUNCIL OF EUROPE (1977), National Youth Committee Report.

COUNTER INFORMATION SERVICES (1975), *Cutting the welfare state – who profits?* CIS/CDP, November, Poland Street, London.

CRAIG, M. and FURST, P. W. (1965), 'What happens after treatment?', *Social Services Review*, 39, pp. 165–71.

CRAWFORD, P. L., MALAMUD, D. I. and DUMPSON, J. R. (1950), *Working with teenage gangs*, Welfare Council of New York City, New York.

CRICHTON, A. *et al.* (1962), 'Youth and leisure in Cardiff, 1960', *Sociological Review*, 10.

CURLE, A. (1972), *Mystics and militants – a study of awareness, identity and social creation*, Tavistock. London.

DALLA COSTA, M. and JAMES, S. (1972), *The power of women and the subversion of the community*, Falling Wall Press, Bristol.

DANIEL, S. and MCGUIRE, P. (eds) (1972), *The paint house – words from an East End gang*, Penguin, Harmondsworth.

DAVIS, B. (1969), 'Non swinging youth', *New Society*, 3.7.69.

DAVIS, F. (1967), 'Focus on the flower children – why all of us may be hippies one day', *Transaction*, vol. 5, no. 2, reprinted in Douglas, J. (1970), *op. cit.*

DAVIS. F. and MUNOZ, L. (1968), 'Heads and freaks – patterns and meaning of drug use among hippies', *Journal of Health and Social Behaviour*, June, pp. 156–63, reprinted in Douglas, J., (1970), *op. cit.*

DEAN, A. J. H. (1976), 'Unemployment among school leavers, an analysis of the problem', *National Institute Economic Review*, 18 November, pp. 63–8.

DE BEAUVOIR, S. (1972), *The second sex*, Penguin, Harmondsworth.

DE LA MATER, J. (1968), 'On the nature of deviance', *Social Forces*, 46, pp. 455–65.

DEPARTMENT OF EDUCATION AND SCIENCE (1978), *Higher Education in the 1990s*, February.

DEUZIN, N. K. (1970), *The Research Act in Sociology*, Butterworth, London.

DISTLER, L. S. (1970), 'The adolescent and the emergent of a matristic culture', *Psychiatry*, Summer.

DODD, D. (1978), 'Police and thieves on the streets of Brixton', *New Society*, 16.3.78.

DOUGLAS, J. D. (ed.) (1970), *Observations of deviance*, Random House, New York.

DOUGLAS, J. D. (1972), 'The absurd and the problem of social order', in Douglas, J. D. and Scott, R. A., *op. cit.*

DOUGLAS, J. D. and SCOTT, R. A. (1972), *Theoretical perspectives in deviance*, Basic Books, New York.

DOUGLAS, J. W. B. (1971), 'Delinquency and social class' in Carson, W. G. and Wiles, P., *op. cit.*

DOUGLAS, M. (1970), *Purity and danger*, Penguin, Harmondsworth.
DOUGLAS, M. (1972), 'Self evidence', *Proceedings of the Royal Anthropological Institute*, pp. 27–43.
DOWNES, D. (1966), *The delinquent solution*, Routledge & Kegan Paul, London.
DOWNES, D. (1968), 'Review of D. Hargreaves "Social relations in a secondary school"' *B.J.C.* 12, pp. 399–401.
DRIVER, C. (1964), *The disarmers*, Hodder & Stoughton, London.
DUBIN, R. (1959), 'Deviant behaviour and social structure', *A.S.R.*, 24, pp. 147–64.
DURKHEIM, E. (1951), *Suicide*, Free Press of Glencoe, Chicago.
EDWARDS, R., REICH, M. and WEISKOPF, T. (eds) (1972), *The capitalist system – a radical analysis of American society*, Prentice-Hall, Englewood Cliffs, New Jersey.
EISEN, J. (1970), *Altamont – the death of innocence in the Woodstock Nation*, Avon, New York.
EISENSTADT, S. N. (1956), *From generation to generation*, Free Press, Chicago.
EMPEY, L. T. and RABOW, J. (1961), 'The Provo experiment in delinquency rehabilitation', *A.S.R.*, 26, October, pp. 679–95.
ENGELS, F. (1962), *Conditions of the working class in England in 1844*, Allen & Unwin, London.
ENGLAND, R. W. Jnr (1967), 'A theory of middle class delinquency', in Vaz, E. W., *op. cit.*
ERIKSON, K. (1966), *Wayward puritans, a study in the sociology of knowledge*, John Wiley, New York.
EYSENCK, H. J. (1970), *Crime and personality*, Paladin, London.
FELDMAN, E. and GARTENBERG, M. (eds) (1959), *The beat generation and the angry young men*, Citadel, New York.
FERDINAND, T. N. (ed.) (1977), *Juvenile delinquency – little brother grows up*, Sage, Beverly Hills.
FIGUEORA, P. (1969), 'School leavers and the colour barrier', *Race*, April, pp. 506–7.
FINESTONE, H. (1957), 'Cats, kicks and colour', *Social Problems*, vol. 5, pp. 3–13.
FIRTH, R. (1951), *Elements of social organisation*, Routledge & Kegan Paul, London.
FISCHER, C. S. (1972), 'Urbanism as a way of life – a review and an agenda', *Sociological Methods and Research*, vol. 1, no. 2, November, pp. 187–243.
FISCHER, C. S. (1973), 'On urban alienation and anomie', *A.S.R.*, 38, June, pp. 311–26.
FISCHER, C. S. (1975), 'Towards a subcultural theory of urbanism', *A.J.S.*, 80, no. 6, pp. 1319–41.
FLACKS, R. (1970), 'Social and cultural meanings of student revolt', *Social Problems*, vol. xvii, Winter.
FLACKS, R. (1971), *Youth and social change*, Markham Press, Chicago.
FLETCHER, C. (1966), 'Beats and gangs on Merseyside', in Raison, T., *op. cit.*

FOOTE, N. (1951), 'Identification as the basis for a theory of motivation', *A.S.R.*, February, pp. 14–41.

FORD, C. S. (1942), 'Culture and human behaviour', *Scientific Monthly*, vol. 44, pp. 546–57.

FORD, J., BOX, S. and YOUNG, D. (1967), 'Functional autonomy, role distance and social class', *B.J.S.*, 18, pp. 370–81.

FOX, J. (1969), 'The Scapegoat Kids', *Sunday Times*, 21 September.

FRIEDENBERG, E. Z. (1966), 'Adolescence as a social problem' in Becker, H. (ed.), *Social problems; a modern approach*, John Wiley, New York.

FRITH, S. (1978), *The sociology of rock*, Constable, London.

FYVEL, T. R. (1963), *The insecure offenders – a rebellious youth in the welfare state*, Penguin, Harmondsworth.

GAGNON, J. (1977), *Human sexualities*, Scott, Foreman, Illinois.

GALBRAITH, J. K. (1974), *The new industrial state*, Penguin, Harmondsworth.

GANS, H. (1962), *The urban villagers*, Free Press, New York.

GARDINER, J. (1976), 'Political economy of domestic labour in capitalist society', in Barker, D. and Allen, S., *op. cit.*

GAYFORD, J. (1975), 'Wife battering, a preliminary of 100 cases', *British Medical Journal*, 25.1.75, pp. 194–7.

GELLES, J. (1972), *The violent home – a study of physical aggression between husbands and wives*, Sage, London.

GEOFFREY, S. and GRAFTON, T. (1967), 'Hippies in College – teeny bopper to drug freaks', *Transaction*, vol. 5, pp. 27–32.

GIALLAMBARDO, R. (1972), *Juvenile Delinquency – a book of readings*, J. Wiley, New York.

GIBBONS, D. (1970), *Delinquent behaviour*, Prentice-Hall, Englewood Cliffs, New Jersey.

GIDDENS, A. (1976), *New Rules of the Sociological Method*, Hutchinson, London.

GIOSCIA, V. (1969), 'LSD subcultures; acidity versus orthodoxy', *American Journal of Orthopsychiatry*, 39, pp. 428–36.

GLASER, B. G. and STRAUSS, A. (1971), *Status passage – a formal theory*, Routledge & Kegan Paul, London.

GLASER, D. (1966), 'Criminality theories and behavioural images', *A.J.S.*, 61, March.

GLASS, D. (1954), *Social mobility in Britain*, Routledge & Kegan Paul, London.

GLEASON, R. (1970), 'Rock for sale', in Eisen, J., *op. cit.*

GLEASON, R. (1971), 'Like a rolling stone', in Gaviglio, G. and Raye, M. (eds), *Society as it is*, Macmillan, New York.

GLESSING, R. J. (1970), *The underground press in America*, Indiana University Press.

GOLDMAN, N. (1963), 'The differential selection of juvenile offenders for court appearance', National Council for Crime and Delinquency, New York.

GORDON, M. (1947), 'The concept of the subculture and its application', *Social Forces*, October.

GORDON, M. (1951), 'A system of class analysis', *Drew University Studies no. 2*, August.

GORDON, R. A. (1967), 'Issues in the ecological study of delinquency', *A.S.R.*, 32, December, pp. 927–44.

GRAMSCI, A. (1973), *Prison notebooks*, Lawrence & Wishart, London.

GREELEY, A. and CASEY, J. (1963), 'An upper middle class deviant gang', *American Catholic Sociological Review*, spring, xxiv, pp. 33–41.

GREER, H. (1965), *Mud Pie – the CND story*, Max Parrish, London.

GRIFFITHS, J. (1978), *The Politics of the Judiciary*, Fontana, London.

HALL, S. (1969), 'The hippies, an American moment', in Nagel, J. (ed.), *Student power*, Merlin Press.

HALL, S. and JEFFERSON, T. (1976), *Resistance through rituals*, Hutchinson University Library, London. Also published (1975) in *Working Papers in Cultural Studies, 7/8*, Centre for Contemporary Cultural Studies, University of Birmingham.

HALL, S., CRITCHER, C., JEFFERSON, T., CLARKE, J. and ROBERTS, B. (1978), *Policing the crisis – Mugging, the state and law and order*, Macmillan, London.

HAN, WAN SANG (1969), 'The conflicting themes – common values versus class differential values', *A.S.R.*, 34, pp. 679–90.

HARGREAVES, D. (1967), *Social relations in a secondary school*, Routledge & Kegan Paul, London.

HARRINGTON, M. (1962), *The other America*, Macmillan, New York.

HARRIS, M. (1973), *The dilly boys*, Croom Helm, London.

HARROP and ZIMMERMAN (1977), *Report on Greater London Council elections 1977*, Department of Government, University of Essex, June.

HEBDIGE, D. (1976a), 'The meaning of mod', in Hall, S. and Jefferson, T., *op. cit.*

HEBDIGE, D. (1976b), 'Reggae, rastas and rudies', in Hall, S. and Jefferson, T., *op. cit.*

HERSKOVITZ, H., LEVENE, M. and SPIVAK, G. (1959), 'Anti-social behaviour of adolescents from higher socio-economic groups', *Journal of Nervous and Mental Diseases*, cxxv, November, pp. 1–9.

HILL, W. W. (1935), 'The study of the transvestites and hermaphrodites in Navajo culture', *American Anthropologist*, June, vol. 37.

HIMMELWEIT, S. and MOHUN, S. (1977), 'Domestic labour and capital', *Cambridge Journal of Economics*, vol. 1, no. 1, March.

HINCKLE, W. (1967), 'The coming of the hippies', *Ramparts Magazine*, New York.

HINDELANG, M. (1970), 'Commitments of delinquents to their misdeeds; do delinquents drift?', *Social Problems*, vol. 17, no. 4, pp. 502–9.

HINES, V. (1973), *Black youth and the survival game in Britain*, Zulu Publications, London.

HIRO, D. (1973), *Black British, White British*, Penguin, Harmondsworth.

HIRSCHI, T. (1969), *The causes of delinquency*, University of California Press.

HJELMSLEV, A. (1959), 'Essais linguistics', *Travaux du cercle linguistic de Copenhagen*, vol. xiii, pp. 59 ff.

H.M.S.O. (1975), *Parliamentary select committee on violence in marriage*, Session 1974–5, Report HC 533 i, H.M.S.O., London.

H.M.S.O. (1976), *Public Expenditure*, Cmnd., H.M.S.O. Publications, London.

HODGES, E. F. and TAIT, C. T. (1965), 'A follow up study of potential delinquents', *American Journal of Psychiatry*, 120, pp. 449–53.

HOFSTADTER, R. (1955), *The age of reform*, Knopf, New York.

HOLLINGSHEAD, A. B. (1949), *Elmstown's youth*, John Wiley, New York.

HOLMES, J. C. (1960), 'The philosophy of the beat generation', in Krim, S., *op. cit.*

HOLT, J. (1969), *How children fail*, Penguin, Harmondsworth.

HOPE, M. (1978), 'Youth unemployment – some perspectives', M.A. thesis, unpublished, University of Kent.

HORTON, J. (1964), 'The dehumanisation of alienation and anomie – a problem in the ideology of sociology', *B.J.S.*, 15, pp. 283–300.

HORTON, J. (1966), 'Order and conflict theories of social problems as competing ideologies', *A.J.S.*, vol. 71, May.

HOUGHTON, M. and HEAD, D. (1974), *Free ways to learning*, Penguin, Harmondsworth.

HOURIET, R. (1973), *Getting back together*, Abacus, London.

HUMPHREY, P. and JOHN, G. (1972), *Police, Power and Black People*, Panther, London.

ILLICH, I. (1973), *Deschooling society*, Penguin, Harmondsworth.

ISHERWOOD, C. (1974), *Down There on a Visit*, White Lion, London.

JEFFERSON, T. (1976), 'The teds – a political resurrection', in Hall, S. and Jefferson, T., *op. cit.*

JEPHCOTT, P. (1967), *A time of one's own*, Oliver & Boyd, Edinburgh.

JEPHCOTT, P. and CARTER, M. P. (1954), 'The social background of delinquency', unpublished, University of Nottingham.

JOHN, G. and HUMPHREY, D. (1971), *Because they're black*, Penguin, Harmondsworth.

JOHNSTON, J. (1973), *Lesbian nation*, Simon & Schuster, New York.

JOHNSTON, N., SAVITZ, L. and WOLFGANG, M. E. (1967), *The sociology of punishment and correction*, John Wiley, New York.

JOHNSTON, N., SAVITZ, L. and WOLFGANG, M. E. (1970), 2nd edn, *The sociology of punishment and correction*, John Wiley, New York.

JOINT DOCKS ACTION RESOURCE TEAM (1976), *Jobs now – the way forward*, 58 Watney St, London E1.

JOINT DOCKS ACTION RESOURCE TEAM (1977), *Rebuilding docklands – cuts and the need for public investment*, 58 Watney St, London E1.

JONES, G. S. (1971), *Outcast in London*, Oxford University Press, London.

KEILL, C. (1966), *Urban Blues*, University of Chicago Press.

KENISTON, K. (1972), *Youth and dissent*, Harcourt, Brace & Jovanovich, New York.

KEROUAC, J. (1957), *On the Road*, Viking, New York.

KEROUAC, J. (1959), 'Beatific – on the origins of a generation', *Encounter*, August, vol. 13, pp. 57–61.
KERR, M. (1958), *The people of Ship Street*, Routledge & Kegan Paul, London.
KITSUSE, J. I. and DIETRICH, D. C. (1959), 'Delinquent boys – a critique', *A.S.R.*, April, pp. 208–15.
KITZINGER, S. (1978), 'West Indian adolescents; an anthropological perspective', *Journal of adolescence*, pp. 35–46.
KLEIN, M. W. (1967), *Juvenile gangs in context*, Prentice-Hall, Englewood Cliffs, New Jersey.
KLEIN, M. (1971), *Street gangs and street workers*, Prentice-Hall, Englewood Cliffs, New Jersey.
KLEIN, M. and MEYERHOF, B. G. (eds) (1963), 'Juvenile gangs in context, research, theory and action', University of Southern California Youth Studies Centre mimeo.
KNAPP, D. and POLK, K. (1971), *Scouting the war on poverty*, D. C. Heath, Lexington.
KOBRIN, S. (1967), 'The Chicago area project', in Johnston *et al.*, *op. cit.*
KOMAROVSKY, M. (1967), *Blue collar marriage*, Vintage Books, New York.
KOZOL, J. (1972), *Free schools*, Penguin, Harmondsworth.
KRIM, S. (ed.) (1960), *The beats*, Fawcett Publications, Greenwich, Connecticut.
KROEBER, A. L. and KLUCKHOHN, S. (1952), 'Culture – a critical review of concepts and definitions', *Papers of the Peabody Museum of American Archaeology and Ethology*, vol. 47, no. 1.
KUHN, M. (1964), 'The reference group reconsidered', *Sociological Quarterly*, Winter, pp. 6–21.
LAING, D. (1969), *The sound of our time*, Sheed & Ward, London.
LAING, R. D. (1966), *The divided self*, Penguin, Harmondsworth.
LAING, R. D., PHILLIPSON, H. and LEE, A. R. (1966), *Interpersonal perception – a theory and method of research*, Tavistock, London.
LAMBERT, J. (1970), *Crime, police and race relations*, London, University Press.
LAND, H. (1976), 'Women – supporters or supported?' in Barker, D. and Allen, S., *op. cit.*
LANDÈR, B. (1954), *Towards an understanding of juvenile delinquency*, Columbia University Press, New York.
LAUFER, R. S. and BENGSTON, V. L. (1974), 'Generations, ageing and social stratification; on the development of generational units', *Journal of Social Issues*, vol. 30, no. 3.
LEAMER, L. (1972), *The paper revolutionaries – the rise of the underground press*, Simon & Schuster, New York.
LEARY, T. (1968), *The politics of ecstasy*, Putnam, New York.
LEE, A. M. (1945), 'Levels of culture as levels of social generalisation', *A.S.R.*, August.
LEE, A. M. (1949), 'A sociological discussion of consistency and inconsistency in inter-group relations', *Journal of Social Issues*, 5, pp. 12–18.

LEMERT, E. (1951), *Social pathology*, McGraw Hill, New York.
LEMERT, E. (1967), *Human deviance, social problems and social control*, Prentice-Hall, Englewood Cliffs, New Jersey.
LERMAN, P. (1967a), 'Argot, symbolic deviance and subcultural delinquency', *A.S.R.*, vol. 1, 32, pp. 209–24.
LERMAN, P. (1967b), 'Gangs, networks and subcultural delinquency', *A.J.S.*.
LEWIS, O. (1952), 'Urbanisation without breakdown', *Scientific Monthly*, 75, July, pp. 31–41.
LEWIS, R. (1972), *Outlaws of America – the underground press and its context*, Penguin, Harmondsworth.
LICHTMANN, R. (1970), 'Symbolic interactionism and social reality – some Marxist queries', *Berkeley Journal of Sociology*, January.
LIEBOW, E. (1967), *Tally's corner*, Little, Brown, Boston, Mass.
LINDESMITH, A. R. (1947), *Opiate addiction*, Principa Press, Indiana.
LIPTON, L. (1960), *The holy barbarians*, W. H. Allen, London.
LITTLE, A., MABEY, C. and WHITTAKER, G. (1968), 'The education of immigrant pupils in Inner London Primary Schools', *Race*, ix, pp. 439–52.
LIVINGSTONE, P. (1978), *The leisure needs of Asian boys aged 8–14 in Slough*, Scout Association, London.
LUKES, S. (1974), *Power*, Macmillan, London.
LYDON, M. (1971), 'Rock for sale', in Ramparts (eds), *op. cit.*
MCALL, G. J. and SIMMONS, J. L. (1966), *Identities and interactions*, Free Press, New York.
MCCABE, P. and SCHONFIELD, R. (1973), *Apple to the core – the unmaking of the Beatles*, Sphere, London.
MCCORD, J. and MCCORD, W. (1959), 'A follow up of the Cambridge-Somerville Youth study', *Annals*, pp. 321–33, pp. 89–96.
MCDONALD, L. (1969), *Social class and juvenile delinquency*, Faber & Faber, London.
MCEACHERN, A. W. and BAUZER, R. (1963), 'Factors related to disposition in juvenile police contacts', in Klein, M. and Meyerhof, B. G., *op. cit.*
MCINTYRE, A. (1967), 'Winch's idea of a social science', *Proceedings of the Aristotelean Society*, Supplement.
MCROBBIE, A. (1978), 'Working class girls and the culture of femininity' in Women's Studies Group, *op. cit.*
MCROBBIE, A. and GARBER, J. (1976), 'Girls and subcultures – an exploration', in Hall, S. and Jefferson, T., *op. cit.*
MAILER, N. (1961), 'The white negro' in *Advertisements for myself*, André Deutsch, London.
MANKOFF, M. (1972), 'Societal reaction and career deviance – a critical analysis,' *Sociological quarterly*, 12, pp. 204–18.
MANNHEIM, H. (1948), *Juvenile Delinquency in an English Middletown*, Routledge & Kegan Paul, London.
MANNHEIM, K. (1952), *Essays on the Sociology of Knowledge*, Routledge & Kegan Paul, London.
MARCUSE, M. (1964), *One dimensional man*, Routledge & Kegan Paul, London.

MARSH, A. (1977), 'Who hates the blacks?' *New Society*, 23.9.77.

MARSH, P., ROSSER, E. and HARRE, R. (1978), *The Rules of Disorder*, Routledge & Kegan Paul, London.

MARX, K. (1951), 'The 18th Brumaire of Louis Bonaparte'.

MATZA, D. (1961), 'Subterranean traditions of youth', *American Academy of Political and Social Science*, 338, pp. 102–18.

MATZA, D. (1962), 'Position and behaviour patterns of youth', in E. Faris (ed.), *Handbook of modern sociology*, Rand McNally, New York.

MATZA, D. (1964), *Delinquency and drift*, John Wiley, New York.

MATZA, D. (1966), 'The disreputable poor', in Bendix, R. and Lipsett, S. M., *Class, status and power*, Routledge & Kegan Paul, London.

MATZA, D. (1969a), 'Reply to Charles Valentine's "Culture and Poverty"', *Current Anthropology*, 10, (2–3), April–June, pp. 192–4.

MATZA, D. (1969b), *Becoming deviant*, Prentice-Hall, New Jersey.

MATZA, D. and SYKES, G. (1957), 'Techniques of neutralisation', *A.S.R.*, 22, December, pp. 664–70.

MATZA, D. and SYKES, G. (1961), 'Juvenile delinquency and subterranean values', *A.S.R.*, 26, pp. 712–19.

MAXINE, D. (1936), *The lost generation – portrait of American youth today*, Macmillan, New York.

MAYO, M. (1977), *Women in the Community*, Routledge & Kegan Paul, London.

MAYS, J. B. (1954), *Juvenile Delinquency*, Jonathan Cape.

MAYS, J. B. (1964), *Growing up in the City*, Liverpool University Press.

MAYS, J. B. (1967), *Crime and the social structure*, Faber & Faber, London.

MAYS, J. B. (1972), *Juvenile delinquency, the family and the social group*, Longman, London.

MEAD, M. (1928), *Coming of age in Samoa*, Penguin edition, 1971.

MELLY, G. (1972), *Revolt into Style*, Penguin, Harmondsworth.

MERTON, R. K. (1938), 'Social structure and anomie', *A.S.R.*, 3, October, pp. 672–82.

MERTON, R. K. (1957), *Social theory and social structure*, John Wiley, New York.

MIDWINTER, E. (1972), *Priority Education*, Penguin, Harmondsworth.

MILLER, A. (1973), 'On the road – hitching on the highway', *Transaction*, vol. 10., no. 5.

MILLER, W. B. (1958), 'Lower class culture as a generting milieu of gang delinquency', *Journal of social issues*, 14, pp. 5–19.

MILLER, W. B. (1962), 'The impact of a "total-community" delinquency control project', *Social Problems*, fall, pp. 168–91.

MILLER, W. B. (1966), 'Violent crimes in city gangs', *Annals*, March, pp. 364–97.

MILLS, C. W. (1943), 'The professional ideology of social pathologists', *A.J.S.*, 49, 2 September.

MILLS, C. W. (1957), *The Power Elite*, Oxford University Press, London.

MILLS, R. W. (1970), *The young outsiders – a study in alternative communities*, Tavistock, London.

MITCHELL, J. (1971), *Women's estate*, Penguin, Harmondsworth.

MONOD, J. (1967), 'Juvenile gangs in Paris – towards a structural analysis' *Journal of Research in Crime and Delinquency*, vol. 4, August, pp. 168–91.

MOORE, R. (1975), *Racism and black resistance in Britain*, Pluto Press, London.

MORRIS, T. (1957), *The criminal area*, Routledge & Kegan Paul, London.

MORSE, M. (1965), *The unattached*, Penguin, Harmondsworth.

MUNGHAM, G. and PEARSON, G. (1976), *Working class youth cultures*, Routledge & Kegan Paul, London.

MURDOCK, G. (1973), 'Culture and classlessness – the making and unmaking of a contemporary myth', *Symposium on Work and Leisure*, University of Salford.

MURDOCK, G. (1974), 'Mass communication and the construction of meaning' in Armistead, N. (ed.), *Reconstructing social psychology*, Penguin, Harmondsworth.

MURDOCK, G. and MCCRON, R. (1973), 'Scoobies, skins and contemporary pop', *New Society*, vol. 23, no. 247.

MURDOCK, G. and MCCRON, R. (1976), 'Consciousness of class and consciousness of generation' in Hall, S. and Jefferson, T. *op. cit.*

MURDOCK, G. and PHELPS, G. (1972), 'Youth culture and the school revisited', *B.J.S.*, 23, 2, June, pp. 478–82.

MUSGROVE, F. (1964), *Youth and the Social Order*, Routledge & Kegan Paul, London.

MUSGROVE, F. (1969), 'The problems of youth and the social structure', *Youth and Society*, 11, pp. 38–58.

MUSGROVE, F. (1974), *Ecstasy and holiness, counter culture and open society*, Methuen, London.

NAIRN, T. and QUATTROCCHI, A. (1968), *The beginning of the end*, Panther, London.

NEILL, A. S. (1968), *Summerhill*, Penguin, Harmondsworth.

NEWHAM COMMUNITY DEVELOPMENT PROJECT (1976), *Prosperity or decline – social audit*, CDP Publications, Home Office, London.

NUTTALL, J. (1969), *Bomb culture*, Paladin, London.

NYE, I. (1958), *Family relationships and delinquent behaviour*, John Wiley, New York.

O'BRIEN, J. E. (1971), 'Violence in divorce prone families', *Journal of Marriage and the Family*, 33, November, pp. 692–98.

PALMER, T. (1971), *The trials of Oz*, Blond & Briggs, London.

PARK, R., BURGESS, E. and MCKENZIE, R. D. (1925), *The city*, University of Chicago Press.

PARKER, H. J. (1974), *View from the boys, a sociology of down town adolescents*, David & Charles, Newton Abbott.

PARKIN, F. (1968), *Middle class radicalism*, Manchester University Press.

PARKIN, F. (1971), *Class inequality and political order*, MacGibbon & Kee, London.

PARKINSON, T. (ed.) (1961), *A casebook on the beat*, Crowell, New York.

PARSONS, T. (1954), 'Age and sex in the social structure of the United States'. In his *Essays in sociological theory*, pp. 89–103, Free Press, Chicago.

PARTRIDGE, W. L. (1973), *The hippy ghetto – the story of a subculture*, Holt, Rinehart & Winston, New York.

PATRICK, J. (1973), *A Glasgow gang observed*, Eyre-Methuen, London.

PEARCE, F. (1973a), 'Crime, corporations and the American social order' in Taylor, I. and Taylor, L. (eds), *Politics and deviance*, Penguin, Harmondsworth.

PEARCE, F. (1973b), 'How to be immoral, pathetic, dangerous and sick all at the same time', in Young, J. and Cohen, S. (eds), *Mass media and social problems*, Constable, London.

PEARCE, F. (1974), 'Crime and the American social order', M.Ph. unpublished, University of Leeds.

PEARCE, F. (1976), *Crimes of the powerful*, Pluto Press, London.

PEARSON, G. and MUNGHAM, G. (eds) (1976), *Working class youth cultures*, Routledge & Kegan Paul, London.

PEPINSKY, H. (1976), 'Police patrolmen's role – offence reporting behaviour', *Journal of research in crime and delinquency*, vol. 12, no. 1, January.

PHILLIPSON, C. M. (1971), 'Juvenile delinquency and the school,' in Carson, W. G. and Wiles, P., *op. cit.*

PILIAVIN, I. and BRIAR, S. (1964), 'Police encounters with juveniles', *A.J.S.*, vol. 70, September, pp. 206–14.

PINE, G. (1965), 'Social class, social mobility and delinquent behaviour', *Personnel and Guidance Journal*, April, pp. 770–4.

PIVEN, F. F. and CLOWARD, R. (1974), *Regulating the poor – the functions of social welfare*, Tavistock, London.

PIZZEY, E. (1975), *Scream quietly or the neighbours will hear*, Penguin, Harmondsworth.

PIZZORNO, E. (1959), 'Accumulation, loisirs et rapports de classe', *Esprit*, June.

PLANT, M. (1975), *Drugtakers in an English town*, Tavistock, London.

PLUMMER, K. (1975), *Sexual stigma – an interactionist account*, Routledge & Kegan Paul, London.

POLK, K. (1957), 'Juvenile delinquency and social areas', *Social Problems*, v, Winter, pp. 214–17.

POLK, K. and HALFERTY, D. S. (1966), 'Adolescence, commitment and delinquency', *Journal of Research in Crime and Delinquency*, vol. 3, no. 2, July, pp. 82–96.

POLSKY, N. (1971), *Hustlers, beats and others*, Penguin, Harmondsworth.

POSTMAN, N. and WEINGARTNER, C. (1971), *Teaching as a subversive activity*, Penguin, Harmondsworth.

POWELL, E. H. (1962), 'Beyond Utopia – the "Beat generation" as a challenge for the sociology of knowledge', in Rose, A. M., *Human behaviour and social processes – an interactionist perspective*, pp. 360–77, Routledge & Kegan Paul, London.

POWER, M. J. (1962), 'Trends in juvenile delinquency', *The Times*, 9 August.

POWER, M. J. (1965), 'An attempt to identify at first appearance before the courts those at risk', *Proceedings of the Royal Society of Medicine*, vol. 58, 9, pp. 704–5.

POWER, M. J., BENN, R. T. and MORRIS, J. (1967), 'Neighbourhoods, schools and juveniles before the court', *B.J.C.*, 12, 2, pp. 111–32.

POWER, M. and SIREY, E. C. (1972), 'A commentary', *B.J.C.*, 12, pp. 402–3.

POWERS, E. and WILMER, H. (1950), *An experiment in the prevention of delinquency*, Columbia University Press, New York.

RAINWATER, L. (1966), 'The problem of lower class culture', *Pruitt-Igoe Occasional Paper 8*, Washington University.

RAISON, T. (1966), *Youth in New Society*, Hart-Davis, London.

RAMPARTS (eds), (1971), *Conversations with the new reality*, Harper & Row, Canfield Press, San Francisco.

RECKLESS, W. C. (1961), *The crime problem*, Appleton-Century-Crofts, New York.

RECKLESS, W. C. and DINITZ, S. (1972), *The prevention of juvenile delinquency – an experiment*, Ohio State University Press, Columbia.

REICH, C. A. (1970), *The greening of America*, Random House, New York.

REICH, C. and WENNER, J. (1972), *Garcia – the Rolling Stone interview*, Straight Arrow, San Francisco.

REID, I. (1977), *Social class differences in Britain*, Open Books Ltd, London.

REISS, A. (1961), 'The social integration of queers and peers', *Social Problems*, 9, pp. 102–19.

REISS, A. and RHODES, A. L. (1961), 'Delinquency and the social class struggle', *A.S.R.*, 26, pp. 720–32.

RESISTANCE THROUGH RITUALS (1975), *Working Papers in cultural studies, 7/8*, Centre for Contemporary Cultural Studies, University of Birmingham. Also published as Hall, S. and Jefferson, T., (1976), *op. cit*.

REX, J. and MOORE, R. (1967), *Race, community and conflict*, Oxford University Press and Institute of Race Relations, London.

REYNOLDS, D. J. (1976), 'When pupils and teachers refuse a truce – the secondary school and the creation of delinquency', in Mungham, G. and Pearson, G., *op. cit*.

RICOEUR, P. (1963), 'Structure et hermétique', *Esprit*, November.

RICOEUR, P. (1972), 'The model of the text – meaningful action considered as a text', *Social Research*, April.

RIESEMAN, D. (1951), *The lonely crowd*, Yale, New Haven.

RIGBY, A. (1973), *Alternative realities*, Routledge & Kegan Paul, London.

ROBERTSON, G. (1974), *Whose conspiracy?*, National Council for Civil Liberties, London.

ROBINS, D. and COHEN, P. (1978), *Knuckle sandwich*, Penguin, Harmondsworth.

ROCK, P. and COHEN, S. (1970), 'The teddy boy', in Bognador, V.

and Skodalsky, V., *The age of affluence 1951–61*, Macmillan, London.

RODMAN, H. (1965), 'The lower class value stretch' in Ferman, L., *Poverty in America*, University of Michigan Press, Ann Arbor.

ROSS, A. M. and HILL, H. (1967), *Employment, race and poverty*, Harcourt Brace, New York.

ROSZAK, T. (1970), *The making of a counter culture*, Faber & Faber, London.

ROWBOTHAM, S. (1973), *Women's World, Women's Consciousness*, Penguin, Harmondsworth.

ROWBOTHAM, S. (1974), *Women's consciousness – men's world*, Penguin, Harmondsworth.

RUNCIMAN, W. G. (1966), *Relative deprivation and social justice*, Routledge & Kegan Paul, London.

RUTTER, M. (1971), 'Why are London children so disturbed?', *Proceedings of the Royal Society of Medicine*, 66, pp. 1221–5.

SAINSBURY, P. (1955), *Suicide in London*, Institute of Psychiatry, London.

SARSBY, J. (1972), 'Love and marriage', *New Society*, 28.9.72.

SASSURE, P. (1960), *Course in general linguistics*, Peter Owen, London.

SCHOFIELD, M. (1965), *The sexual behaviour of young people*, Longman, London.

SCHOFIELD, M. (1973), *The sexual behaviour of young adults*, Allen Lane, London.

SCHOOLS BULLETIN (1970), West Riding Education Committee, July.

SCHUR, E. (1973), *Radical Non-Intervention*, Prentice-Hall, Englewood Cliffs, New Jersey.

SCHWENDINGER, H. and J. (1967), 'Delinquent stereotypes of probable victims', in Klein, M. W., *op. cit*.

SCOTT, J. and VAZ, E. W. (1967), 'A perspective on middle class delinquency', in Vaz, E. W., *op. cit*.

SCOTT, M. B. and TURNER, R. H. (1965), 'Weber and the anomie theory of deviancy', *Sociological Quarterly*, vi, pp. 223–40.

SCOTT, P. (1967), 'Gangs and delinquent groups in London', *B. J. Delinquency*, 1, pp. 525–6.

SCOTT, R. A. (1972), 'A proposed framework for analyzing deviancy as a property of social order', in Douglas, J. and Scott, R., *op. cit*.

SHANLEY, F. J. (1967), 'Middle class delinquency as a social problem', *Sociology and Social Research*, 11, January, pp. 185–98.

SHANLEY, F. J., LEFEVER, D. W. and RICE, R. E. (1966), 'The aggressive middle class delinquent', *Journal of Criminal Law, Criminology and Police Science*, June, pp. 145–57.

SHARPE, S. (1976), *Just like a girl*, Penguin, Harmondsworth.

SHAW, C. R. and MCKAY, H. (1927), *Juvenile delinquency and urban areas*, University of Chicago Press.

SHAW, J. (1976), 'Finishing school – some implications of sex segregated education', in Barker, D. and Allen, S., *op. cit*.

SHIBUTANI, T. (1955), 'Reference groups as perspectives', *A.J.S.*, ix, May, pp. 562–9.

SHIBUTANI, T. (1966), *Improvised news – a sociological study of rumour*, Bobbs-Merrill, New York.

SHORT, J. and STRODBECK, F. L. (1965), *Group process and gang delinquency*, University of Chicago Press.

SIMMONS, J. L. (1965), 'Public stereotypes of deviants', *Social Problems*, Fall, pp. 223–32.

SIMON, G. and TROUT, G. (1967), 'Hippies in college – from teeny boppers to drug freaks', *Transaction*, vol. 5, pp. 27–32.

SIVANANDAN, A. (1976), *Race, class and the state, the black experience in Britain*, Race and Class, Institute of Race Relations, London.

SKOLNIK, J. (1966), *Justice without trial*, John Wiley, New York.

SKOLNIK, J. (1960), *The politics of protest*, Simon & Schuster, New York.

SMART, C. (1976), *Women, crime and criminology*, Routledge & Kegan Paul, London.

SMART, C. and SMART, B. (1978), *Women, sexuality and social control*, Routledge & Kegan Paul, London.

SMITH, C. (1966), *Young people at leisure*, Bury Department of Youth Work Report, University of Manchester.

SMITH, D. H. (1970), *Marijuana – the new social drug*, Prentice-Hall, Englewood Cliffs, New Jersey.

SMITH, D. H. and GAY, G. (1972), *Heroin – it's so good don't even try it once*, Prentice-Hall, Englewood Cliffs, New Jersey.

SMITH, D. H. and LUCE, J. (1971), *Love needs care*, Harper & Row, San Francisco.

SMITH, D. H., SCHICK, J. E. F. and MEYERS, F. H. (1968), 'Use of marijuana in the Haight Ashbury', in Smith, D. H., *op. cit.* (1970).

SMITH, D. J. (1977), *Racial disadvantage in Britain*, Penguin, Harmondsworth.

SMITH, E. A. (1962), *American youth culture*, Free Press, New York.

SMITH, L. SCHACKLADY (1978), 'Sexist assumptions and female delinquency', in Smart, C. and Smart, B. *op. cit.*

SPECTOR, M. (1971), 'On "Do delinquents drift?"' in *Social Problems*, 18 March, pp. 420–22.

SPINLEY, M. (1953), 'The Deprived and the Privileged', Routledge & Kegan Paul, London.

SPROTT, W. J., JEPHCOTT, P. and CARTER, M. (1954), The Social Background of Delinquency, University of Nottingham.

STERLING, J. W. (1962), 'The juvenile offender from community to court – two stages of decision', Unpublished, read at Illinois Academy of Criminology, 31 November.

STERN, S. (1975), 'Altamont – Pearl Harbor to the Woodstock Nation', in Ramparts (eds), *op. cit.*

STEWART, J. (1971), 'Communes in Taos' in Ramparts (eds), *op. cit.*

STIMPSON, G. (1969), 'Interview with skinheads', *Rolling Stone*, 26 July.

STOLTENBERG, J. (1975), 'Towards gender justice', *Social Policy*, May/June.

SUGARMAN, B. (1967), 'Involvement in youth culture, academic

achievement and conformity in school', *B.J.S.*, June, pp. 151–64.
SUTHERLAND, E. H. and CRESSY, D. R. (1966), *Principles of Criminology*, J. P. Lippincott, Philadelphia (7th edn).
SWINGEWOOD, A. (1977), *The myth of mass culture*, Macmillan, London.
TAYLOR, I. (1970), 'Soccer consciousness and soccer hooliganism' in Cohen, S., *Images of deviance*, Penguin, Harmondsworth.
TAYLOR, I. and WALL, D. (1976), 'Beyond the skinheads – comment on the emergence and significance of glamrock', in Mungham, G. and Pearson, G., *op. cit.*
TAYLOR, I., WALTON, P. and YOUNG, J. (1973), *The new criminology*, Routledge & Kegan Paul, London.
TAYLOR, I., WALTON, P. and YOUNG, J. (1975), *Critical criminology*, Routledge & Kegan Paul, London.
TAYLOR, L. (1968), *Deviance and society*, Michael Joseph, London.
TAYLOR, S. (1978), 'Racism and youth,' *New Society*, 3 August, pp. 249–50.
TENNENT, T. G. (1971), 'School non attendance and delinquency', *Educational Research* 13, 3, pp. 185–90.
TERRY, R. M. (1965), 'The screening of juvenile offenders – a study in the societal reaction to deviant behaviour', unpublished Ph.D. thesis, University of Wisconsin.
TERRY, R. M. (1970), 'Discrimination in the handling of juvenile offenders by social control agencies', in Garabedian, P. and Gibbons, D., *Becoming delinquent*, Aldine Press, New York.
TESELLE, S. (1972), *Family, communes and utopian society*, Harper & Row, New York.
THOMPSON, E. P. (1969), 'Time, work discipline and industrial capitalism', *Past and Present*, no. 38.
THRASHER, F. M. (1927), *The gang*, University of Chicago Press.
TITMUSS, R. (1958), 'Industrialisation and the family', in his *Essays on the Welfare State*, Allen & Unwin, London.
TITMUSS, R. (1962), *Income distribution and social change*, Allen & Unwin, London.
TOLSON, A. (1977), *The limits of masculinity*, Tavistock, London.
TOWNSEND, P. and ABEL-SMITH, B. (1965), *The poor and the poorest*, Bell, London.
TRASLER, G. (1962), *The explanation of criminality*, Routledge & Kegan Paul, London.
TRUZZI, M. (1972), 'The occult revival as popular culture, the old and nouveau witch', *Sociological Quarterly*, winter, 13.
TYLOR, E. B. (1871), *Primitive culture*, John Murray, London.
TYRELL, C. (1975), *Rates of Decline*, Association of Community Workers, January.
VALENTINE, C. (1968), *Culture and poverty*, University of Chicago Press.
VAZ, E. W. (1967a), *Middle class delinquency*, Harper & Row, New York.
VAZ, E. W. (1967b), 'Juvenile delinquency in the middle class youth culture', in Vaz, E. W., *op. cit.*

VENESS, T. (1962), *School leavers, their expectations and aspirations*, Methuen, London.

WARREN, M. Q. (1970), 'The community treatment project', in Johnston, N. *et. al., op. cit.*

WEBER, M. (1930), *The Protestant Ethic and the Spirit of Capitalism*, Allen & Unwin, London.

WEIR, S. (1978), 'Youngsters in the Front line', *New Society*, 27 April, pp. 189–93.

WERTHMAN, C. and PILIAVIN, I. (1967), 'Gang members and the police', in Bordua, D. (ed.), *The police*, John Wiley, New York.

WEST, D. J. and FARRINGTON, D. (1973), *Who becomes delinquent?*, Heinemann, London.

WESTERGAARD, J. and RESLER, H. (1975), *Class in a capitalist society*, Heinemann, London.

WESTHUES, W. (1972), 'Hippiedom – some tentative hypotheses', *Sociological Quarterly*, Winter, pp. 81–9.

WESTLEY, W. and ELKIN, F. (1955), 'The myth of adolescent culture', *A.S.R.*, December xx, pp. 680–4.

WESTLEY, W. and ELKIN, F. (1967), 'The protective environment and adolescent socialisation', in Vaz, E. W., *op. cit.*

WEST RIDING EDUCATION COMMITTEE (1970), *Schools Bulletin*.

WHITEHEAD, A. (1976), 'Sexual antagonism in Hertfordshire', in Barker, D. and Allen, S., *op. cit.*

WHYTE, W. F. (1943), *Street corner society, the social organisation of a Chicago slum*, University of Chicago.

WIEDER, D. L. and ZIMMERMAN, D. H. (1974), 'Generational experience and the development of freak culture', *Journal of Social Issues*, vol. 30, no. 2.

WIENER, R. (1970), *Drugs and schoolchildren*, Longman, London.

WILES, P. (1976), *Sociology of Crime and Delinquency in London*, Vol. 2, Martin Robertson, London.

WILKINS, L. (1964), *Social Deviance*, Tavistock, London.

WILLENER, A. (1970), *The action image of society – on cultural politicisation*, Tavistock, London.

WILLIS, P. (1970), 'Subcultural meaning of the motor bike', *Working papers in Cultural Studies*, University of Birmingham, Birmingham.

WILLIS, P. (1972), 'Pop music and youth groups', Ph.D. thesis, unpublished, Centre for Contemporary Cultural Studies, University of Birmingham.

WILLIS, P. (1977), *Learning to labour*, Saxon House, London.

WILLIS, P. (1978), *Profane culture*, Routledge & Kegan Paul, London.

WILLMOTT, P. (1966), *Adolescent boys of East London*, Routledge & Kegan Paul, London.

WILLMOTT, P. and YOUNG, M. (1957), *Family and kinship in East London*, Penguin, Harmondsworth.

WILSON, A. (1978), *Finding a voice – Asian women in Britain*, Pluto Press, London.

WILSON, D. (1978), 'Sexual codes and conduct – a study of teenage girls', in Smart, C. and Smart, B., *op. cit.*

WILSON, E. (1977), *Women and the Welfare State*, Tavistock, London.
WILSON, J. Q. (1963), 'The police and their problems, a theory', *Public Policy*, xii, pp. 189–216.
WIRTH, L. (1938), 'Urbanism as a way of life', *A.J.S.*, 44, July, pp. 187–243.
WOLFGANG, M. E. and FERRACUTI, F. (1967), *The subculture of violence*, Tavistock, London.
WOMEN'S STUDIES GROUP (1978), *Women take issue*, Centre for Contemporary Cultural Studies, University of Birmingham, Hutchinson, London.
WOODS, P. (1977), *Youth, generations and social class*, Open University Press, Milton Keynes.
WRIGHT, N. (1977), *Progress in education*, Croom Helm, London.
WRIGHT, P. (1968), *The coloured worker in British industry*, Oxford University Press, London.
YABLONSKY, L. (1967), *The violent gang*, Penguin, Harmondsworth.
YABLONSKY, L. (1969), *The hippy trip*, Pegasus, New York.
YINGER, J. M. (1960), 'Contraculture and subculture', *A.S.R.*, pp. 625–35.
YOUNG, J. (1971), *The drugtakers*, Paladin, London.
YOUNG, J. (1973), 'The hippies – an essay in the politics of leisure' in Taylor, I. and Taylor, L., *op. cit*.
ZARETSKY, E. (1976), *Capitalism, the Family and Personal Life*, Pluto, London.
ZETTERBURG, H. (1968), 'The secret ranking', in Truzzi, M. (ed.), *Sociology and everyday life*, Prentice-Hall, Englewood Cliffs, New Jersey.

Index